BREAKTHROUGH SPANISH

THIRD EDITION

Sandra Truscott
Co-ordinator, The Languagewise Programme,
University of Manchester

Brian Hill
General Editor
Head of the School of Languages
University of Brighton

palgrave
macmillan

First published 1987 by Pan Books Ltd
First Palgrave Macmillan edition published 1998
Reprinted nine times
Second edition 1998
Reprinted four times
Third edition 2003

Published by
PALGRAVE MACMILLAN
Houndmills, Basingstoke, Hampshire RG21 6XS and
175 Fifth Avenue, New York, N.Y. 10010
Companies and representatives throughout the world

PALGRAVE MACMILLAN is the global academic imprint of the Palgrave Macmillan division of St. Martin's Press, LLC and of Palgrave Macmillan Ltd. Macmillan® is a registered trademark in the United States, United Kingdom and other countries. Palgrave is a registered trademark in the European Union and other countries.

ISBN 1-4039-1679-9 book
ISBN 1-4039-1680-2 two cassettes
ISBN 1-4039-1678-0 book and cassette pack

A catalogue record for this book is available from the British Library.

This book is printed on paper suitable for recycling and made from fully managed and sustained forest sources.

Designed by design@djhunter
Audio production: first and second editions Gerald Ramshaw, Max II; additional audio production for the third edition Brian Hill.
Actors: Carlos Fernández Pando, Marisa Julián, Guillermo Reinlein, Esther Gurruchaga, Maika Gil, Rosa Hernández, Janette Grabham, Angel García Rodríguez, Jesús Colom Bataller, Roberto Martin Arrabal, Diana Bejarano Coca

10   9   8   7   6   5   4   3
12   11   10   09   08   07   06   05   04

Printed in China

Acknowledgements

The author and publishers would like to thank the following for illustrative material: Cabitel, p.164; El País, p.145; Editorial Prensa Alicantina, S.A., p. 145; Tim Fox, pp. 32, 79, 96, 112, 114, 129, 135, 160, 179, 190; design@djhunter, p. 111; Helen O'Donnell, pp. 46, 49, 55, 81, 94, 97, 123, 127, 132, 155, 158, 61; Supertele, Madrid, p. 5; Susannah Tipple, pp. 21, 45, 146. All other photographs supplied by the author, 22, 23, 24 & 25.

Every effort has been made to trace all the copyright holders but if any have been inadvertently overlooked the publishers will be pleased to make the necessary arrangements at the first opportunity.

Contents

MAKING THE MOST OF THIS COURSE

Welcome to *Breakthrough Spanish 2*, which is intended for both self-study learners and classroom use. If you are using Breakthrough on your own, please do take the time to read through this introduction. You'll be able to get more out of the course if you understand how it has been structured and what is expected of you.

Breakthrough Spanish 2 is designed to take you on from *Breakthrough*, or indeed any similar beginner's course. We have consulted with hundreds of language learners on what they need at this level and the course has been built on their advice. Above all, people want a course which will enable them to cope in real situations. *Breakthrough Spanish 2* combines authentic spoken Spanish and authentic written Spanish, so that you are prepared both for the informality of real speech and for the more formal style of the written language.

There are twelve units, each based on a theme which reinforces and extends your knowledge of real Spanish. The emphasis is on the language used to understand and communicate effectively in a range of common situations. Each unit has the same basic structure.

The introductory page

This sets the scene, tells you what you will learn, reminds you of some key points from the previous unit and gives you a few tips on how to learn and what to watch out for.

Conversations

In each unit there are three Conversations in which the new vocabulary and structures are introduced. They have been specially recorded on location in Spain and cover different aspects of the unit theme. Please DO NOT expect to understand them immediately. By their nature, each one is introducing new vocabulary and structures. Try playing the Conversation through once or twice (reading the transcript at the same time if it helps). Then go through the Conversation using your PAUSE button and consulting the linked notes which explain things you may not yet have come across. Don't be afraid to make your own notes in the book or to underline things which are important to you. Finally, listen to the Conversation once or twice straight through without looking at the book before you move on to the Practice section.

Practice

Each Conversation has a number of exercises attached to it. These pick up the main points from the Conversations and give you practice in reading, listening, speaking and, to a lesser extent, writing. Instructions on how to do each exercise are given in the book, with answers, where appropriate, listed at the end of each unit. You will probably need to go through these exercises several times, particularly the speaking practice, before you feel you have mastered them. It's wise to spend as much time as you need here so that you really do learn the main words and structures.

Key words and phrases

To help you pull together the most important points, each unit has a Key Words and Phrases page which follows the Conversation and Practice sections. Read these through, checking back to the notes linked to the Conversations if you need to refresh your memory. Then work through the list, first covering up the English column to see if you can translate the Spanish phrases. Then try it the other way round, from English into Spanish.

Grammar

This is not a grammar course. The Conversations have been selected on the basis of the topic and the vocabulary they introduce. However, it is often valuable, and indeed interesting, to see how the language works. This can increase your confidence in generating language of your own. Each unit explains a few important aspects of grammar which should help you develop a firmer foundation. Interspersed are exercises to practise the points which have been introduced. If you can't get on with grammar, look at this section more for reference rather than feeling you need to have mastered everything before moving on.

And finally...

Each unit ends with two or three activities including an exercise designed to encourage working with a partner. You can of course also work on them alone. The aim is to reinforce key points that have cropped up during the unit.

At the end of the book are a Verb list, a Vocabulary list, a Grammar contents by unit and a Grammar index.

A few hints and tips:

- Be patient with yourself … above all don't get discouraged. Everybody goes through sticky patches when they feel they are not getting anywhere. Try looking back to some earlier Conversations to see just how much you have learned.

- If you can, practise regularly. Thirty to forty minutes a day is usually better than a block of four hours once a week.

- It helps to speak out loud in Spanish as much as possible. This may seem strange at first but actually using the words, with a friend or to yourself, is a good way of practising and remembering.

- There is a lot of material to take on board. Have confidence in us. Real language is quite complex and the course has been designed to build up your knowledge slowly, selecting what is important at each stage.

¡Buena suerte!

Brian Hill

1

EXPRESSING PREFERENCES

WHAT YOU WILL LEARN

- ▶ how to talk about your favourite leisure activities
- ▶ how to describe your favourite radio programme
- ▶ how to say if you prefer shopping at a corner shop or supermarket – and why
- ▶ you will also review verbs like **me gusta**, stem-changing verbs and nouns and adjectives

BEFORE YOU BEGIN

Although you already have some knowledge of Spanish, it may be some time since you studied it and you may feel that you have forgotten all you learnt. Take heart – it's all still there, somewhere, but it can take a little time to retrieve. That's why we start this course with some revision rather than plunging immediately into the unknown. To get back into the swing of things, try listening to the cassette (in the car or at home) just to get used to the sound of the language once again. You'll soon find that you recognise many of the words. This unit covers material that you may already be familiar with – likes and dislikes and verbs which work like **me gusta**. Some of the vocabulary will be new, however, and some of the accents unfamiliar. This course uses a number of native speakers of Spanish from South America. You will find that their speech has a different rhythm from that of a Spaniard, but you will also find they tend to speak more slowly. So, good luck!

A survey

Gustavo	Bueno, yo prefiero ir a una taberna a oír música, a conversar con un amigo.
Claudia	A mí me gusta ... a veces, en las tabernas hay pista de baile, entonces me gusta tomar un sifón y bailar también.
Veronica	En verano, prefiero salir a caminar, cerca de la costa.
Andrés	Ir de bares.
Carmen	Ir de copas.
Marga	Me gusta ir a cenar fuera con los amigos, después, ir a tomar una copa a un pub y luego ir a una discoteca.
Maite	Me interesa bastante mejorar mi inglés entonces veo la televisión bastante por las noches.
José Luis	A mí me encanta la natación. Por eso todos los viernes voy a la piscina y nado durante una hora.

LISTEN FOR...

prefiero salir a caminar	I prefer to go walking
me gusta ir a cenar fuera	I like going out for a meal

yo prefiero ir a una taberna a oír música
I prefer to go to a pub to hear music. Later, Marga uses the word **pub** – this describes a more fashionable type of establishment than the **taberna**. You can also use the phrase **escuchar música** to listen to music. **Prefiero** (from **preferir**, to prefer) is a stem-changing verb. (See Grammar section in this unit.)

a mí me gusta I like (it pleases me). Claudia is stressing what she likes (as opposed to Gustavo). That is why she adds **a mí** to me. **A mí me gusta el whisky, pero a Raúl no** *I* like whisky but Raúl doesn't. (See Grammar section in this unit.)

una pista de baile a dance floor; **una pista de esquí** a ski slope

a veces sometimes. You can also say **algunas veces**.

un sifón a draught beer (in South American Spanish). Here's a good example of the difference between South American and peninsular Spanish. In Spain, **un sifón** would probably mean 'soda water' – and a **caña** is a draught beer. In practice, many drinks and snacks change their name

according to region, so it's best to ask if you're not sure.

caminar to walk; **un camino** a path

bailar to dance; **un baile** a dance

ir de bares and **ir de copas** both mean the same – to go bar hopping or on a pub crawl!

a cenar fuera to dine out; **fuera** out; **dentro** in

me interesa bastante mejorar mi inglés
I am quite interested in improving my English. **Me interesa** works just like **me gusta**. (See Grammar section in this unit.)

mejorar to improve (**mejor**, better)

a mí me encanta la natación I love swimming. Another phrase which works like **me gusta**. Literally, swimming enchants me. **Nado** I swim.

y por eso and because of this. A very useful connecting phrase.

PRACTICE

1 Man or woman? **¿Hombre o mujer?** Listen to Conversation 1 again. Was it a man or a woman who made the following remarks?

		hombre	mujer
a	Me gusta tomar un sifón.	☐	☐
b	Me gusta ir a tomar una copa a un pub.	☐	☐
c	Prefiero ir a una taberna.	☐	☐
d	A veces en las tabernas hay pista de baile.	☐	☐
e	Ir de bares.	☐	☐
f	En verano prefiero salir a caminar.	☐	☐
g	Me encanta la natación.	☐	☐
h	Me interesa el inglés.	☐	☐

Answers p. 16

2 What does Guillermo like doing? On the recording you hear Guillermo saying what he likes to do in the evening. Each activity is numbered. Jot in the number beside its English translation.

a   I like to go dancing. _____

b   I like to go drinking. _____

c   I like to go out walking. _____

d   I like going out for a meal. _____

e   I like to talk to my friends. _____

f   I like to listen to music. _____

Answers p. 16

g   I like to go to a disco. _____

3

Dislikes. There are lots of things that Marisa doesn't like doing. Listen to what she says and check off each statement in the grid below. You will notice that some activities she mentions do not appear on the grid and vice versa.

a	No me gusta escuchar música clásica.	
b	A mí no me gusta ir a los pubs.	
c	Odio bailar en las discotecas.	
d	No me gusta comer sola en casa.	
e	A mí no me gusta hablar con personas que no conozco.	
f	Odio caminar en el campo.	
g	Odio la música popular.	
h	No me interesa aprender nuevos idiomas.	

Answers p. 16

4

It's your turn to speak. Marisa will ask you what you like to do in the evening. You will be prompted with an answer in English. Pause the recording to create your answers in Spanish and then carry on with the recording to hear the correct answer. You will be using the words and phrases you learnt in the conversation such as **me gusta**, **salir**, **caminar** and **salir de copas**. You will also need **los fines de semana** weekends, and **una buena película** a good film.

Unit 1   Expressing preferences

CONVERSATION 2

Have you a favourite radio programme?

Marga	Sí, *Sin Prisa*, un programa de música lenta.
Verónica	De música selecta.
Carmen	Me gusta escuchar música por la noche cuando estoy estudiando.
Rafael	Prefiero escuchar los informativos.
Eduardo	Un programa, *Directo Directo*.
Martín	Mm, no sé, temas musicales, y temas deportivos y telediarios.
Gustavo	Generalmente tengo la radio sintonizada en la Radio Nacional que divulga constantemente música clásica.
Claudia	Yo la tengo en una emisora que se llama la emisora Montserrat, que solamente es música romántica.
Daniel	Normalmente, si no estoy muy cansado, me gustan los programas informativos.

LISTEN FOR...

los informativos	the news
temas deportivos	sports programmes
una emisora	a radio station

Sin Prisa *In No Hurry* (literally, without any hurry). Here it's the name of a radio programme. **No tengo prisa** I'm not in a hurry.

selecta fine, choice or especially chosen, select

escuchar música to listen to music. Note that **escuchar** means to listen *to* so you don't need to use **a**. **No me gusta escuchar música popular** I don't like listening to pop music.

cuando estoy estudiando when I'm studying. You can use **estar** and this form of the verb to stress that you are doing something *now*. **Estoy haciendo la cama** I'm making the bed. (See Unit 4.)

los informativos the news. You can also use **las noticias**. The television news is **el telediario**.

Directo Directo is a magazine-type programme which combines news, interviews, comment and features.

temas musicales musical topics. **Tema** looks feminine but is masculine – **el tema** topic, subject.

tengo la radio sintonizada en la Radio Nacional I have the radio tuned to **Radio Nacional**; **sintonizar** to tune (into).

que divulga constantemente música clásica which broadcasts classical music non-stop. **Divulgar** is a more formal word than **emitir** to broadcast.

una emisora a radio station.

si no estoy muy cansado if I'm not very tired. Don't confuse the word **cansado** tired, with **casado** married.

me gustan – **gustan** has an extra **n** because what Daniel likes (**los programas informativos**) is in the plural. (See Grammar section in this unit.)

PRACTICE

5 Who likes what? Listen to the conversation again and then on the grid below, indicate which sort of programme each person liked. Remember that some people had more than one preference.

	Classical music	Easy listening	News	Sports	Magazine programmes
Eduardo					
Martín					
Carmen					
Daniel					
Rafael					
Verónica					
Claudia					
Marga					
Gustavo					

Answers p. 16

6 Listen to Marisa talking about her favourite radio programmes. Then number these sentences in the order in which she said them.

a   Por la mañana, cuando me ducho, suelo poner las noticias. _____

b   Y así me duermo enseguida. _____

c   También me gusta mucho la música latina. _____

d   No me gusta leer el periódico. _____

e   Vuelvo a poner las noticias. _____

Answers p. 16   f   Depende un poco de lo que estoy haciendo. _____

7 Football crazy! There is a lot of football shown on Spanish television these days and many people (including **estudiantes** students, and **jubilados** retired people) are tired of seeing it. Read through their opinions and answer the questions which follow.

Juan Antonio Camino, 20 años, estudiante de ingeniería:
Me gusta el fútbol pero con tantos partidos estoy bastante cansado. Pones la radio o la televisión, lees el periódico y todo es fútbol y más fútbol. Lo veo en casa, solo normalmente.

José María Cestari, 73 años, jubilado:
A mí me encanta ver todos los partidos porque tengo tiempo para verlos. Soy forofo del Real Madrid. Veo los partidos en el bar pero si son importantes prefiero verlos en casa.

Celia Martínez, 31 años, empleada de banco en paro (unemployed bank clerk):

Es horrible, me parece muy mal que pongan tanto fútbol en televisión y a una hora cuando no hay otra opción. Hemos discutido mucho mi marido y yo por el fútbol.

Fernando Moreno, 20 años, estudiante de informática (computer science):

A mí me parece excesivo. De todas formas, yo no veo mucho fútbol, sólo me interesa algún partido cuando juega la selección española.

Angela Barona, 24 años, estudiante de física:

En mi casa mi padre y mi hermano siempre ven el fútbol y como al resto de la familia no nos gusta, no podemos ver la televisión todos juntos.

a Who is only interested in a game when the Spanish team is playing?

b Whose family can't watch television together any more?

c Who normally watches football at home, alone?

d Who has quarrelled with their spouse because of football?

Answers p. 16 e Who sometimes watches the games in a bar?

8 Your turn to speak. This time, Guillermo asks you about what you like to listen to in your spare time. Use **me gusta** if you only like one thing, or **me gustan** if you like several. You'll need **las noticias** the news, **música rock** rock music, **faenas de la casa** housework, and **emite** it broadcasts.

Which do you prefer, the corner shop or the supermarket?

Claudia	Generalmente, en mi pueblo se compra en una plaza de mercado, que es mejor, para mejor escoger ¿no?

LISTEN FOR...

una plaza de mercado	a market place
sin ir de un sitio para otro	without going from one place to another
guardar la cola	to queue up

Verónica	Prefiero el supermercado, porque uno queda libre, compra todo lo que necesita de una sola vez.
Andrés	Prefiero en un supermercado, porque puedo encontrar todas las cosas sin ir de un sitio para otro.
Carmen	En un supermercado, porque no me gusta tener que guardar la cola y esperar a que me atiendan.
Rafael	Prefiero en un supermercado por la variedad de cosas que puedo comprar.
Paqui	Depende. Si es en el pueblo, prefiero la tienda porque conozco a la gente.
Ventura	Prefiero el supermercado porque hay más cantidad en diferentes artículos.
Araceli	Si voy con prisa me gusta la tienda pequeña, pero si voy con tiempo me gusta el supermercado.

en mi pueblo se compra en una plaza de mercado in my home town (or village) you (one) buy(s) in the market square. The idea of the **pueblo** is important for many Spaniards and South Americans. Paqui also mentions her **pueblo** later on.

para mejor escoger to choose better

uno queda libre one is free/able to. Verónica could have said **se queda libre**; **compra todo lo que necesita** you buy all you need (**lo que** that which) **de una sola vez** at one go; **una vez** once.

puedo encontrar todas las cosas I can find everything. Here **encontrar** means 'to find'. It is a stem-changing verb. (See Grammar section in this unit.)

sin ir de un sitio para otro without going from one place to another. Note how you use the infinitive after connecting words like **sin, con, para** etcetera. **Una casete sin grabar** a blank tape (without recording); **un casete** (masculine) means 'cassette player'.

no me gusta tener que guardar la cola I don't like to have to queue; **tener que** to have to: **tengo que encontrar ese libro** I have to find that book. **La cola** means a 'tail', or here, 'a queue'. Carmen says **'guardar la cola'**, but **'guardar cola'** (without **'la'**) is more widely-used.

esperar a que me atiendan to wait for them to serve me. **Atender** to serve – not 'to attend'.

por la variedad de cosas because of the variety of things. Use **por** to mean 'because of', 'on account of'. You have already met **por eso** because of this.

depende it depends; **depende de** it depends on; **todo depende de María** it all depends on María.

hay más cantidad there is more quantity; **más calidad** more quality

si voy con prisa if I am in a rush; **si voy con tiempo** if I've got time; **voy** I go.

9 Who shops where. Listen to the recording again and then tick the boxes to show at which type of outlet the interviewees prefer to shop.

	tienda	supermercado	plaza de mercado
Claudia	☐	☐	☐
Verónica	☐	☐	☐
Andrés	☐	☐	☐
Carmen	☐	☐	☐
Rafael	☐	☐	☐
Paqui	☐	☐	☐
Ventura	☐	☐	☐
Araceli	☐	☐	☐

Answers p. 16

10 Complete these sentences, so that you have two reasons why you prefer to do your shopping in a local shop and four reasons for shopping at the supermarket.

a Me gusta la tienda pequeña porque conozco a

_____ .

b Si _____ , prefiero la tienda pequeña.

c Me gusta el supermercado, si

_____ .

d Prefiero el supermercado por

_____ .

e Me gusta el supermercado porque no tengo que

_____ .

f Prefiero el supermercado porque uno

Answers p. 16   _____ .

11

Where does Guillermo do his shopping? Listen to Guillermo telling you where he likes to shop. Note down three reasons, in English, why he prefers to shop in the supermarket.

a _____

b _____

Answers p. 16 c _____

12

Your turn to speak. You prefer the supermarket too! Reply to Guillermo's questions on the recording. You'll be using **puedo** (I can) + an infinitive, **tengo que** (I have to) + infinitive and **hay** there is, there are.

```
5[641835   3 00188 7402328 090103/17:53

124677 PALETA COCIDA
  0,300 Kg.      6,91  € /Kg. B    2,07
107540 JAMON COCIDO
  0,290 Kg.      8,50  € /Kg. B    2,47
224956 PECHUGA PAVO
  0,160 Kg.      9,56  € /Kg. B    1,53
179036 TRUFADO POLLO
  0,100 Kg.      7,50  € /Kg. B    0,75
118398 QUESO GGUDA
  0,245 Kg.     13,16  € /Kg. A    3,22
116301 QUESO DIETET          1 A   2,48
116301 QUESO DIETET          1 A   2,31
71188 NATA LIGERA            1 B   0,94
                     SUBTOTAL.    15,77
(*) TOTAL COMPRA SUPER         15,77
                 EFECTIVO     17,00
                   CAMBIO      1,23
                   COBRADO    15,77
(*) 2624 PTAS              D/    0,00
A 4/     8,01 B 7/    7,76 C16/    0,00
                          0188 00

 GRACIAS POR SU VISITA  -  PRECIADOS
```

KEY WORDS
AND PHRASES

(a mí) me gusta/me encanta ...	I like/I love ...
escuchar música	listening to music
salir a caminar	going out walking
ir de bares	going to bars
ir de copas	going drinking
ir a cenar fuera	going out for a meal
conversar con amigos	chatting with friends
ir a bailar a una discoteca	going dancing in a disco
(a mí) me gustan ...	I like ...
los informativos	the news
los programas de música romántica	programmes of romantic music
los temas deportivos	sports programmes
los telediarios	television news
me interesa el alemán	I am interested in German
no me interesa el francés	I am not interested in French
me interesan los idiomas	I am interested in languages
no me interesan las noticias	I am not interested in the news
si no estoy cansado(a)	if I'm not tired
cuando estoy estudiando	when I am studying
prefiero ...	I prefer ...
el supermercado	the supermarket
la tienda pequeña	the small shop
porque ...	because ...
hay más cantidad de cosas	there is more quantity of things
hay más variedad	there is more variety
no tengo que ...	I don't have to ...
ir de un sitio para otro	go from one place to another
guardar (la) cola	queue
conozco a la gente	I know the people
puedo comprar todo de una sola vez	I can buy everything at once
puedo escoger mejor	I can choose better
puedo encontrar todas las cosas	I can find everything
si voy con prisa	if I am in a hurry
si voy con tiempo	if I have time
depende	it depends

Likes and dislikes – using impersonal verbs

Gustar to like
- Instead of saying 'I like wine' in Spanish you say 'Wine pleases (to) me' – **me gusta el vino**.
- If what you like is plural – Spanish wines – then make **gusta** plural too:
  me gustan los vinos españoles.

Look at the box below to refresh your memory about how impersonal verbs like **gustar** work:

(No)	me te le	gusta	leer bailar la playa	I like reading you like dancing s/he/you (formal) likes the beach
	nos os les	gustan	las ciudades	we like cities you like cities they/you (formal plural) like cities

Interesar 'to be interested in', **encantar** 'to love' and **apetecer** 'to feel like' work the same way.

Me interesa el arte contemporáneo.	I am interested in contemporary art (literally, contemporary art interests me).
Le encanta esquiar.	He adores skiing.
¿Te apetece una cerveza?	Do you feel like a beer?
¿Le interesan las biografías?	Are you (**usted**) interested in biographies?

If you want to
- stress who likes what
- contrast who likes what

then use these pronouns:

a mí	**(me gusta esquiar) pero**	*I* like skiing, but
a ti	**(te gusta mirar la tele)**	*you* like watching TV
a él	**(le gusta el golf) pero**	*he* likes golf, but
a ella	**(le gusta el baloncesto)**	*she* likes basket ball
a Carlos (le gusta el cine) pero		*Carlos* likes the cinema, but
a Carlota (le gusta el teatro)		*Charlotte* likes the theatre
a nosotros (nos gustan los vinos franceses) pero		*we* like French wines, but
a vosotros (os gustan los vinos alemanes)		*you* like German wines
a ellos (les gustan las mujeres españolas) pero		*they* (m.) like Spanish women, but
a ellas (les gustan los hombres franceses)		*they* (f.) like French men

13 How do you say the following?

a I like the small shop.
b I like supermarkets.
c I don't like the market square.
d I like small towns.
e Pablo likes the city.

Answers p. 16

- If you want to agree with someone about what they like, you can reply **a mí también**:
  a **A mí me gusta este vestido.**   I like this dress.
  b **A mí también.**   So do I.

- If you want to agree with someone who *doesn't* like something, add **a mí tampoco**:
  a **No me gusta esta sopa.**   I don't like this soup.
  b **A mí tampoco.**   Neither do I.

14 So reply to these statements out loud.

Guillermo   **A mí me gusta el tenis.**

You   _____

Guillermo   **A mí no me gusta el voleibol.**

You   _____

Guillermo   **A mí me gusta el fútbol.**

You   _____

Guillermo   **A mí no me gusta nada el golf.**

You   _____

Guillermo   **A mí no me gusta nadar.**

You   _____

- Three other common verbs work in the same way – **interesar** to interest, **encantar** to love, and **apetecer** to feel like.
  a **A mi hermano le interesan los coches antiguos.**   My brother is interested in old cars (literally, old cars interest my brother).
  b **A Teresa le encanta esquiar.**   Teresa loves skiing (literally, it charms/enchants Teresa to ski).
  c **A José Luis le apetece tomar una bebida.**   José Luis feels like a drink.

15 Translate these sentences:

a I feel like a coca cola. _____

b Diana loves dancing. _____

c She's interested in French films. _____

d I love going drinking. _____

e I am interested in classical music. _____

Answers p. 16

Nouns and adjectives

All nouns in Spanish are either masculine or feminine. Nouns ending in **-o** are usually masculine and those ending in **-a** are feminine. Other common feminine endings are **-dad** (**la ciudad**) and **-ión** (**la nación**). As always, there are exceptions – and three cropped up in Conversation 2: **el tema** matter, topic, subject, **el programa** programme, and **la radio**. Another very common exception is **el problema**. **¡No hay problema!** No problem! **Día** is also masculine: **¡buenos días!** good morning, good day!

Adjectives which describe nouns must also be feminine, masculine, singular or plural as appropriate: **pueblos pequeños**, **ciudades grandes**.

Stem-changing verbs (e ▷ ie, o ▷ ue)

Some verbs in Spanish gain an extra 'i' before the 'e' in some parts of the present tense. Other verbs change the 'o' to 'ue' in the same circumstances. Look at these two examples to see how they work.

preferir to prefer   **encontrar** to find

prefiero	**encuentro**
prefieres	**encuentras**
prefiere	**encuentra**
preferimos	**encontramos**
preferís	**encontráis**
prefieren	**encuentran**

Similar verbs are:

sentir to feel	**¡Lo siento!**	I'm sorry!
pensar to think	**¡Eso pienso yo!**	That's what I think!
volver to return	**¡Vuelvo enseguida!**	Coming immediately!
dormir to sleep	**Siempre duermo muy bien.**	I always sleep very well.
jugar to play	**Juego al tenis y al squash.**	I play tennis and squash.

16 Your turn to speak. This time Marisa asks you about what you like to do at the weekend. You'll be using vocabulary from Conversation 1, so you may want to look at it again.

17 Talk through the pros and cons of corner shops and supermarkets. If you are working with a partner let one of you be in favour of the corner shop and the other prefer the supermarket. Be prepared to fight your corner! Marshal as many arguments as you can, using the ideas and phrases on page 11 and any more that occur to you. Here are some more ideas.

La tienda	El supermercado
Es más cara que el supermercado.	Hay demasiados productos. Es difícil escoger.
Si no compramos en la tienda, cerrará (it will close) y se muere el barrio.	Es más caro porque compras más de lo que necesitas.
Puedes ir a pie.	Tienes que ir en coche.
Hay poca variedad.	Es difícil encontrar lo que necesitas por ser muy grande.

Using the leading question **¿Qué te gusta hacer cuando sales de noche?** work out how you would say what you like to do on a night out. If you are working with a partner, interview each other. Here are some ideas.

VOCABULARY

ligar   to pull/to be on the make

ir a cenar en casa de amigos
salir al teatro y después cenar en un buen restaurante
ir a un cine a ver una película romántica/de suspense/de horror
ir a una discoteca a beber, bailar y ligar

Restaurante
Casa Manolo

PESCADOS, MARISCOS Y CARNES

Real, 14 - Teléfono 244 89 23 • Benalmádena-Pueblo

EXERCISE 1

(a), (b), (d), (f), (h) were said by women, the others by men.

EXERCISE 2

(a) 4   (b) 2   (c) 6   (d) 7   (e) 5   (f) 1   (g) 3

EXERCISE 3

(b), (d), (e), (g) were said.

EXERCISE 5

Eduardo, magazine programmes. Martín, music, news and sports programmes. Carmen, easy listening. Daniel, news. Rafael, news. Verónica, classical music. Claudia, easy listening. Marga, easy listening. Gustavo, classical music.

EXERCISE 6

(f), (c), (a), (d), (e), (b)

EXERCISE 7

(a) Fernando Moreno   (b) Angela Barona
(c) Juan Antonio Camino   (d) Celia Martínez
(e) José María Cestari

EXERCISE 9

Claudia – plaza de mercado. Verónica – supermercado. Andrés – supermercado. Carmen – supermercado. Rafael – supermercado. Paqui – tienda. Ventura – supermercado. Araceli – tienda y supermercado.

EXERCISE 10

(a) la gente   (b) voy con prisa   (c) tengo tiempo
(d) la variedad de cosas que tiene   (e) guardar la cola   (f) queda libre

EXERCISE 11

(a) He doesn't know anyone, so it's quicker.
(b) You get everything in one shop.   (c) More variety

EXERCISE 13

(a) Me gusta la tienda pequeña.   (b) Me gustan los supermercados.   (c) No me gusta la plaza de mercado.   (d) A mí me gustan los pueblos pequeños.   (e) A Pablo le gusta la ciudad.

EXERCISE 15

(a) Me apetece una coca cola.   (b) A Diana le encanta bailar.   (c) Le interesan las películas francesas.   (d) Me encanta ir de bares/copas
(e) Me interesa la música clásica.

Unit 1   Expressing preferences

2 EVERYDAY LIFE

WHAT YOU WILL LEARN

▶ how to talk about your job
▶ how to make a **paella valenciana**
▶ how to discuss your fitness and beauty régime!

POINTS TO REMEMBER

● likes and dislikes: **a mí (no) me gusta, me encanta, me apetece, me interesa**
● stem-changing verbs: **prefiero, siento, juego, vuelvo, encuentro, duermo**

BEFORE YOU BEGIN

To keep the new Spanish you have learned fresh in your mind, keep going over the key words and phrases in your head or preferably out loud. Pretend to tell a Spaniard what you like doing in the evening, which radio programmes you listen to and where you prefer to do your shopping. Get into the habit of translating shop signs, notices and adverts when you are travelling around. Try inventing little dialogues sparked off by what you see.

Talking about your job

¿cuánto tiempo llevas trabajando aquí?	how long have you been working here?
¿cuántos soléis tener allí?	how many (people) do you usually have there?

Marga	Oye, ¿cuánto tiempo llevas trabajando aquí?
Joven	Tres años.
Marga	Y ¿cuántos sois en la tienda?
Joven	En la tienda de aquí somos seis ahora mismo.
Marga	Y ¿qué? ¿Tienes otra tienda?
Joven	Tenemos una en Gijón y otra en Avilés.
Marga	Y ¿cuántos soléis tener allí más o menos? ¿Seis también?
Joven	Pues no, vamos, en Gijón sobre unas veinte personas y en Avilés otras cinco o seis aproximadamente.
Marga	Mm ... y ¿qué horario tenéis?
Joven	Pues el horario es de diez a una y cuarto y de cuatro a ocho.
Marga	Y ¿cuántas vacaciones tenéis?
Joven	Treinta días o cuarenta, depende.
Marga	Y ¿os suelen pagar el sueldo a final de mes?
Joven	Sí, el último día del mes.
Marga	Ya, y ¿soléis hacer puentes festivos?
Joven	No, puentes nunca se hacen.
marga	¿Nunca?
Joven	Nunca.
Marga	¿O sea que trabajáis los sábados por la tarde?
Joven	Sábado por la tarde o sábado por la mañana. Depende del horario.

¡oye! hey! Marga uses the familiar form (**tú**) of the verb because she is talking to a young man, **un joven**. Use **oiga** normally.

¿cuánto tiempo llevas trabajando aquí? how long have you been working here? Use **llevar** + the '**-ando** form' of the word to express the amount of time spent on an activity. **Llevo una hora esperando aquí** I have been waiting here for an hour. **Llevar** usually means to carry or wear. You will be looking at '**-ando/-iendo** forms' in Unit 3.

ahora mismo right now; **voy ahora mismo** coming right away

y ¿cuántos soléis tener allí más o menos? how many do you usually have there, more or less? **Soler** to be usual, normal. As you see, it is a stem-changing verb. **Suelo ir todos los días** I usually go every day.

sobre unas veinte personas about twenty people more or less. **Sobre** usually means 'on' but can mean 'about'. **Unos/unas** also means 'approximately'; **unos diez kilómetros** about 10 kilometres.

el horario schedule, time-table. Notice the late opening hours, typical of Spanish shops.

¿os suelen pagar el sueldo a final de mes? do they usually pay your wage at the end of the month? **Sueldo** means either 'wage' or 'salary'.

puentes festivos festival bridges (literally). **Hacer el puente** refers to the practice of taking a holiday on the working days between one day off and another, e.g. at Christmas and New Year. **No, puentes nunca se hacen** no, 'bridges'/days off are never taken; **nunca vamos al teatro** we never go to the theatre.

o sea that is to say. A frequent filler phrase in Spanish.

depende del horario it depends on the schedule; **depende del día** it depends on the day.

PRACTICE

1 Read Conversation 1 again and find the equivalent Spanish phrases to the English sentences below.

a How many are there of you in the shop?

_____

b Do you have another shop?

_____

c About twenty people

_____

d How much holiday do you have?

_____

e The last day of the month

_____

f Do you work on Saturday afternoon?

Answers p. 32

_____

2 Read Teresa's account of her son's first job.

> **Sí, Tomás ya está trabajando – después se seis meses de buscar, fíjate. Que no está mal. Hay muchos jóvenes que llevan buscando trabajo mucho más tiempo que él. Está trabajando en una tienda de vídeo en la calle del Pino. ¿La conoces? Vende todo lo que tiene que ver con música, televisión, discos, discos compactos, DVD, videojuegos, etcétera. Está encantado porque tú sabes cómo le encanta la música moderna. Lleva al menos tres años tocando con su grupo, Los Bárbaros. ¿Sabes que ahora tocan en discotecas y que les pagan? O sea que con el sueldo de la tienda y el del grupo, no está mal. No, que tienen pocas vacaciones – es que sólo son tres en la tienda y es bastante grande con una clientela que viene de todo Oviedo. Y el horario es largo – empieza a las nueve y media y no termina hasta las ocho de la tarde. Pero, nada, está bien – y yo, encantada.**

a How long has Tomás been looking for a job?

_____

b Is his experience typical?

_____

c What sort of shop does he work in?

_____

d Why does he get two sets of wages?

_____

_____

e Why doesn't he have much holiday?

_____

_____

f What hours does he work?

Answers p. 32

_____

3

Listen to Marisa talking about her job and then answer the questions which follow in English.

a Where does Marisa work? _laboratoria._

b To whom does the company belong? _German_

c How many people work for the company in Barcelona? _200_

d And how many in her particular team? _4_

e What nationality is Marisa's boss? _American_

f What are their normal hours of work? _2 - 5·30   8·30 - 1_

g What happens on Fridays? _4_

h How many weeks holiday do they have? _6_

i How many weeks holiday do they have in summer? _4_

j Why do they have to work sometimes on Saturday? _____

falta, mucho trabajas,

Answers p. 32

4

Now Guillermo asks you about _your_ job. You will be using **somos**, **trabajo** and **trabajamos**.

Making paella valenciana

Paqui

Para hacer una paella, necesitas aceite, ajo, pimiento, cebolla,

necesitas aceite, ajo y pimiento you need oil, garlic and pepper
se añade el arroz you add the rice

calamares, gambas, pollo, azafrán, arroz, sal y pimienta. Primero, calientas el aceite y fríes el ajo en el aceite hasta que se dore. Luego, se añade el pollo con el pimiento etcétera. Una vez que, pasados diez minutos, se añade el resto, como es los calamares o las gambas: se mezcla todo otra vez y luego se añade el arroz. Se añade el arroz y el azafrán, se mezcla bien y se le añade el agua, por taza de arroz dos de agua y nada más. Se decora con gambas etcétera, con limón, con huevo cocido y está lista para servir.

para hacer una paella in order to make a paella. Use **para** + infinitive to mean 'in order to'. **Para ir a Valencia, tienes que …** in order to go to Valencia, you have to …

necesitas aceite, ajo, pimiento you need oil, garlic, pepper. **Pimiento** (with an 'o' on the end) refers to the vegetable. **Pimienta** (with an 'a' to go with s<u>a</u>l, salt) is pepper, the condiment.

cebolla, calamares, gambas onion, squid, prawns

azafrán y arroz saffron and rice. Two ingredients essential to Southern Spanish cooking. Both are masculine.

calientas el aceite y fríes el ajo you heat the oil and fry the garlic. Notice how Paqui uses the 'you form' (as in English) to give instructions. **Calentar** 'to heat' and **freír** 'to fry' are both stem-changing verbs. **Calentar** behaves like **preferir** ('e' to 'ie') and **freír** like **pedir** ('e' to 'i').

hasta que se dore until it goes golden brown; **dorarse** to go golden brown. The phrase **hasta que** 'until' takes a special form of the verb called the subjunctive. Don't worry about this for the moment.

luego se añade el pollo then you add the chicken; **añadirse** to add. Paqui now switches from the 'tú' form of the verb to

giving instructions with **se**. (See Grammar section in this unit.) Note for now that if you add two things, you should say **se añaden – se añaden los huevos** you add the eggs.

una vez que, pasados diez minutos once that, after ten minutes have passed. Paqui changes her mind as to what to say in mid-sentence. Don't be fazed by this – it's very common in normal speech.

se mezcla todo otra vez you mix everything again; **mezclarse** to mix; **otra vez** (literally) another time.

por taza de arroz, dos de agua for (each) cup of rice, two of water. Use **por** when talking about measurements. **Lo venden por metro** they sell it by the metre.

huevo cocido hard-boiled egg (literally, 'egg cooked'); **huevos revueltos** scrambled eggs; **huevo frito** fried egg; **huevo pasado por agua** soft-boiled egg.

lista para servir ready to serve. **Estoy listo/a** I'm ready.

5 How many of these can you remember? Label each drawing with its Spanish equivalent.

a _____   b _____

c _____   d _____

e _____   f _____

Answers p. 32

6 Marisa is discussing a top model called Cristina Barreiros. Listen carefully and then note down in the two columns below what she can and cannot eat.

Permitido	Prohibido

Answers p. 32

7

Now listen to Guillermo telling you how to prepare **una tortilla española** (a Spanish omelette) and see if you can answer the questions.

a What four ingredients do you need to make the tortilla?

_____

b What is the first ingredient that you prepare?

_____

c What do you add to this ingredient?

_____

d What ingredient do you heat?

_____

e How long do you have to fry the **tortilla** before taking it off the heat?

Answers p. 32

_____

8

This time Marisa asks you how you make **una tortilla francesa** (a simple omelette). You will use the following phrases: **se necesita(n)**, **se bate(n)** (you beat), **se añade**, **se calienta** and **se fríe**.

You look gorgeous!

Marga ¡Estás guapísima!
¿Qué haces para
mantenerte así?

Carmen ¡Uy bueno! Pues, no

LISTEN FOR...	
¡estás guapísima!	you look gorgeous!
procuro tomar bastantes frutas	I try to eat a lot of fruit

sé, la verdad es que no hago mucho. Pero sí, que soy bastante cuidadosa con el tipo de comida que tomo y eso. Por ejemplo, procuro tomar bastantes frutas y verduras frescas y ensaladas y cosas así y no tomar mucha grasa, porque no, creo que no son muy buenas para la piel y eso, sobre todo. Y además también me gusta hacer un poco de ejercicio de vez en cuando, por ejemplo, eh una vez a la semana voy por las tardes a clase de yoga.

Marga Y ¿practicas algún deporte más?

Carmen No, la verdad es que no tengo mucho tiempo para practicar más deporte. A veces, juego al squash pero no con mucha frecuencia.

¡estás guapísima! you look gorgeous! **guapo/a** handsome, beautiful; **guapísimo/a**, very handsome/very beautiful. This is a good example of where using **estar** or **ser** changes the meaning of the sentence. **Ser guapo/a** means that you are beautiful (always) but **estás guapo/a** means that you look particularly good today. **¡Tu nuevo novio es muy guapo!** your new boyfriend is really good-looking!

¿qué haces para mantenerte así? what do you do (in order) to keep yourself like that?

¡uy bueno! heavens, well … Carmen uses a lot of useful words in this conversation to keep the ball rolling: **y eso** and all that; **pues** well; **por ejemplo** for example; **cosas así** things like that.

soy bastante cuidadosa I am quite careful. **Cuidado** care; **ten(ga) cuidado** take care.

el tipo de comida the type of food; **la comida** food or meal

procuro tomar bastantes frutas I try to eat/take quite a lot of fruit. **Fruta** is usually used in the singular. **Le gusta mucho la fruta** he really loves fruit. **Procurar** to try.

verduras frescas fresh greens. Spaniards differentiate between **verduras** green vegetables, and **legumbres** vegetables like peas, beans (legumes).

no tomar mucha grasa not to eat much fat. **Grasiento/a** fatty.

la piel the skin. Facial skin or complexion is **la tez**.

además besides

¿practicas algún deporte? do you play any sport?

de vez en cuando from time to time. The plural of **vez** is **veces**: **a veces/algunas veces** sometimes; **tres veces a la semana** three times a week.

---

9 According to what Carmen says in Conversation 3 about how she tried to keep fit and well, which of these statements would you consider to be true (**verdad**) and which false (**mentira**)?

		verdad	mentira
a	Como muchas cosas fritas – huevos fritos, patatas fritas – cosas así.	☐	☐
b	No me gustan nada las coles de Bruselas, la lechuga, la coliflor, ni las judías verdes.	☐	☐
c	Me encanta todo tipo de fruta – uvas, manzanas, ciruelas, naranjas.	☐	☐
d	Intento hacer un poco de ejercicio todos los días – algunas veces es sólo ir a pie a la oficina, pero …	☐	☐
e	Soy una fanática del deporte – juego al bádminton todos los días y los fines de semana hago cien largos en la piscina.	☐	☐

Answers p. 32

10 Guillermo has lost a lot of weight and now is really quite slim (**delgado**). Listen to Guillermo and Marisa talking about his diet and then tick the four statements which were actually said.

a Me quedo allí una hora, nadando. ☐

b No como ni pan, ni patatas ni pasteles. ☐

c ¡Qué delgado estás! ☐

d ¿No me ves más delgado? ☐

e No tengo ningún secreto. ☐

f Me siento muchísimo mejor. ☐

g Bueno, por la noche, como fruta o una galleta. ☐

h ¡Soy muy disciplinado! ☐

i También hago ejercicio por lo menos cinco veces a la semana. ☐

Answers p. 32

j He perdido diez kilos desde junio. ☐

11

Read this short report about a new American product and then answer the questions which follow.

> Una empresa estadounidense está produciendo ya la patata frita **light**, o sea, una patata frita hecha con muy poco aceite. Tampoco tiene mucha sal. También se está estudiando la posibilidad de fabricar una patata frita hecha con un sustituto de grasa. Con un producto así, una persona a dieta podría comer un plato **light** pero atractivo cuando le apetece, sin ingerir demasiadas calorías.

a What two ingredients is this new product low on?

_____

b What new product does this company have in mind?

_____

c What two advantages would this product have for the dieter?

_____

Answers p. 32

12

Now you talk about your diet and fitness régime to Guillermo. You'll be using **como** and **bebo**.

KEY WORDS
AND PHRASES

llevo 3 meses trabajando aquí	I've been working here for 3 months
somos seis	there are six of us
¿qué horario tenéis?	what schedule do you have?
¿cuántas vacaciones tenéis?	how much holiday do you have?
el sueldo	salary, wage
hacer el puente	to 'make the bridge'
depende del horario	it depends on the schedule
para hacer una paella …	to make a paella …
necesitas …	you need …
(el) aceite	oil
(el) ajo	garlic
(el) pimiento	pepper (vegetable)
(el) sal	salt
(la) pimienta	pepper (condiment)
(los) calamares	squid
(las) gambas	prawns
(el) arroz	rice
(el) azafrán	saffron
(el) huevo cocido	hard-boiled egg
se añade	you add
se mezcla	you mix
se decora	you decorate
se dora	you brown
una tortilla española	a Spanish omelette
una tortilla francesa	a plain omelette
¡estás guapísimo/a!	you look wonderful!
¡es un chico muy guapo!	he's a good-looking boy!
procuro tomar fruta y verdura	I try to eat fruit and greens
no tomo mucha grasa	I don't eat much fat
¿practicas algún deporte?	do you play any sport?
juego al squash	I play squash
voy a clase de yoga	I go to a yoga class

GRAMMAR AND EXERCISES

Se

This little word crops up all over the place in Spanish and has a variety of meanings. Here are two.

■ Use it with reflexive verbs – that is, verbs which reflect back on themselves: **se levanta siempre a las siete de la mañana** he always gets (himself) up at seven in the morning; **se acuesta a la medianoche** she goes (gets herself) to bed at midnight.

■ Use it to convey the meaning 'you' or 'one' in sentences like those which Paqui used in Conversation 2.

Se añade el arroz.   You add rice.

If the noun is plural, make the verb plural too.

Se añaden los huevos.   You add the eggs.

13 Your friend gives you directions for going to his new house, using the '**tú** form'. You convey the same directions to someone else – but this time, use **se** + the third person. The first example would be **se tiene que hacer lo siguiente** you must do the following.

a   Bueno, para ir al nuevo piso, tienes que hacer lo siguiente.

_____

b   Desde la universidad, puedes coger el autobús número 192.

_____

c   Si prefieres, puedes ir andando (pero está un poquito lejos).

_____

d   Si coges el autobús, bajas justo fuera del hospital.

_____

e   Cruzas la calle y subes la calle Montero hasta el parque.

_____

f   Pasado el parque coges la calle Serrano, a la derecha.

_____

g   Sigues todo recto hasta el número 27, que es mi casa. ¡No puedes perderte!

_____

| Answers p. 32 |

Negatives

To make a sentence negative, simply place **no** in front of the verb.

Voy a Madrid este verano.   I'm going to Madrid this summer.

No voy a Madrid este verano.   I'm not going to Madrid this summer.

There are other negative words too, like **nunca** never, **nadie** no one, **nada** nothing, **ni ... ni ...** neither ... nor ...

If you use these *after* the verb, you also need to use **no** before.

No voy nunca a Madrid.   I never go to Madrid.
No me conoce nadie.   No-one knows me.
No veo nada.   I can't see anything.
No están ni Carlos ni María.   Neither Carlos nor María are here.

If you use these words *before* the verb, you don't need to use **no** before. This is a little less colloquial than using the double negative.

Nunca voy a Madrid.   I never go to Madrid.
Nadie viene por la tarde.   Nobody comes in the afternoon.
Nada más gracias.   No more thank you.

You can often use these negatives on their own.

¿Quién viene conmigo? Nadie.   Who's coming with me? No-one.
¿Qué tienes allí? Nada.   What do you have there? Nothing.
¿Vas muy a menudo a Valencia? Nunca.   Do you often go to Valencia? Never.

14   Write down the opposites of these statements, using the simple, single, negative form.
For example: **Voy siempre al cine. Nunca voy al cine.**

a   Voy a Barcelona este fin de semana.

_____

b   La familia siempre va al cine los jueves.

_____

c   Todo el mundo va al teatro los lunes por la tarde.

_____

d   Juan y Tomás están en casa.

_____

e   ¿Quién está allí? Susana.

_____

Answers p. 32

15   Now for negatives *after* the verb. Translate the word in brackets.

a   No juego (never) al squash ahora. _____

b   No viene (no-one) a vernos. _____

c   No ha pasado (nothing). _____

d   No han venido (neither) Javier (nor) Pablo. _____

e   No me dice (never) si va a salir. _____

Answers p. 32

Paying compliments (hacer cumplidos)

In Conversation 3, Marga told Carmen she looked **guapísima**. You can pay people compliments in several ways.

- Use **estás** (or **eres** if you mean 'always') + **muy** + adjective. ¡**Estás muy guapa**! ¡**Estás guapísima**! (add **ísimo/a/os/as** to most adjectives to mean 'very', extremely). ¡**Eres muy inteligente**!
- Or you can simply use ¡**Qué ...**! ¡**Qué guapa estás**! ¡**Qué inteligente eres**!

16 You have just seen your neighbour's new baby son. Write down six compliments about him for his proud mother, using some of the following adjectives, e.g. ¡**Qué guapo está**!
Remember that sometimes both **es** or **está** are appropriate. All answers use the '**qué** construction'.

guapo	inteligente	espabilado (alert)	gordo	grande
	delgado	lindo (lovely)	rico (sweetie)	

_____ _____

_____ _____

_____ _____

Answers p. 32

Stem-changing verbs (e ▷ i)

Some verbs change their stem from '**e**' to '**i**' in the present tense. (They are often called 1236 verbs – look at the forms to see why). **Pedir** 'to ask for' or 'to order' is the most common example of this, but Paquita used **freír** 'to fry' in her recipe, and **medir** 'to measure' is another common verb with this change. **Mi hermano mide 1.85** my brother is 1.85 metres tall.

You may also want to know **reír** to laugh, and **sonreír** to smile. With **freír**, **reír** and **sonreír**, there is an accent on the '**i**'. **Río** I laugh.

pedir – to ask for, order

1	pido	2	pides	3	pide
4	pedimos	5	pedís	6	piden

17 Use the correct form of the verb in each sentence.

a Yo (medir) 1.74. _____

b Y tú ¿cuánto (medir)? _____

c Se (freír) la cebolla primero. _____

d Se (freír) los huevos. _____

e Yo siempre (pedir) coca cola y mi marido casi siempre (pedir) un whisky. _____

_____

f ¡Qué niño más rico! – (sonreír) todo el día. _____

Answers p. 32

AND FINALLY...

18 You get caught up in a survey. Guillermo asks you about your everyday life, your work, eating habits and level of fitness. You will be using the words and phrases from Conversations 1, 2 and 3.

19 Here is a quiz about your life-style. If you are working with a partner, ask each other the questions in the questionnaire below and tick off the appropriate responses. You'll notice that the questionnaire uses **usted**, but if you prefer, use the '**tú** form'. If you are working alone, read the questions out loud and then give your own answers out loud too.

¿Cuánto tiempo lleva trabajando en su trabajo actual?

menos de un año ☐   un año ☐   dos años ☐   tres años ☐

más de tres años ☐   no trabajo ☐

¿Con cuántas personas trabaja usted?

trabajo solo ☐   con una persona ☐   con dos ☐

con cuatro ☐   con más de cuatro ☐

¿Cuántas horas trabaja usted por semana?

no trabajo ☐   menos de 20 ☐   20-30 ☐   30-40 ☐   más de 40 ☐

¿Trabaja usted los fines de semana?

nunca ☐   algunas veces ☐   siempre ☐

¿Cuántas veces por semana hace algún tipo de ejercicio?

no hago ejercicio ☐   una vez ☐   dos veces ☐   tres veces ☐

más de tres veces ☐

¿Cuántas veces al día come usted fruta y verduras?

no como ni fruta ni verduras ☐   una vez ☐   dos veces ☐

más de dos veces ☐

¿Cuántas veces al día toma usted comida frita?

no tomo comida frita ☐   una vez ☐   dos veces ☐

más de dos veces ☐

¿Cuántas veces a la semana toma usted bebidas alcohólicas?

nunca ☐   una vez ☐   dos veces ☐   tres veces ☐

más de tres veces ☐

¿Cuántos cigarillos fuma usted al día?

no fumo ☐   menos de 5 ☐   5-10 ☐   más de 10 ☐   más de 20 ☐

EXERCISE 1

(a) ¿Cuántos sois en la tienda? **(b)** ¿Tienes otra tienda? **(c)** Sobre unas veinte personas. **(d)** ¿Cuántas vacaciones tenéis? **(e)** El último día del mes. **(f)** ¿Trabajáis los sábados por la tarde?

EXERCISE 2

(a) 6 months. **(b)** No, other young people have to look for longer. **(c)** A video and television shop. **(d)** He gets a wage from the shop and money for playing in the band. **(e)** There are only 3 in the shop and there is a large clientele. **(f)** 9.30-8.00.

EXERCISE 3

(a) in a laboratory **(b)** A German company **(c)** 200 **(d)** 4 **(e)** American **(f)** 8.30 to 1.00 and 2 to 5.30 **(g)** they leave at 4.00 **(h)** 6 **(i)** 1 month **(j)** If they have a lot of work or someone is absent or ill

EXERCISE 5

(a) ajo **(b)** sal y pimienta **(c)** pimiento **(d)** cebolla **(e)** calamares **(f)** gambas

EXERCISE 6

allowed: fruit, water, tomato juice and wine; forbidden: meat, milk, cheese, coffee and tea

EXERCISE 7

(a) potatoes, eggs, oil and salt **(b)** potatoes **(c)** salt and pepper **(d)** oil **(e)** till golden

EXERCISE 9

False: **(a)**, **(b)**, **(e)**; the rest are true

EXERCISE 10

(a), **(c)**, **(e)**, **(i)** were all said

EXERCISE 11

(a) oil and salt **(b)** chips made with substitute fat **(c)** You can eat chips when you feel like them without consuming too many calories.

EXERCISE 13

(b) se puede coger **(c)** se puede ir **(d)** si se coge/se baja **(e)** se cruza/se sube **(f)** se coge **(g)** se sigue

EXERCISE 14

(a) No voy a Barcelona este fin de semana. **(b)** La familia nunca va al cine los jueves. **(c)** Nadie va al teatro los lunes por la tarde. **(d)** Ni Juan ni Tomás están en casa. **(e)** ¿Quién está allí? Nadie.

EXERCISE 15

(a) No juego nunca al squash ahora. **(b)** No viene nadie a vernos. **(c)** No ha pasado nada. **(d)** No han venido ni Javier ni Pablo. **(e)** No me dice nunca si va a salir.

EXERCISE 16

Here are some possibilities: ¡Qué inteligente es! ¡Qué espabilado es/está! ¡Qué gordo es/está! ¡Qué rico es! ¡Qué lindo es/está! ¡Qué delgado es/está!

EXERCISE 17

(a) mido **(b)** mides **(c)** fríe **(d)** fríen **(e)** pido/pide **(f)** sonríe

3

DESCRIBING OBJECTS, EVENTS AND ACTIONS

WHAT YOU WILL LEARN

▶ how to describe objects, using measurements and shapes
▶ how to describe events, using different sorts of adjectives
▶ how to describe actions

POINTS TO REMEMBER

● giving compliments: **¡Qué guapa estás! ¡Eres muy inteligente!**
● using **se** to mean 'you': **se decora con limón**
● how to use negatives: **no voy nunca a Madrid, no hay nadie**
● stem-changing verbs where 'e' becomes 'i': **pido, mido**

BEFORE YOU BEGIN

Why not try writing out some of the key words, phrases or grammar points on index cards, post-its or scraps of paper? Put them up somewhere that you will see them – near the desk or table where you work, on the fridge or on a kitchen cupboard. Each time you look at them, say them out loud. This activity will keep jogging your memory and won't take up any of your precious time.

My Nikon ...

Gustavo

Sí, tengo una cámara de 35 milímetros, Nikon,

tengo un lente con zoom y teleobjetivo	I have a zoom/telephoto lens
es un modelo reciente de la Nikon	it's a recent Nikon model

con microprocesador. Es un modelo reciente de la Nikon que permite operación programada. Tengo un lente normal de 50 milímetros y tengo un lente con zoom y teleobjetivo de 35 a 125 milímetros. Desafortunadamente es un lente que requiere mucha luz, por la distancia focal. Tengo además un lente gran angular, de 28 mm. Todo el equipo se puede operar también con flash electrónico y por supuesto, poseo todos los aditamentos de limpieza que se requieren para mantener un equipo de fotografía en condiciones de operación.

tengo una cámara de 35 milímetros I have a 35 millimetre camera. The easiest way to say something is an amount of mm long/wide etc. is to say: **la caja tiene 115 mm de largo** (long), **55 mm de ancho** (wide), **150 mm de alto** (high), **15 mm de hondo** (deep).

la Nikon. Names of companies are always feminine in Spanish. **Trabajo con la Ford, con la Seat**. This is because **la empresa/la compañia** is understood.

que permite which allows. Use **que** to mean 'which' or 'that'. Later examples are **que requiere** which requires and **que se requieren** which are needed/one needs.

tengo un lente normal I have a normal lens; **lente** can be either masculine or feminine; **lentillas** (f.p.) are contact lenses.

un teleobjetivo a telephoto lens

desafortunadamente unfortunately; **afortunadamente** fortunately. Sometimes, you can place the prefix **des** in front of a word to create its opposite: **agradable** agreeable; **desagradable** disagreeable.

es un lente que requiere mucha luz it's a lens which needs a lot of light; **requerir** to require. **La luz** (**las luces**) is like **la vez** (**las veces**).

por la distancia focal because of the focal distance. **Por** is used in several different contexts (**por favor** please, **por aquí** along here). Here, it is a neat way of giving a reason. **Lo hago por mi hijo** I'm doing this because of, on account of, my son.

tengo además un lente gran angular I also have a wide-angle lens; **además** besides.

todo el equipo all the equipment. **Equipo** often means a team (**un equipo de fútbol**) but here it means equipment or kit: **Mi equipo de sonido** my sound system.

por supuesto of course. You can also say **claro**.

poseo todos los aditamentos de limpieza I own all the cleaning equipment; **aditamentos** accessories, equipment; **poseer** to possess, to own.

para mantener (in order) to maintain. Always use the infinitive of the verb after **para**: **para aprender español** (in order) to learn Spanish, **para ir a Buenos Aires** to go to Buenos Aires.

1 Dimensions. Look at the drawings (**b–e**) of four household objects and complete the sentences which describe them, as shown in example **a**. Try saying each sentence out loud when you've finished. You'll need **centímetro**, **vídeo**, **teléfono**, **calculadora** and **estantería** (shelves).

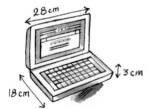

a *El computador tiene 18 cm de hondo, 28 cm de ancho y 3 cm de alto.*

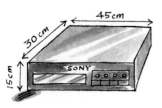

b _____

_____

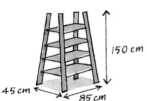

c _____

_____

d _____

_____

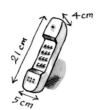

e _____

_____

Answers p. 48

2 Listen to Guillermo and Marisa describing objects. Write the number under the object it describes.

a _____   b _____

c _____   d _____

e _____   Answers p. 48

3 Read the following description of a television and tick if this model has the features listed below. Write in the Spanish equivalent.

T E L E V I S O R

Tubo de imagen Black Line 84 cm. Tecnología digital 100 hz. Consumo en standby, 1 watt. 100 memorias de programas. Multinorma: Pal, Secam, NTSC. Teletexto. Guía de usuario. Mando a distancia. Protección de uso de cualquier canal. Potencia de sonido 2x25 W. Ampliable con sintonizador satélite estéreo interno. Estante de cristal. Vídeo opcional no incluido. Disponible en negro y gris

FEATURES

glass stand _____

teletext _____

special digital effects _____

available in black and grey _____

users' guide _____

wide-angle screen _____

Answers p. 48   optional video not included _____

4 Now Guillermo asks you about your new camera. You'll be using: **una lente, un zoom, un teleobjetivo** and **un flash**.

The bambuco

Gustavo

Sí, mira, en Neiva se celebra la fiesta del bambuco. La

LISTEN FOR...

es un ritmo típico colombiano	it's a typical Colombian rhythm
son colores vistosísimos	they are very bright colours
la gente toma muchísimo aguardiente	the people drink a lot of rum

fiesta del bambuco se celebra para festejar el ritmo del bambuco, que es un ritmo típico colombiano y en esta fiesta se corona a la reina del bambuco, que se escoge por atributos físicos, y talento artístico, ya que se supone que debe bailar y cantar muy bien el bambuco. Además, la gente obviamente toma grandes cantidades de aguardiente en esta fiesta.

Claudia

Otra fiesta importantísima es los carnavales de Barranquilla. Esto se prepara con mucho tiempo de anticipación. La gente, las familias completas, ensayan sus danzas folklóricas durante mucho tiempo, preparan sus disfraces para las comparsas, son colores vistosísimos. La gente baila mucho en las calles, toma muchísimo aguardiente. Además, se echa mucha maizena ¿no?

Gustavo

Eh, la maizena es harina de maíz.

Claudia

Es harina blanca, es muy fina, que se la echa en la cabeza, en el pelo.

Neiva is a town in Colombia.

se celebra la fiesta del bambuco the bambuco festival is celebrated. The **bambuco**, as Gustavo explains later, is a particular dance rhythm from Colombia. Notice how both he and Claudia use the '**se**/one form' to convey the passive (is celebrated, is crowned etc.).

para festejar in order to celebrate

se corona a la reina you/they/one crown(s) the queen (or, the queen is crowned). Notice how Spanish needs to use what is called the personal '**a**' before an object, if this is a person: **Juan ve a su hermana** Juan sees his sister, but **Juan ve el coche** Juan sees the car.

que se escoge por atributos físicos y talento artístico who they choose (or is chosen) because of her physical attributes and her artistic talent.

ya que se supone que debe bailar since it's taken for granted that she must dance. **Ya**

que is a useful connecting phrase meaning 'given that', 'since'. **Suponer** to suppose; **Supongo que está en casa** I suppose s/he is at home.

aguardiente burning water (literally)! This refers to all sorts of spirits, depending on which country you are in, but since Gustavo is Colombian, he is probably referring to rum, **aguardiente de caña**.

otra fiesta importantísima another very important festival

los carnavales the carnival. Carnival time is in February, just before Lent. The most famous Carnivals in the Latin world are in the Canary Islands and in Río.

mucho tiempo de anticipación a long time in advance. Most Spaniards would use the word **antelación** rather than **anticipación**.

ensayan sus danzas folklóricas they practise their traditional dances; **ensayar** to practise.

---

preparan sus disfraces para las
comparsas they prepare their costumes (literally, disguises) for the parades. Notice again how 'z' changes to 'c' in the plural (**disfraz, disfraces**).

son colores vistosísimos they are very vivid colours; **vistoso** vivid, lively.

se echa mucha maizena they throw a lot of maize flour (or, a lot of maize flour is thrown); **echar** to throw.

harina flour. Those of you who know French will recognise this from 'farine', French for 'flour'. An 'f' in French often changes to 'h' in Spanish: 'fuir' in French becomes **huir** to escape, flee in Spanish.

PRACTICE

5 Can you remember how to say:

They/one crown/s _____

They/one prepare/s _____

They/one throw/s _____

They/one choose/s _____

They/one celebrate/s _____

Answers p. 48 They/one suppose/s _____

6 Listen to Guillermo and Marisa discussing two important festivals in Cataluña, **carnavales** and **Sant Jordi**. Then decide whether the following statements are true or false.

	verdad	mentira
In the past it was forbidden to celebrate Carnival.	☐	☐
Carnival is usually in March.	☐	☐
Many activities take place in the street.	☐	☐
The **entierro de la sardina** winds up the proceedings.	☐	☐
Sant Jordi's day is the 23rd April.	☐	☐
On Sant Jordi's day you give a book and a carnation to the person you love.	☐	☐

Answers p. 48

7

Fiestas. Read the following description of the **fiestas** in a small town in Galicia and then answer, in English, the questions which follow.

Las fiestas del Carmen, en Portoviejo, tienen lugar el cuarto fin de semana de agosto. Hay un curioso acto folklórico que consiste de un desfile de carros de la región en los que se representan temas propios del campo como La Vendimia y La Cosecha. Todo eso lo podemos ver el primer día de fiestas. En cambio, el último día se celebra la llamada Fiesta de la Empanada, en la cual todo el pueblo se congrega en la plaza del mercado a comer uno de los platos típicos de Galicia, la empanada. Otra fiesta también popular es la Romería del Faro que tiene lugar el ocho de septiembre en la cual se sube a la Virgen del Faro a una ermita situada en la cima del Monte Faro.

El segundo fin de semana de marzo se celebra la tradicional Feria del Vino en la cual se puede degustar el vino nuevo de los distintos vinicultores de la región, en la cual hay premios para los productores de los mejores vinos.

VOCABULARY	
un desfile de carros	a procession of carts
la vendimia	the grape-harvest
la cosecha	the cereal harvest
la empanada	type of pie or pasty filled usually with fish or pork
la ermita	a hermitage, shrine

a When are the **fiestas del Carmen**?

_____

b What happens on the first day of the **fiestas**?

_____

c What happens on the last day?

_____

d Where is the statue of Our Lady of the Lighthouse taken on the 8th of September? _____

_____

e What is special about the wine served at the **Feria del Vino**?

_____

_____

f Who receives the prizes?

Answers p. 48

_____

8

Now Guillermo asks you about a festival you have in your home town – the Queen of Flowers **la reina de las flores**. You'll be using: **se llama, se celebra, se corona, se echa** and **vistosísimo**.

Latin gestures

		LISTEN FOR...
	de arriba para abajo	up and down
	me tienen hasta acá arriba	I'm fed up to here!

Carmen Hm, sí, cuando se hace así, que es poniendo la mano hacia arriba, y haciendo movimientos intermitentes, de unir y separar los dedos, los cuatro dedos juntos contra el dedo gordo. Eso significa que hay mucha gente, que un sitio está lleno de gente.

Andrés Mover la mano de arriba para abajo, golpeando los dedos. Esto significa gran cantidad de algo, mucho, demasiado.

Daniel Hay varios gestos, uno de ellos es poner la mano unos treinta centímetros sobre la cabeza. El significado de esto es decir me tienen hasta acá arriba, en la coronilla.

Verónica Por ejemplo, para preguntar a alguna persona que está en una feria, vendiendo algo, cuánto cuesta, uno coloca tres dedos juntos y los roza, uno con otro, diciendo ¿cuánto vale?

These gestures are widely used throughout Spanish-speaking countries.

cuando se hace así when you do this; **así** means 'like this'.

poniendo putting, **haciendo** doing. More about present participles (words ending in '-ing') on page 46.

hacia arriba upwards; **hacia abajo** downwards; **hacia** on its own means 'towards'.

de unir y separar los dedos bringing together (uniting) and separating the fingers; **un dedo** a finger or toe; **el dedo gordo** the thumb or big toe. After a preposition (small connecting words like **a**, **de**, **con**), the verb is almost always in the infinitive: **va a ir a Londres** he is going to go to London.

un sitio está lleno de gente a place is full of people. **Lleno** and its opposite **vacío** (empty) always take the verb **estar**.

golpeando los dedos knocking the fingers together; **golpear en la puerta** to hammer on the door. Andrés is describing the gesture where you shake your hand up and down.

algo something. This word is invariable (never changes its form) and is linked with the adjective **alguno/a** some. Later on, Verónica uses the phrase **alguna persona** some person.

demasiado too much

sobre la cabeza over the head

me tienen hasta acá arriba I'm fed up to here (literally they have me up here above). Another common expression is **estoy hasta la coronilla**, which means the same; **la coronilla** literally means the 'crown of your head'.

para preguntar (in order) to ask

una feria a fair or market

vendiendo algo selling something

uno coloca tres dedos juntos y los roza one places three fingers together and rubs them; **colocar** is an alternative to **meter** or **poner**, to put or place; **rozar** to rub.

diciendo saying

PRACTICE

9 '-ando' and '-iendo'. Link up the Spanish with its English equivalent.

vendiendo	doing/making
preguntando	dancing
diciendo	knocking
bailando	singing
poniendo	selling
cantando	asking
haciendo	putting
golpeando	saying

Answers p. 48

10 More gestures. Listen to the description of these gestures and match them up with the appropriate photo.

You'll hear the word **suerte** luck, **el dedo índice** the index finger, **la sien** temple, **la nariz** nose, and **sospechar** to suspect.

a _____

b _____

c _____

d _____

e _____

f _____

Answers p. 48

11 Read this description of a gesture and then decide what you think it means.

Si, por ejemplo, sueles acercar la mano con los dedos unidos hacia la boca, sueltas un beso y en el momento que das un beso, alejas la mano, este gesto significa que:

a **quieres comer algo**

b **una cosa te gusta mucho**

c **estás diciendo adiós a un/a amigo/a**

VOCABULARY	
la boca	the mouth
soltar un beso	to blow a kiss
alejar	to move away

Answers p. 48

12 Look at the sketches below and label each part. You'll find the vocabulary you need in the box.

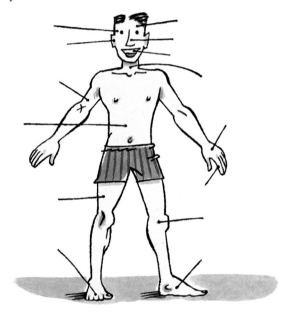

el dedo	la cara	el pie	la pierna
la boca	el estómago	el brazo	el tobillo
la mano	los ojos	la rodilla	la nariz
el cuello	la oreja		

Answers p. 48

KEY WORDS AND PHRASES

tengo una cámara de 35 mm	I have a 35 mm camera
tengo un(a) lente normal de 50 mm	I have a normal 50 mm lens
tiene 25 mm de ancho	it is 25 mm wide
tiene 15 mm de hondo	it is 15 mm deep
tiene 30 mm de largo	it is 30 mm long
tiene 20 mm de alto	it is 20 mm high
en ... se celebra la fiesta de ...	in ... they celebrate the feast of ...
es un ritmo típico colombiano	it's a typical Colombian rhythm
otra fiesta importantísima	another very important fiesta
son colores vistosísimos	they are very vivid colours
la gente baila mucho en las calles	the people dance a lot in the streets
la gente toma muchísimo aguardiente	the people drink a lot of rum
la cabeza	head
el estómago	stomach
el dedo	finger
el dedo gordo	thumb or big toe
cuando se hace así	when you go like this
eso significa que ...	that means that ...
hay mucha gente	there are a lot of people
un sitio está lleno de gente	a place is full of people
de arriba para abajo	up and down
gran cantidad de algo	a lot of something
demasiado	too much
algo	something
afortunadamente	fortunately
desafortunadamente	unfortunately
por supuesto	of course
además	also, besides
estoy hasta la coronilla	I've had it up to here
golpeando	knocking, shaking
poniendo	putting
haciendo	doing/making
vendiendo	selling
diciendo	saying

More about adjectives

- Shortened adjectives. When placed *before* a noun in the singular, a few adjectives drop their final letter(s):
- **grande** becomes **gran** before masculine and feminine singular nouns
  un gran hombre – a great man (**un hombre grande** would mean 'a large or tall man')
  una gran mujer – a great woman
- Before a masculine singular the following changes take place:

bueno ▷ **buen**	**un buen día**
malo ▷ **mal**	**un mal día**
primero ▷ **primer**	**el primer piso**
tercero ▷ **tercer**	**el tercer piso**
alguno ▷ **algún**	**algún día**
ninguno ▷ **ningún**	**no hay ningún problema; no ... ningún** no/none at all works just like **nada**, **nadie**, **nunca** etc.

13 Translate the following phrases:

a a great/large fiesta _____

b good weather _____

c bad weather _____

d the third man _____

e the first book _____

f some problem _____

Answers p. 48

- Position of adjectives. Most adjectives go after the noun they refer to except some of the more common ones (like those listed above). Some adjectives change their meaning according to whether they go before or after the noun – like **grande**. Other examples are **antiguo**: **mi antiguo colegio** my former school, but **un colegio antiguo** an ancient school; **pobre**: **un pobre hombre** a wretched man, but **un hombre pobre** a poor (not rich) man.

- '**ísimo, ísima, ísimos, ísimas**'. In Conversation 3, Claudia used these forms with adjectives to intensify their meaning:
  colores vistosos vivid colours; **colores vistosísimos** very vivid colours.
  mucho aguardiente a lot of rum; **muchísimo aguardiente** an awful lot of rum.
  Look out for the spelling change with words which end in '**co**' to '**quísimo**': **rico** rich, **riquísimo** very rich; **poco** few, little; **poquísimo** very few, very little.

14 Your brother has a new girl friend whom he thinks is wonderful. Change each of the adjectives below to ones ending in '**ísimo/a/os/as**', omitting the **muy** along the way.

Belén es una chica muy linda, muy inteligente, muy simpática, muy preciosa. Tiene los ojos muy oscuros, la voz muy suave y unas manos muy delicadas.

_____

_____

_____

_____

_____

_____

_____ | Answers p. 48 |

Measurements

The easiest way to give measurements is as follows:
La caja (box) **tiene 25 centímetros de largo** (long).
                                15   **de ancho** (wide).
                                10   **de hondo** (deep).
                                10   **de alto** (high).

Other ways of talking about measurements are:
Mi dormitorio mide/tiene 8 metros por 6.
Yo mido 1.75.
Peso (I weigh) **62 kilos.**

Most adjectives which describe objects are similar to the English:
ovalado, triangular, rectangular, cuadrado (square) and **redondo** (round)

15 Your neighbour's baby son is six months old. Here she is describing him. Work out the correct form of the word in brackets.

Javier tiene seis meses y ya (measures) **70 cms.** (He weighs) **8 kilos. Tiene una cara** (round), **y los dedos** (wide). **Su cabeza es** (square). **¡Es riquísimo!**

| Answers p. 48 |

Present participles (verb + '-ing')

To express the English verb + '-ing' (going, walking, jumping etc.), form the present participle in these ways:

- '-ar verbs' add '-ando'. **Andar, andando** (walking)
- '-er and -ir verbs' add '-iendo'. **Coger, cogiendo** (catching), **subir, subiendo** (going up)

Some stem-changing verbs also change the vowel in the present participle:
durmiendo sleeping, **prefiriendo** preferring, **pidiendo** ordering, **viniendo** coming

16 You're very busy in the kitchen but none of your family wants to help you. They're all busy doing something else. Describe exactly what they are doing by putting the verb in brackets into the '-ing form' (present participle).

a   Tu marido está (dormir) la siesta _____

b   Tu hijo pequeño está fuera, (jugar) con sus amigos _____

c   Tu hija mayor se está (lavar) el pelo _____

d   Tu amiga Almudena está (llamar) a su novio _____

e   Tu vecino está (cortar) el césped _____

f   Su mujer está (fregar) los platos _____

¡Tú estás hasta la coronilla!

Answers p. 48

17 Your chance to speak. You've been to a fiesta in Spain and you want to tell Guillermo all about it. You will be describing the people (**la gente**), the costumes (**el disfraz/los disfraces**) and the processions (**las comparsas**). You will also be describing what goes on – so you will need the verbs **bailar**, **beber** and **cantar**.

18 Look at the photographs of Magdalena using a lot of body language. Describe out loud what she is doing. If you are working with a partner, see if they can guess which picture you are describing.

Useful words and phrases:

eso significa que   **¡estoy hasta la coronilla!**   **poner la mano hacia arriba**   **los dedos**

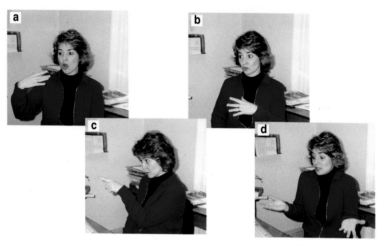

19 Look at these pictures and try saying as much as you can about each one. If you are working with a partner, you could ask them to guess which one you are describing.
Here are some useful words: **lavadora** washing machine, **cafetera** coffee machine, **tostador** toaster.

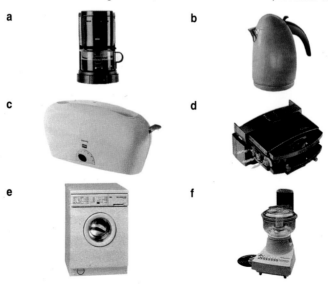

EXERCISE 1

(b) El vídeo tiene 30 cm de hondo, 45 cm de ancho y 15 cm de alto.   (c) La estantería tiene 85 cm de ancho, 45 cm de hondo y 150 cm de alto.   (d) La calculadora tiene 10 cm de ancho, 13 cm de hondo y 1 cm de alto.   (e) El teléfono tiene 21 cm de largo, 5 cm de ancho y 4 cm de alto.

EXERCISE 2

(a) 4   (b) 3   (c) 1   (d) 5   (e) 2

EXERCISE 3

It has teletext, users' guide, glass stand, optional video not included, available in black and grey.

EXERCISE 5

se corona/se prepara/se echa/se escoge/se celebra/se supone

EXERCISE 6

True: forbidden to celebrate Carnival; activities in streets; the entierro de la sardina finishes the proceedings; Sant Jordi's day is the 23rd April. The other two are false (a rose, not a carnation, is given).

EXERCISE 7

(a) 4th weekend in August   (b) a procession of carts   (c) everyone eats **empanada**   (d) to a shrine on the top of Monte Faro   (e) it is new, and made by local wine-makers   (f) the producers of the best wines

EXERCISE 9

vendiendo, selling; preguntando, asking; diciendo, saying; bailando, dancing; poniendo, putting; cantando, singing; haciendo, doing; golpeando, knocking

EXERCISE 10

(a) 3   (b) 1   (c) 6   (d) 2   (e) 4   (f) 5

EXERCISE 11

(b) una cosa te gusta mucho

EXERCISE 12

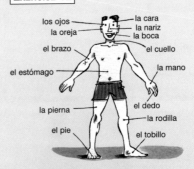

los ojos — la cara
la oreja — la nariz
— la boca
el brazo — el cuello
el estómago — la mano
la pierna — el dedo
— la rodilla
el pie — el tobillo

EXERCISE 13

(a) una gran fiesta   (b) buen tiempo   (c) mal tiempo   (d) el tercer hombre   (e) el primer libro   (f) algún problema

EXERCISE 14

lindísima, inteligentísima, simpatiquísima, preciosísima, oscurísimos, suavísima, delicadísimas

EXERCISE 15

mide/pesa/redonda/anchos/cuadrada

EXERCISE 16

(a) durmiendo   (b) jugando   (c) lavando   (d) llamando   (e) cortando   (f) fregando

4 EXPRESSING OPINIONS

WHAT YOU WILL LEARN
- ▶ how to express opinions
- ▶ how to express surprise
- ▶ how to express continuity

POINTS TO REMEMBER
- ● talking about measurements: **tiene 30cm de ancho, 45cm de alto y 5cm de hondo**
- ● using present participles: **vendiendo, poniendo, haciendo, diciendo**
- ● expressing 'one' or 'they': **se celebra, se corona, se prepara**
- ● saying 'very' with '**ísimo**': **lindísimo, riquísimo, guapísimo**

BEFORE YOU BEGIN
Because there is a lot of new vocabulary to learn once you have reached a second stage language course, it is a good idea to look out for certain language patterns which will increase your vocabulary power. In Unit 3 you saw that adding the prefix '**des**' to a word will create the opposite meaning: **aparecer** to appear, **desaparecer** to disappear; **agradable** agreeable, **desagradable** disagreeable. 'In' has a similar meaning – **justo, injusto**. Keep an eye out for patterns like these.

We travel agents ...

Ismael

Los agentes de viajes tenemos una gran facilidad para efectuar viajes transatlánticos alrededor del mundo, y entre ellos yo he conocido, pues, Brasil, Argentina, Rio de Janeiro, Santo Domingo, hace poco ... Entonces, considero que dentro de estos países sudamericanos que acabo de conocer en un plazo de un año, considero que el más bonito para mí, a mi entender, como paisaje y como amabilidad de la gente, y como encantadores que son, considero que es Rio de Janeiro. Rio de Janeiro es una ciudad preciosa, tiene unos encantos naturales fenomenales y aparte de eso, la gente, como he dicho antes, es fantástica. Es una gente muy agradable, y luego para el español, tiene un funcionamiento de vida bastante económico para nosotros que considero que es interesante hacer unas vacaciones allí.

LISTEN FOR...	
una gran facilidad	great ease
acabo de conocer	I have just got to know
encantos naturales	natural charms

los agentes de viajes tenemos una gran facilidad para efectuar viajes transatlánticos we travel agents can very easily undertake transatlantic journeys. Ismael uses the '**nosotros** form' because he is an **agente de viajes** also. (Literally the travel agents, we ...)

alrededor del mundo around the world; **todo el mundo** everyone

entre ellos yo he conocido amongst these I have known, I have been to. **Conocer** to know, to meet for the first time: **esta mañana he conocido a tu jefe** this morning I met (for the first time) your boss.

hace poco a little while ago. Use **hace** + a time expression to mean 'ago': **hace un año** a year ago

dentro de estos países among these countries

los países sudamericanos que acabo de conocer the South American countries I've just been to. **Acabar de** means 'to have just done something': **acabo de ir al hospital** I've just been to the hospital; **acaba de volver de Argentina** he has just come back from Argentina.

en un plazo de un año in the space of a year; **un plazo** a period; **tenemos un plazo de un mes para pagar la cuenta** we have a month to pay the bill.

considero que I think that; **a mi entender** in my opinion. These phrases express points of view. (See Grammar section in this unit.)

como paisaje as landscape, countryside. Don't confuse this with **el campo** the country. **Voy al campo este fin de semana** I'm going into the country this weekend, but **¡el paisaje de Escocia es fantástico!** the Scottish countryside is fantastic!

como amabilidad de la gente as for the friendliness of the people. Like most nouns ending in '**-dad**', **amabilidad** is feminine.

como encantadores que son as they (the people **gente**) are so charming; **encantadores** charming; **el encanto** charm; **¡este pueblo tiene un encanto!** this town has (such) charm!

como he dicho antes as I said before. This past tense (**he dicho** I have said) is explained in Unit 9.

y luego para el español and then for the Spaniard. Remember that **español/francés/alemán** can refer both to the people and to the language: **los españoles hablan español** Spaniards speak Spanish.

un funcionamiento de vida bastante

económico a fairly economic way of living. An easier way to say this might be **un coste de vida bastante económico**. The opposite would be **bastante alto** quite high.

para nosotros for us

interesante interesting, but also, in the context of prices, 'good value'.

PRACTICE

1 Many places in South, Central and North America were named by Spanish **conquistadores** and settlers in the 15th and 16th century. Match their names with their English equivalent.

a	Palo Alto	1	holy cross
b	Colorado	2	the angels
c	Nevada	3	snowy
d	Santa Cruz	4	tall mast
e	Río Tinto	5	the crossing
f	Florida	6	big river
g	Los Angeles	7	silver river
h	Las Vegas	8	holy faith
i	Río de la Plata	9	the plains
j	Río Grande	10	flowery
k	Santa Fe	11	red
l	El Paso	12	red river

Answers p. 64

2 **Reservas por internet.** Read this short publicity slogan and complete the exercise below.

¿Eres un vago? ¿Estás muy ocupado con tus estudios? ¿Trabajas 25 horas al día? Si contestas que sí o simplemente no quieres desplazarte a tu agencia de viajes, AVCO te lo pone fácil: desde hoy puedes hacer tus reservas directamente desde casa y pagar el viaje dentro de un plazo de dos meses. Mira, mejor no te lo contamos todo, así que visitas nuestras páginas en //WWW.AVCO. ¡Te esperan muchas sorpresas!

Find the Spanish equivalent for:

a are you lazy?

_____

b within a two month period

_____

c to make your reservations

_____

d lots of surprises await you!

_____

e you don't want to go

_____

f it's better we don't tell you

Answers p. 64

3 Listen to Marisa talking about her visit to Madrid.

In the grid below, note down three advantages and two disadvantages to life in Madrid – in Spanish, if you can.

Ventajas	Desventajas
1	1
2	2
3	

Answers p. 64

4 Listen to the recording again and complete these sentences with the correct adjective.

a Fui por _____ vez.

b Una ciudad _____.

c Los madrileños son muy _____.

d El Museo de Arte _____.

e Una ciudad tan _____.

f El coche es muy _____.

5 In this exercise Guillermo asks you all about Valencia and its attractions. You'll be using the following words and phrases:

un coste de vida alto	**gente agradable**	**una ciudad preciosa**
	museos **teatros** **cines**	

Unit 4 Expressing opinions

Problems with English

Marga

Estoy estudiando inglés desde hace un año y medio aproximadamente y lo estoy haciendo porque realmente me gusta, no porque lo necesite para mi

LISTEN FOR...

estoy estudiando inglés	I'm studying English
un inglés coloquial	colloquial English
tu propio idioma	your own language

trabajo, ya que en el trabajo solamente utilizamos un inglés técnico y no es imprescindible conocer un inglés coloquial. Eh, para mí es bastante fácil traducir del inglés al español: lo que ocurre es que cuando intentas hablar en inglés, no dispones de esa fluidez que tienes en tu propio idioma.

estoy estudiando inglés desde hace un año y medio I have been studying English for a year and a half. Note the construction: 'I am studying English since ...' (See Grammar section in this unit – **estoy** + '**-ando**', '**-iendo**'.)

lo estoy haciendo I am doing it (English); **lo** refers to **el idioma** the language.

no porque lo necesite para mi trabajo not because I need it for my work. Marga uses a form of the verb called the subjunctive (**necesite** instead of **necesito**) because she's expanding on a negative idea.

ya que en el trabajo ... given that at work ... **Ya que** is a useful linking phrase. Use **dado que** and **puesto que** to mean the same thing: **dado que no hablo bien francés ...** given that, seeing that, I don't speak French well ...

no es imprescindible it isn't vital. This is quite an emphatic statement. You could just say **no es necesario**, it isn't necessary.

lo que ocurre what happens (literally, that which happens) **lo que pasa** means the same thing.

no dispones de esa fluidez you don't have that fluency (literally, you do not dispose of that fluency); **disponer de** to dispose of

PRACTICE

6 You know that **estoy estudiando** means 'I am studying'. What do you think these phrases mean?

a Estoy traduciendo.

_____

b Estoy utilizando.

_____

c Estoy intentando.

_____

d Estoy hablando.

_____

e Estoy trabajando.

Answers p. 64

_____

7 Listen to Guillermo describing his attempts to learn German and then answer the questions. You'll hear **esto me ayuda mucho** this helps me a lot, and **conocimientos** (m.p.) knowledge.

Now answer these questions:

a How long has Guillermo been learning German?

_____

b Why does he find it quite difficult?

_____

c Why is he studying German? (2 reasons)

_____

_____

d Is he fluent yet?

_____

e What four things does he do to help him with the language?

_____

_____

_____

Answers p. 64

_____

8 **La Escuela de Idiomas.** Read this publicity item about the language school which Marga attended.

En un mundo lleno de oportunidades, el conocimiento de un segundo o tercer idioma es un factor clave para el éxito en la universidad y la expansión de los contactos comerciales dentro y fuera de España. Esta escuela ofrece una amplia gama de cursos de idiomas para facilitar a estudiantes y a otras personas, la comunicación con universitarios y empresarios extranjeros. Entre nuestros clientes se incluyen departamentos de gobierno y agencias, para los que personalizamos y adaptamos nuestros cursos con el objeto de ajustarnos a sus necesidades específicas. Aunque estamos abiertos a cualquier tipo de necesidad, debido a la demanda del mercado, nos especializamos en la enseñanza de los siguientes idiomas:

| inglés británico | inglés americano |
| francés | alemán |
| catalán para extranjeros |
| castellano para extranjeros |

Nuestro personal está formado exclusivamente por profesores nativos, licenciados y con una amplia experiencia profesional. Los alumnos están organizados en grupos pequeños, teniendo en cuenta la edad, el nivel cultural, la profesión y los intereses personales y sociales. Enseñamos según el sistema comunicativo a entender, hablar, leer y escribir. Como soporte, tenemos CD Rom, biblioteca, videoteca y audioteca. ■

Answers p. 64

VOCABULARY

dentro y fuera	inside and out
una amplia gama	a wide selection
un empresario	a business man
la enseñanza	the teaching
el gobierno	the government

Now answer these questions:

a What skill is a key factor (**un factor clave**) for success at university and in commerce?

_____

b What sort of clients does the language school have?

_____

c Which of the six languages taught are spoken in Spain?

_____

d Which three qualities do the teachers have?

_____

e Which four skills do you learn if you follow the **sistema comunicativo**?

_____

f If a **biblioteca** is a 'library', what are a **videoteca** and an **audioteca**?

Answers p. 64   _____

9 Now Marisa asks you about the best way to learn a language. You'll be using these words and phrases: **practicar mucho, la gramática, ir a una clase, una vez.**

A way of defending yourself against women!

Andrés En el País Vasco la gastronomía es una de las aficiones más importantes. Los jóvenes y los hombres vascos tienen sus sedes gastronómicas, las sociedades gastronómicas. Todos ellos, o la mayoría, pertenecen a una de las sociedades.

Carmen Y ¿qué es una sociedad gastronómica?

Andrés Es un local que los hombres alquilan y tienen sus ritos para entrar. Solamente pueden entrar hombres.

Carmen ¿Ah sí? Y ¿eso por qué es?

Andrés Pienso que esto es una derivación, una forma de protegerse. La sociedad vasca es una sociedad, es un matriarcado. Y una forma de defenderse de las mujeres es ...

Carmen ¿Una forma de defenderse de las mujeres? ¡Eso sí que tiene gracia! ¡Vamos, hombre! Ahora resulta que las mujeres estamos aquí reprimiendo a los hombres.

Andrés No, ¡no me esperaba esto!

LISTEN FOR...	
una forma de defenderse de	a way of protecting
las mujeres	yourself from women
¡eso sí que tiene gracia!	that really is funny!
¡no me esperaba eso!	I wasn't expecting that!

el País Vasco the Basque country. This **autonomía**, or 'historic region', is on the Northern coast, bordering on France. It has its own language, culture and traditions – including the **sociedad gastronómica** or 'dining club' which is discussed in this conversation.

las aficiones más importantes the most important hobbies, interests. (More about this kind of adjective, known as the superlative, in Unit 5.)

una sede gastronómica a place where the dining club members meet. **La sede** literally means a 'headquarters': **la sede de Hunosa** the headquarters/head office of Hunosa.

la mayoría the majority. Also, **la mayoría de edad** full legal age.

un local que los hombres alquilan premises which the men rent. **Alquilar** is the verb 'to rent', but **alquiler** is a masculine noun meaning 'hire': **alquiler de coche** car hire.

tienen sus ritos para entrar they have their ceremonies (in order) to enter; **un rito** a rite/ceremony.

pienso que ... I think that ... This is a good way of starting to express an opinion:

pienso que no es aceptable consumir drogas I don't think it is acceptable to take drugs.

una derivación, una forma de protegerse A derivation, a way of protecting oneself. The **se** here means 'yourself' or 'oneself' and as you can see, is tacked on to the end of the infinitive. Later on, Andrés uses the phrase **una forma de defenderse** a way of defending oneself. (See Grammar section in Unit 2.) By derivation, Andrés means that Basque society is derived from **un matriarcado** a matriarchy, a society where women are dominant.

¡eso sí que tiene gracia! that really is funny! A very colloquial phrase. **Gracia** can mean 'charm' or 'wit'; **ella tiene gracia** she has a certain something about her. Use the **sí** for emphasis.

¡vamos hombre! well really! (See Grammar section in this unit.) You don't need to be talking to a man to use **hombre**. **¡Hombre!** is an expression of surprise in any situation.

ahora resulta que ... now it turns out that ...; **resulta que no vamos a Madrid** it turns out that we aren't going to Madrid (after all).

estamos reprimiendo a los hombres we are repressing men; **reprimir** to repress. Notice how you need to add the personal 'a' when the object is a person.

¡no me esperaba eso! I wasn't expecting that! **esperar** to wait for; **estoy esperando a mi mujer** I'm waiting for my wife; **esperarse** to expect.

PRACTICE

10 Match up these dictionary definitions with the vocabulary in the box. Each word has been taken from the dialogue.

a gusto, inclinación _____

b esposa, señora _____

c encanto _____

d sitio _____

e ser propiedad de _____

Answers p. 64 f defenderse _____

> mujer   gracia   protegerse
>
> pertenecer a   afición   local

11 Listen to Guillermo and Carlos discussing traditions in the north of Spain. They mention two fiestas, the **romería** and the **sardinada**. You'll hear the words **santuario** shrine and **gratis** free. Jot down at least three facts about those festivals in English.

La romería	La sardinada
1	1
2	2
3	3

Answers p. 64

12 **Un concurso gastronómico.** Read the rules for a cooking competition in the **País Vasco** and then answer the questions. The answers are all numbers.

111 CONCURSO GASTRONÓMICO DE VILLAFRANCA

día	martes, 8 de agosto, 1998
hora	9.30
lugar	Plaza Nueva de Villafranca

1 Puede participar una pareja de cocineros por sociedad gastronómica.

2 Cada pareja debe dar a la organización un sobre cerrado, indicando el nombre de los participantes, la sociedad a la que representan, conteniendo en su interior la receta, indicando el nombre del plato, sus ingredientes con cantidades aproximadas y la forma de realizar. (Se pueden publicar las recetas en el futuro.)

3 Los participantes disponen de 2 horas para la elaboración del plato.

4 Cantidad a preparar – 4 a 6 raciones.

5 La organización pone a disposición de los participantes espacio, mesa y cocina.

6 El jurado estará compuesto por Mikel Anton, Patxi Larrauri y Juan José Aranguiz.

a How many people are there in each cooking team?

_____

b How many hours are they allowed to cook for?

_____

c For how many people do they have to prepare the meal?

_____

d How many things/items are provided by the organisation?

_____

e How many judges are there?

Answers p. 64

_____

13 In this speaking exercise you explain what Thanksgiving is all about to a Spanish friend. You'll use phrases like **una tradición**, **se come pavo** one eats turkey, **se bebe vino**, **Estados Unidos**.

KEY WORDS
AND PHRASES

acabo de conocer	I have just got to know
acabo de ver	I have just seen
todo el mundo	everyone
la gente	people
dentro	within
fuera	outside
el paisaje	the landscape
una ciudad preciosa	a gorgeous city
en un plazo de un año	within the space of a year
la agencia de viajes	the travel agency
el agente de viajes	the travel agent
hacer la reserva	to make a reservation
un local	a place/premises
alquilar	to hire, rent
estoy estudiando	I am studying
estoy haciendo	I am doing
creo que ...	I think that ...
considero que ...	I think that ...
pienso que ...	I think that ...
en mi opinión	in my opinion
a mi entender	in my opinion
sí, es verdad	yes, that's true
sí, claro	yes, of course
eso no es verdad	that isn't true
no es cierto	it isn't true
lo que ocurre/pasa es ...	what happens is that ...
ya que ...	given that, seeing that ...
¡eso sí que tiene gracia!	that really is funny!
¡no me esperaba eso!	I wasn't expecting that!
¡vamos, hombre!	well, really!

GRAMMAR AND EXERCISES

The continuous tense in the present

In Conversation 2, Marga said **estoy estudiando** I am studying, and **estoy haciendo** I am doing, rather than **estudio** or **hago**. This is because she wants to emphasise that she is doing both these things now. The example below makes things clear:

Hablo inglés y francés   I speak both English and French –
pero ahora, estoy hablando en español   but now, I am speaking in Spanish.

In some cases you can use either tense: the continuous simply emphasises the idea of 'at the moment' or 'right now'.

Forming these tenses is easy. Simply use the appropriate tense of **estar** and add the present participle (the '-ing form') which you learned in Unit 3.

¿Qué estás haciendo?   What are you doing?
Estoy preparando la cena.   I'm making the evening meal.
Estoy leyendo una revista.   I'm reading a magazine.

In later units, you will see how you can use other forms of **estar** as well as the present tense, to make sentences like 'I was doing', 'I will be going' and so on.

14   Look at these sentences in English and decide if you would use **estoy + '-iendo/ando'** or not, in Spanish.

a   I have problems with my health.   _____

b   I speak some German but no Dutch.   _____

c   She's typing a letter at the moment.   _____

d   He's reading a book now in the library.   _____

e   What are you doing?   _____

Answers p. 64

15   Put the verbs in the following sentences into the continuous tense.

a   ¿Qué haces?   _____

b   Abro una carta.   _____

c   Me arreglo.   _____

d   Cuido a los niños.   _____

e   Escucho música.   _____

f   Firmo estos documentos.   _____

g   Limpio el coche.   _____

h   Lavo la ropa.   _____

i   Real Madrid juega en Manchester.   _____

Answers p. 64

Unit 4   Expressing opinions

Expressing opinions

You can say what you think by using the following expressions.

Yo creo que ...	I think that ...
Yo creo que sí.	I think so.
Yo creo que no.	I don't think so.
A mí me parece que ...	It seems to me that ...
A mí me parece que sí.	It seems so to me.
A mí me parece que no.	It doesn't seem so to me.
En mi opinión ...	In my opinion ...
A mi entender ...	In my opinion ...
Para mí ...	In my opinion ...

And you can agree, or disagree, by using phrases like these:

Sí, es verdad.	Yes, that's true.
Sí, claro.	Yes, of course.
Sí, (estoy) de acuerdo pero ...	Yes, OK, but ...
No, eso no es verdad/no es cierto.	No, that's not true.

16 Look at these statements and decide whether you agree or disagree. Use one of the phrases listed above to state your opinion.

Hay que ...

a   legalizar las drogas blandas como el hachís.

b   prohibir el fumar en sitios públicos, como los teatros, el cine, los restaurantes.

Los jóvenes de hoy ...

c   son muy vagos. No quieren ni trabajar ni estudiar.

d   tienen demasiado dinero.

e   Los adultos ven demasiada televisión.

f   La gente de hoy no hace suficiente ejercicio.

g   Se vive mejor hoy día que en el pasado.

VOCABULARY

hay que	one must
blando/a	soft
joven	young/youth

Acabar de

This expression means 'to have just' done something. The verb which follows is always in the infinitive.

Acabo de comprarme un nuevo abrigo.   I have just bought myself a new coat.

17 Pairing off. Match up the Spanish phrase with its English equivalent.

a   We've only just arrived!

b   They've just missed the train!

c   He's not here. He's just gone out.

d   I've just opened this parcel.

e   Her mother has just died.

f   She's coming – she's just finished!

1   Su madre acaba de morir.

2   Si acabamos de llegar!

3   No está. Acaba de salir.

4   Ya viene – ¡acaba de terminar!

5   Acabo de abrir este paquete.

6   ¡Acaban de perder el tren!

Answers p. 64

Expressing surprise

In Conversation 3, Andrés was surprised by Carmen's vehemence. He expressed this by saying **¡No me esperaba esto!** I wasn't expecting that!
Here are a few more expressions you can use in similar situations:

¡vaya!	well!
¿en serio?	seriously?
¡no me digas!	you don't say!
¡no me lo puedo creer!	I can't believe it!
¡hombre!	well, really!

Link words (or conjunctions)

In the conversations, you learned one or two connecting words which you can use to make more complex sentences. Look at these:

ya que/puesto que/dado que	given that
pero	but
en cambio	on the other hand
así que	so that

18 Now link up each sentence in the pairs below. You will find that there are several possibilities.

a A mí me gustan las fiestas. A Elena, no. _____

_____

b Estoy estudiando el portugués. Voy muy a menudo a Portugal. _____

_____

c Carolina no está. Lo dejo para mañana. _____

_____

d No conozco Londres. Conozco muy bien Roma. _____

_____

e Hay mucha polución. Es una ciudad encantadora. _____

_____

f No voy al trabajo en coche. Mi oficina está a 1 kilómetro de casa. _____

_____

Answers p. 64

19 Your turn to speak. In this conversation you talk about a future holiday to South America and the reasons for your learning Spanish. You'll be using: **voy a, estoy estudiando, creo que, una colombiana** a Colombian girl.

20 Here are some statements. Read them out loud and express an opinion, either agreeing or disagreeing. Look back at the Grammar section in this unit to help you with this. Don't use sentences beginning with **no creo que** or **no pienso que** because you will need to use a subjunctive – a form you learn later on in this course. Instead, say **No estoy de acuerdo** + a new sentence.

If you are working with a partner, one of you agrees and the other disagrees with the statement, like this:

El internet es maravilloso.
Partner A: **Yo creo que el Internet es maravilloso.**
Partner B: **No estoy de acuerdo. Creo que es peligroso ya que ponen mucha pornografía.**

a   La censura es mala.
b   Las drogas blandas son muy peligrosas.
c   Hay que prohibir el alcohol.
d   Hay que prohibir y controlar la prostitución.
e   Las mujeres son más débiles que los hombres.
f   El español es más fácil que el francés.

VOCABULARY	
peligroso/a	dangerous
débil	weak

21 React to each of the phrases below by using some of the 'surprise' expressions in the Grammar section in this unit. If you have a partner, take it in turns to read out the statements and give reactions. See if you can add some more shocking statements with suitable surprise reactions of your own.

Voy a emigrar a Australia el año que viene.
La mujer de Pepe tiene veinte años más que él.
Hay más gente que habla catalán que danés.
A Carlos le han tocado diez mil euros en la lotería.
Patricia es mucho más alta que su madre y sólo tiene once años.
Las mujeres no pueden entrar en las sociedades gastronómicas.
Soy española pero no conozco Madrid.

EXERCISE 1

(a) 4 (b) 11 (c) 3 (d) 1 (e) 12 (f) 10 (g) 2
(h) 9 (i) 7 (j) 6 (k) 8 (l) 5

EXERCISE 2

(a) ¿eres un vago? (b) dentro de un plazo de dos meses (c) hacer tus reservas (d) te esperan muchas sorpresas! (e) no quieres desplazarte (f) mejor no te lo contamos

EXERCISE 3

Ventajas: los madrileños son amables, los parques son muy lindos y los museos son fantásticos.
Desventajas: la vida es cara, y hay mucha polución.

EXERCISE 4

(a) primera (b) fantástica (c) amables
(d) Moderno (e) grande (f) práctico

EXERCISE 6

(a) I am translating (b) I am using (c) I am trying
(d) I am talking/speaking (e) I am working

EXERCISE 7

(a) for 3 years (b) it's very different from Spanish (c) he works for a German firm; he visits Frankfurt once a month (d) no (e) he practises each day, reads a newspaper, talks with German friends, goes to a class at the Goethe Institut

EXERCISE 8

(a) knowing a 2nd or 3rd language (b) students and business people (c) Catalán and Spanish (d) they are native speakers, graduates and experienced teachers (e) listening, speaking, reading and writing (f) videoteca video library, audioteca audio library

EXERCISE 10

(a) gusto, inclinación – afición (b) esposa, señora – mujer (c) encanto – gracia (d) sitio – local (e) ser propiedad de – pertenecer a (f) defenderse – protegerse

EXERCISE 11

Romería: people go on foot to a shrine in the country; they take a picnic; it is religious in character.
Sardinada: people eat sardines in the small town; they drink, dance and eat; the sardines are free!

EXERCISE 12

(a) 2 (b) 2 (c) 4 – 6 (d) 3 (e) 3

EXERCISE 14

You would definitely use the continuous with (c) and (d), and the simple present with (b). With (e) you could use either. In (a) if you say estoy teniendo it suggests you have particular problems at the moment. If you say tengo, it suggests that these problems are chronic.

EXERCISE 15

(a) ¿Qué estás haciendo? (b) Estoy abriendo una carta. (c) Me estoy arreglando/Estoy arreglándome. (d) Estoy cuidando a los niños. (e) Estoy escuchando música. (f) Estoy firmando estos documentos. (g) Estoy limpiando el coche. (h) Estoy lavando la ropa. (i) Real Madrid está jugando en Manchester.

EXERCISE 17

(a) 2 (b) 6 (c) 3 (d) 5 (e) 1 (f) 4

EXERCISE 18

(a) A mí me gustan las fiestas. En cambio, a Elena, no. (b) Estoy estudiando el portugués ya que voy muy a menudo a Portugal. (c) Carolina no está, así que lo dejo para mañana. (d) No conozco Londres. En cambio conozco muy bien Roma. (e) Hay mucha polución pero es una ciudad encantadora. (f) No voy al trabajo en coche, ya que mi oficina está a 1 kilómetro de casa.

5 LIVING AND WORKING IN SPAIN

WHAT YOU WILL LEARN

▶ how to rent a flat
▶ how to open a bank account
▶ how to say something about your job
▶ more uses of **se**

POINTS TO REMEMBER

● expressing opinions with: **yo creo que, pienso que, en mi opinión**
● agreeing: **sí, es verdad, sí, claro**
● disagreeing: **eso no es verdad, no es cierto**
● expressing surprise: **¡vamos, hombre! ¿en serio? ¡no me digas!**
● continuous tenses: **estoy estudiando, estoy haciendo**

BEFORE YOU BEGIN

In order to widen your vocabulary, it is a good idea to think about where words come from. Spanish (like French, Portuguese and Italian) is a Latin-based language, and you will be able to guess the meanings of certain words if you already know something of other related languages. Some words are false friends though – they may look like something you recognise but mean something quite different. **Estoy constipado** doesn't mean 'I'm constipated' but 'I have a cold'! **Conveniente** doesn't really mean 'convenient' but 'suitable, advisable'. English also has many words derived from Latin which you can draw upon. If you have to translate *into* Spanish and don't know a particular word, cast about for one with a similar meaning which may be more formal. Chances are that this has a direct equivalent in Spanish. For instance, in Conversation 2, the bank manager uses the word **suficiente** where an English person would say 'enough' – although we also have the word 'sufficient'.

ACACIAS

Junto a metro, exterior 116 m²
4dormitorios, 2 baños, aseo, suelos de parquet, calefacción central, dos terrazas, garaje, ascensor.

362.338 € Ref. 1-14889-0

ALAMEDA DE OSUNA

Exterior, 90 m². 3 dormitorios, 2 baños, suelos de parquet, calefacción individual de gas, terraza, ascensor, parking, trastero.

243.410 € Ref. 1-14858-0

ARGANZUELA

Exterior, 95 m². 3 dormitorios 2 baños, suelos de parquet, climalit, calefacción individual de gas, ascensor, garaje, trastero, gimnasio, sauna. A estrenar.

264.446 € Ref. 1-14579-0

Renting an apartment in Spain

Extranjera	Hola, buenos días. Mmm … estoy aquí por un año en Madrid. Estoy trabajando en la Complutense con una amiga y queremos alquilar un piso, un piso de dos dormitorios, si es posible.
Empleada	De dos dormitorios exactamente en este momento sólo tengo un ático.
Extranjera	Un ático.
Empleada	Si quieren más, tengo también un apartamento, bueno, un apartamento también en el ático, de tres dormitorios.
Extranjera	No, esto es demasiado. Y ¿tiene salón, cocina, comedor …?
Empleada	Este ático tiene sí un pequeño salón, una cocina pequeña aunque no aparece aquí en la explicación.
Extranjera	Bien. Y ¿cuánto es al mes?
Empleada	Al mes son mil ochocientos euros.
Extranjera	Y esto incluye …
Empleada	No, no incluye ni teléfono, ni gas, ni electricidad, ni gastos de comunidad.
Extranjera	Bien, bien. Y ¿está vacío en este momento?
Empleada	En este momento sí, está vacío. Pero hay dos personas interesadas.
Extranjera	Y ¿lo podemos ver ahora?
Empleada	Sí, en cualquier momento, por ejemplo a las once, ¿le parece bien?
Extranjera	Sí, me parece muy bien.
Empleada	Muy bien, pues, vamos.

LISTEN FOR...

queremos alquilar un piso	we want to rent a flat
no incluye ni teléfono, ni gas	it includes neither telephone nor gas
ni electricidad ni gastos de comunidad	nor electricity nor community charges

la Complutense one of the universities in Madrid

queremos alquilar un piso we want to rent a flat; **queremos alquilar un coche** we want to hire a car

esto es demasiado this is too much. **Esto** means 'this', in general. Use **este, esta, estos, estas**, when talking about particular things: **este ático** this attic.

aunque no aparece aquí en la explicación although it doesn't appear here in the explanation (details); **aparecer** to appear. Don't confuse this with **parecer** to seem, which crops up later in this conversation. **Aunque** means 'although'.

¿cuánto es al mes? how much is it per month? **al año** per year; **a la semana** per week

esto incluye this includes; **incluir** to include. As you can see, this verb has a spelling change in certain forms.

no incluye ni teléfono, ni gas, ni electricidad, ni gastos de comunidad   it includes neither telephone, gas, electricity nor community charges; **no ... ni ... ni ...** neither ... nor ... nor. In Spain **luz** (light) is often used instead of **electricidad: la factura de la luz**   the electricity bill.

¿está vacio?   is it empty? **no, está ocupado** no, it's occupied

me parece muy bien   a very good idea (literally it seems very good to me); **¿te/le parece bien?** do you think it's a good idea?

vamos   let's go

PRACTICE

1   If you want to rent a flat in Spain, there are certain phrases you should know. Do you remember how to say ...

a   I want to rent a flat. _____

b   A flat with one bedroom. _____

c   Does it have a dining room? _____

d   How much is it per month? _____

e   Does it include electricity? _____

f   Is it empty? _____

Answers p. 80   **g**   Can I see it now? _____

2   Read this advertisement about apartments in the **calle Julio Palacios** and decide if the statements on the next page are true or false.

Situados en la calle Julio Palacios, número 4, en el Edificio Palacios 2, inmueble de gran calidad en la zona norte de Madrid. Las características de estos apartamentos son las siguientes.
- amueblados con gran calidad
- dos amplios dormitorios
- cuarto de baño completo, mármol
- salón-comedor con terraza con vistas a los jardines y piscina del edificio y al Parque Norte
- cocina amueblada
- armarios empotrados
- suelos de moqueta
- teléfono instalado
- antena parabólica

El precio de alquiler de estos apartamentos es del orden de 3.000 euros mensuales.
Esta renta cubre las gastos de comunidad. No hay que abonar ningún tipo de comisión.

VOCABULARY	
el inmueble	building
la parabólica	satellite dish
cubrir	to cover

	verdad	mentira

a   These apartments are unfurnished. ☐ ☐

b   The apartment block is very prestigious. ☐ ☐

c   The apartments have a swimming pool. ☐ ☐

d   There is a park in the vicinity. ☐ ☐

e   You can watch satellite television. ☐ ☐

f   There is marble flooring throughout. ☐ ☐

g   The mortgage payment is 145.000 pesetas monthly. ☐ ☐

h   Commission is payable. ☐ ☐

i   No community charge is payable on these properties. ☐ ☐

Answers p. 80

3 Listen to the description of two flats in Murcia which the estate agent thinks might suit you. In the grid below, put a tick if the information is accurate and a cross if incorrect. You may wish to play the recording again and correct the inaccurate statements.

	Calle Fuencarral	**Plaza Marina Española**
número	92	8
piso	tercero	segundo
dormitorios	tres	dos
cocina	semi-independiente	amueblada
conserje	sí	no
ascensor	no	sí, uno
alquiler	1.050 euros al mes	1.530 euros al mes
garaje	no	sí
antena parabólica	no	sí
gas/electricidad/luz etc	pagado aparte	incluido

Answers p. 80

4 It's your turn to try renting a flat in Madrid. You'll be using the following words and expressions: **quiero alquilar un piso**, **¿cuánto es al mes?**

Opening a bank account

Tomás	Mire usted, soy inglés y quiero abrir una cuenta corriente aquí en España. ¿Me puede decir lo que hay que hacer?
Gerente	Sí, sí usted está residiendo en España, solamente con tener la tarjeta de residencia es suficiente.
Tomás	Y ¿necesito una cierta cantidad para abrir la cuenta?
Gerente	No, en principio no hay ninguna cantidad estipulada.
Tomás	Y ¿me puede facilitar un talonario?
Gerente	Sí, lo que es la cuenta corriente, porque hay dos casos, puede ser cuenta de ahorros o cuenta corriente.
Tomás	Y ¿cuál es la diferencia?
Gerente	La diferencia está en que la cuenta corriente tiene más, perdón, la cuenta de ahorros tiene más interés que la cuenta corriente.
Tomás	Sí.
Gerente	La cuenta de ahorros se mueve por otro sistema que la cuenta corriente que usa el talonario.
Tomás	Bueno, y si yo quiero sacar dinero de España para Inglaterra, ¿qué puedo hacer? ¿Es legal?
Gerente	De su cuenta corriente, siempre puede retirar el saldo que tenga, bien en euros, que es la moneda nacional, o en divisas.
Tomás	Muy bien. ¿Lo puedo hacer ahora entonces?
Gerente	Sí, ¿cómo no? ahora mismo.
Tomás	Muchas gracias.
Gerente	A usted.

mire usted look. This is an example of a polite command. Other examples are **vaya** go, **salga** leave, and **ponga** put.

quiero abrir una cuenta corriente I want to open a current account. You'll also meet **una cuenta de ahorros** a savings account, for which you need a **libreta** or 'pass book'.

lo que hay que hacer what you have to do. **Lo que** literally means 'that which'. **Hay que** one/you must. This is an alternative to **se tiene que**. **Hay que tomar el autobús en la Calle Colón** you have to catch the bus in the Calle Colón.

solamente con tener la tarjeta de residencia es suficiente it's enough to have the resident's card. Notice how after prepositions like **con** and **para** you need to use the infinitive: **para sacar dinero ...** (in order) to withdraw money ...

¿necesito una cierta cantidad? do I need a certain quantity/sum? **necesitar** to need

en principio in principle

no hay ninguna cantidad estipulada there is no set/stipulated sum

y ¿me puede facilitar un talonario? and can you provide me with a cheque-book? **un talón** a cheque

porque hay dos casos because there are two cases/types

y ¿cuál es la diferencia? and what is the difference? **¿Cuál?** means 'which one of a set?'. **Cuáles** is the plural: **¿cuál/es quieres?** which do you want?

la cuenta de ahorros tiene más interés the savings account has more interest.

se mueve por otro sistema it works on another system. Notice how **sistema** (and other similar words like **programa** and **problema**) looks feminine but is in fact masculine.

bueno O.K.

si yo quiero sacar dinero If I want to take out money. A false friend: the word **moneda**, which crops up later, means 'currency' or a 'coin': **una moneda de un euro** a 1 euro coin.

siempre puede retirar el saldo que tenga you can always withdraw the balance you have. **Tenga** is an example of the subjunctive and occurs here because it conveys an indeterminate amount. Don't worry about this here – this structure is dealt with on page 172.

bien en euros ... o en divisas either in euros or in foreign currency. In this construction, **bien** is often repeated: **bien en francés, o bien en inglés** either in French or in English.

¿cómo no? ahora mismo certainly, right now

PRACTICE

5 Here are some phrases which Isabel and the manager did not use in the bank. Read them through, cross out the incorrect word or phrase and insert the actual words which they used. If you can do this without looking back at the conversation, so much the better!

a Mire, soy argentino …

_____

b Solamente con tener el documento nacional de identidad (el DNI) es suficiente.

_____

c ¿Me puede facilitar talones?

_____

d Puede ser listín de ahorros o cuenta corriente.

_____

e Siempre puede retirar la cantidad que tenga.

_____

f En euros, que es el dinero nacional, o en efectivo.

_____

g Funciona por otro sistema que la cuenta corriente.

_____

h Si está usted viviendo en España …

Answers p. 80 _____

6 Link up the English with the Spanish expressions.

a Me gustaría cambiar ...
b una cuenta corriente
c una cuenta de ahorros
d ¿A cómo está el dólar?
e cheques de viaje(ro)
f en efectivo
g ¿Puedo abrir una cuenta?
h ¿Tengo que rellenar esta ficha?

1 Can I open an account?
2 in cash
3 travellers' cheques
4 I would like to change ...
5 Do I have to fill in this form?
6 a current account
7 a savings account
8 What is the rate of exchange for the dollar?

Answers p. 80

7 Listen to another conversation on your recording and then fill in the form according to the details. You'll hear **deletrear** 'to spell'.

BANCO CASTELLÓN
DEPARTAMENTO EXTRAJERO

CAJA - PAGOS
NEGOCIACIONES

.... de .... de ....

D. ....
con domicilio en ....
pasaporte...expedido en ....
el ...., nos cede las divisas expresadas a continuación, que le liquidamos en efectivo, según detalle:

MONEDA	CAMBIO	EUROS	
.... Dólares			
Total			
Comisión . . . . [ ]			
Impuesto Tráfico de Empresas % [ ]			
Líquido entregado Euros			

Answers p. 80

8 Now you try changing dollars in the bank. You will be using the following vocabulary:
me gustaría cambiar dólares, un cheque de viajero, ¿a cómo está el dólar? ¿es legal?

CONVERSATION 3

I'm a travel agent

Ismael

Soy agente de viajes. Tengo una agencia de viajes en Oviedo y anteriormente he trabajado con Viajes Melia unos quince años, quince, dieciséis años. Actualmente tengo esta agencia de viajes: he decidido instalarme por cuenta propia. La experiencia después de cinco años me demuestra que efectivamente estaba en lo acertado. Concretamente, estoy muy satisfecho de la labor que estoy realizando en esta agencia de viajes y actualmente, después de cinco años, pues la clientela cada vez es mucho mejor, cada vez es mayor, las ventas van mucho mejor y lo que en principio era un temor tremendo hacer este cambio importante, pues actualmente me siento muy satisfecho y muy feliz de haber dado este paso importante.

LISTEN FOR...	
soy agente de viajes	I'm a travel agent
por cuenta propia	on my own account
estoy muy satisfecho	I'm very satisfied
cada vez es mucho mejor	it's much better all the time

soy agente de viajes I am a travel agent. **Una agencia de viajes** a travel agency.

anteriormente he trabajado con Viajes Melia previously, I've worked with **Viajes Melia** (a large Spanish travel company); you could say 'en' instead of 'con'; **he trabajado** I have worked. You'll be looking at how to form past tenses like this (the perfect) in Unit 9.

actualmente at the moment. This is a good example of a false friend. It does *not* mean 'actually', which you could translate as **en realidad**.

he decidido instalarme por cuenta propia I've decided to set up on my own account/for myself

trabajo por mi cuenta I am self-employed

la experiencia me demuestra que efectivamente estaba en lo acertado experience shows me that I really was right. **Demostrar** is an example of a stem-changing verb. **Tener razón** 'to be right' is a more colloquial way of saying **estoy en lo acertado**. **Tengo razón** I am right.

concretamente specifically

estoy muy satisfecho de la labor que estoy realizando I am very satisfied with the work I'm achieving. **Realizar** is a little

formal. Why not use **estoy haciendo** 'I am doing' instead?

la clientela cada vez es mayor the clientele is growing (literally, the clientele each time is larger).

cada vez más rápido quicker all the time

las ventas van mucho mejor the sales are going much better

lo que era un temor tremendo hacer este cambio what was a tremendous fear of making this change. **Cambio** also means 'exchange', 'bureau de change'.

me siento muy feliz de haber dado este paso importante I feel very happy to have taken (literally, given) this important step. **Sentir** 'to feel', is a stem-changing verb; **lo siento** I am sorry.

9 Jot down the Spanish equivalent of these phrases. They are all taken from Conversation 3. Try not to look back!

a I'm a travel agent.

_____

b Before, I worked with Viajes Melia.

_____

c I decided to set up on my own. _____

_____

d I am very satisfied with the work that I'm doing. _____

_____

e The clientele is much better all the time. _____

_____

f Sales are getting better.

_____

g I feel very satisfied.

| Answers p. 80 | _____

10 Study the mini curriculum vitae of Carolina Álvarez Gómez and then write out your own, using hers as a model.

ALVAREZ GOMEZ, CAROLINA

Zaragoza
Nacido el 2/4/58
Permiso de conducir B1

Experiencia:		
	1980 a 1983	Escuela de Turismo Aragón-Zaragoza Función: Guía turística (nacionales e internacionales)
	1983 a 1985	Varios congresos, Zaragoza, Valladolid Función: Azafata (control y organización)
	1985 a 1986	STE, Valladolid Función: Azafata
	1987 a 1996	Agencia de Viajes Colombia (Valladolid) Función: Agente de Ventas
Estudios		Diploma de Gestión (turismo)
Otros estudios		Macintosh
Idiomas		Francés (alto) alemán (bueno)

VOCABULARY

azafata (la)   (air) hostess
gestión (la)   management

Unit 5   Living and working in Spain   73

11 Here is a **formulario** or 'form' which you need to complete for an employment agency. Fill in as much as you can, either in English or Spanish. Any words which you haven't met before are in the vocabulary section at the end of the book.

Nombre _____ **Apellido(s)** _____

Dirección _____ **Código Postal** _____

Teléfono _____ **DNI** _____

Fecha de nacimiento ____ / ____ / ____ 19 _____

Estado civil   soltero ☐   casado ☐   separado/divorciado ☐   viudo ☐

Sexo   varón ☐   mujer ☐

Servicio Militar   cumplido ☐   exento ☐

Permiso de conducir   sí ☐   no ☐

Situación laboral   desempleado total ☐   desempleado parcial ☐
trabaja ☐   estudia ☐   invalidez ☐

¿Cuál es su profesión? _____

Títulos académicos oficiales

Título	Fecha	Lugar

Idiomas	Nivel

¿En qué ciudades está dispuesto a trabajar? _____

Nº de cuenta bancaria _____

---

12 In this exercise, you apply for a job in Spain as a guide. You'll be using the followings words and phrases: **un(a) guía** (a guide), **diploma de gestión**, **azafata** and **he trabajado** (**en/como**).

Unit 5   Living and working in Spain

KEY WORDS
AND PHRASES

quiero alquilar un piso	I want to rent a flat
¿cuánto es al mes?	how much is it per month?
no incluye ni teléfono, ni gas	it includes neither telephone nor gas
ni electricidad, ni gastos de	nor electricity nor community
comunidad	charges
¿está vacío?	is it empty?
¿lo puedo ver ahora?	can I see it now?
me parece muy bien	a very good idea
el/la guía turístico/a	the tourist guide
la azafata	hostess (air, game show, trade fairs)
el formulario	the form
la gestión	management
las ventas	sales
desempleado/a	unemployed
la clientela es cada vez mayor	there are more and more customers
actualmente	at the moment
concretamente	specifically
trabajo por mi cuenta	I work for myself
(no) tengo razón	I am (not) right
me siento ...	I feel ...
muy satisfecho/a	very satisfied
muy feliz	very happy
el mármol	marble
el suelo de moqueta	fitted carpets (carpeted floor)
los armarios empotrados	fitted wardrobes
la antena parabólica	satellite dish
el conserje	the porter
quiero abrir ...	I want to open ...
una cuenta corriente/bancaria	a current/bank account
una cuenta de ahorros	a savings account
tiene más interés que ...	it has more interest than ...
¿cuál es la diferencia?	what is the difference?
la tarjeta de residencia	the residence card
la libreta de ahorros	the savings book
el saldo	the balance (bank)
en divisas	in foreign exchange
en moneda nacional	in national currency
¿me puede facilitar ...	can you let me have a ...
un talonario?	cheque-book?
un talón?	a cheque?
Pablo es más grande que Luis	Pablo is bigger than Luis
Anabel es más pequeña que Pablo	Anabel is smaller than Pablo
Pablo es el más grande de la familia	Pablo is the biggest in the family
Anabel es la más pequeña de la familia	Anabel is the smallest in the family

GRAMMAR AND EXERCISES

Using the infinitive

The infinitive is the basic form of the verb. In English, it is usually preceded by 'to' – to speak, to return, to go out. In Spanish, the infinitive has three endings: **-ar**, **-er** and **-ir** – **hablar**, **volver** and **salir**.

■ Use the infinitive in Spanish when it follows closely on another verb:

Me gusta ir al cine.	I like going to the cinema.
Sabe nadar muy bien.	S/he knows how to swim very well.

■ Use the infinitive after prepositions (short words like **para**, **por**, **con**, **a**, **de**).

Con tener la tarjeta es suficiente.	To have the card is enough.
Para abrir la cuenta ...	(In order) to open the account ...

■ Use the infinitive with **al** to mean 'on doing something', 'having done something' ...

Al llegar a casa, cena.	On arriving home/having arrived home, s/he has dinner.
Al volver de Madrid, voy a Valencia.	When I get back from Madrid, I go to Valencia.

13 Complete these sentences, using a verb in the infinitive:

a   A mí me gusta _____ en las discotecas los viernes por la noche.

b   Tengo que _____ varias cartas esta tarde.

c   Al _____ mis estudios, quiero _____ en un banco.

d   Mañana, ¿vas a _____ al squash, no?

e   ¿Quieres _____ de compras conmigo a Barcelona?

f   ¿Me ayudas a _____ los platos?

g   ¡No puedo _____ esta lata!

h   Pablito todavía no sabe _____ .

Answers p. 80

andar	bailar	jugar	ir	fregar	abrir	terminar	escribir	trabajar

More uses of 'se'

Use **se** for translating 'each other':

Se quieren mucho.	They love each other a lot.
Se ven sólo durante las vacaciones.	They only see each other in the holidays.

14 How would you translate the following sentences?

a   Ester y Carolina se ven mucho – son muy buenas amigas.

b   Se paga la luz por separado.

VOCABULARY

un beso	a kiss
saludar	to greet

c   ¿Se puede abrir una cuenta corriente ahora mismo?

_____

d   Al saludarse, los franceses se dan uno o dos besos.

_____

e   Se piden veinte mil euros por el coche.

_____

f   El 3° Festival Internacional del Tango se celebra en Buenos Aires del 11 al 14 de julio.

_____

g   Si se desea participar en las clases de baile, el coste adicional es de 35 euros.

_____

h   Los servicios que se ofrecen en este hotel son de calidad exquisita.

_____

Answers p. 80

More about adjectives: comparatives

To compare one thing with another and say it is bigger, better, rounder, stronger etc., Spanish uses **más** + adjective + **que**. If it is less round or less strong, use **menos** + adjective + **que**. Suppose you want to compare cameras. You might say ...

La Nikon es más grande que la Pentax.	The Nikon is bigger than the Pentax.
Es más ligera y más fácil (que ...)	It's lighter and easier (than ...)
Es menos complicada (que ...)	It's less complicated (than ...)

There are some exceptions.

mejor better	**peor** worse	**mayor** older	**menor** younger

La Pentax es mejor que la Nikon pero peor que la Leica.
Cristina es mayor que Juan pero menor que Javier.

If a number follows the comparison use **de** and not **que**.

Tiene más de 10 centímetros de ancho.	It's more than 10 cms wide.
Tiene menos de 25 centímetros de hondo.	It's less than 25 cms deep.

Adverbs (words like 'quickly', 'slowly', 'efficiently') work in the same way:

El AVE va más rápidamente que el TALGO.	The AVE travels faster than the TALGO.
Marta habla más despacio que Eva.	Marta speaks more slowly than Eva.
Juan toca mejor que Pablo.	Juan plays (an instrument) better than Pablo.

15 Read these sentences and choose the first option as your preference. Then give a reason why, using **más/menos** + an adjective, e.g. **prefiero el campo porque es más tranquilo**. Use the vocabulary in the box. There are sample answers in the Answers section.

a   ¿Qué prefieres, el campo o la ciudad?

_____

b   ¿Qué prefieres, el té o el café?

_____

c ¿Qué prefieres, el pescado o la carne?

_____

d ¿Qué prefieres, el fútbol o el rugby?

_____

e ¿Qué prefieres, la noche o la mañana?

_____

f ¿Qué prefieres, la música clásica o la música popular?

_____

g ¿Qué prefieres, los perros o los gatos?

_____

suave	cariñoso	peligroso	tranquilo	estimulante
ligero	emocionante	oscuro	problemático	

Answers p. 80

More about adjectives: superlatives

If you want to say something is the biggest, brightest or best, then follow these rules:
Use the noun (**televisor**), plus its article (**el**), followed by **más** and the adjective (**caro**).

El televisor más caro de la gama.   The most expensive television in the range.

Notice how in English it is 'in the range' and in Spanish 'of the range'.

La cámara más barata de la serie.   The cheapest camera in the range.

If you want to say 'least', then use **menos**.

El vídeo menos complicado es el Astra.   The least complicated video is the Astra.

El ordenador más potente es el Macintosh.   The most powerful computer is the Macintosh.

La calculadora más pequeña es ésta.   The smallest calculator is this one.

16 Make these sentences superlative, by filling in the blanks.

a Madrid es _____ ciudad _____ grande

_____ España.

b Brasil es _____ país _____ grande _____

América Latina.

c El salmón es _____ pescado _____ apreciado

_____ todos.

d El Barça es _____ equipo de fútbol _____ popular

_____ España.

e La Ford es _____ empresa _____ grande de Valencia.

f La Pentax 500 es _____ cámara _____ impresionante

_____ la gama.

Answers p. 80

17 Guillermo asks you all about your job. You'll be using **trabajo por mi cuenta**, **agencia de viajes**, **satisfecho**, **la clientela es cada vez mayor** and **las ventas**.

18 Here are details of five flats to rent. Choose a flat, describe its features and explain why you like it. You'll make comments like:

El piso en la calle _____ tiene _____. Me gusta/lo

prefiero porque _____ .

If you have a partner, take it in turns to choose and compare your choice.

Inmuebles en alquiler	Refer.	Precio
AVDA. REPUBLICA ARGENTINA: Gran piso de 170 m² con 4 dormitorios, 2 salones, cocina amueblada, 3 baños completos, 6 armarios empotrados, mármol, terraza.	1.654	1.081 euros
LOS REMEDIOS: Precioso ático con terraza de 28 m², con 3 dormitorios, salón, cocina, baño amueblado, mármol.	1.655	661 euros
C/ALFONSO XII: Apartamento amueblado inmejorablemente situado de 1 dormitorio, salón, cocina, baño completo, climatizado frío/calor.	1.656	601 euros
EL ARENAL: casa de 4 dormitorios, bien situada, buenas vistas en Semana Santa, baños completos, nueva, estilo sevillano.	1.657	1.020 euros
STA. TRINIDAD; Ático de 80 m² amueblado, 2 dormitorios, baño completo y aseo, aire acondicionado, terraza de 65 m², teléfono.	1.658	570 euros

Exercise 1

(a) Quiero alquilar un piso. (b) un piso con un dormitorio. (c) ¿Tiene comedor? (d) ¿Cuánto es al mes? (e) ¿Esto incluye la electricidad/la luz? (f) ¿Está vacío? (g) ¿Lo puedo ver ahora?

Exercise 2

(b), (c),(d) and (e) are true. The rest are false.

Exercise 3

	Calle Fuencarral	Marina Española
número	92 ✗	8 ✗
piso	tercero ✓	segundo ✗
dormitorios	tres ✗	dos ✓
cocina	semi-independiente ✗	amueblada ✓
conserje	sí ✓	
ascensor	no ✗	sí, uno ✗
alquiler	1.050 euros al mes ✓	1.530 euros al mes ✗
garaje	no ✓	sí ✓
antena parabólica	no ✓	sí ✓
gas/electricidad etc	pagado aparte ✓	incluido ✗

Exercise 5

(a) soy inglés (b) la tarjeta de residencia (c) un talonario (d) cuenta (e) el saldo (f) la moneda (g) se mueve (h) residiendo

Exercise 6

(a) 4 (b) 6 (c) 7 (d) 8 (e) 3 (f) 2 (g) 1 (h) 5

Exercise 7

5 de marzo de 2003; Peter Crawford; Northampton; 011853490; Liverpool; 3 de Agosto 1999; 200 dólares; en efectivo; 96 céntimos; 192 euros; Comisión 2%; 188,16 euros

Exercise 9

(a) Soy agente de viajes. (b) Anteriormente, he trabajado con Viajes Melia. (c) He decidido instalarme por cuenta propia. (d) Estoy muy satisfecho de la labor que estoy realizando. (e) La clientela cada vez es mucho mejor. (f) Las ventas van mucho mejor. (g) Me siento muy satisfecho.

Exercise 13

(a) A mí me gusta bailar en las discotecas los viernes por la noche. (b) Tengo que escribir varias cartas esta tarde. (c) Al terminar mis estudios, quiero trabajar en un banco. (d) Mañana, ¿vas a jugar al squash, no? (e) ¿Quieres ir de compras conmigo a Barcelona? (f) ¿Me ayudas a fregar los platos? (g) ¡No puedo abrir esta lata! (h) Pablito todavía no sabe andar.

Exercise 14

(a) Ester and Carolina see each other a lot. They are very good friends. (b) One pays the electricity separately (c) Can you open a current account right now? (d) When they greet each other, French people give each other one or two kisses. (e) They are asking 20,000 euros for the car. (f) The 3rd International Tango Festival is celebrated in Buenos Aires from the 11 to the 14 of July (g) If you wish to take part in the dancing classes, the additional cost is 35 euros. (h) The services offered in the hotel are of a very high quality.

Exercise 15

(a) Prefiero el campo porque es más tranquilo.
(b) Prefiero el té porque es menos estimulante.
(c) Prefiero el pescado porque es más ligero.
(d) Prefiero el fútbol porque es menos peligroso.
(e) Prefiero la noche porque es más emocionante.
(f) Prefiero la música clásica porque es más suave.
(g) Prefiero los perros porque son más cariñosos.

Exercise 16

(a) Madrid es la ciudad más grande de España.
(b) Brasil es el país más grande de América Latina.
(c) El salmón es el pescado más apreciado de todos.
(d) El Barça es el equipo de fútbol más popular de España. (e) La Ford es la empresa más grande de Valencia. (f) La Pentax 500 es la cámara más impresionante de la gama.

6 TRAVEL PROBLEMS

BEFORE YOU BEGIN

Unit 4 suggested how you can find words you don't know by comparing Spanish with other languages you already know (including English). But there will always be vocabulary which is more difficult to learn because it bears little relation to anything you are familiar with. This is most likely to occur in Spanish with words which come from Arabic: about ten per cent of words in Spanish have this origin. So what do you do? First decide whether you really want to learn the word or not – some vocabulary is so obscure that you may not meet it very often. Does the word have some significance for you in particular? If you are an enthusiastic chess-player for instance, you need the word **ajedrez, (jugar al ajedrez** to play chess) – if not, forget it. Suppose you *do* want to learn it, but find it difficult, try these strategies. Find some other word it resembles – what about the Spanish city, Jerez? Jot down the word you want to know on a post-it and stick it somewhere that you will notice it often – on a mirror or kitchen cupboard. Say it out loud as often as you can bear – put it to music if you are operatically inclined! Anything to transfer it from short to long-term memory.

Moving house

Maite

Sí, bueno. Me mudé el año
pasado. Fue una experiencia
bastante inolvidable. Yo
empaqueté todo, empaqueté
libros, empaqueté ropa etcétera y luego ya contraté una compañía que me transportó
todo, en conjunto. Ahora me pasó una cosa que tampoco la olvidaré, que me
mancharon la alfombra de aceite y además me rompieron la televisión. Y bueno, muy
mal, muy mal. Les tuve que denunciar, les denuncié y al final pues pagué la mitad del
coste del transporte.

LISTEN FOR...

me mudé el año pasado	I moved house last year
empaqueté todo	I packed up everything
me mancharon la alfombra	they stained my carpet

me mudé   I moved; **mudarse** to move house. This verb form is called the preterite and deals with events which ocurred in the past. The 'yo form' of most '-ar' verbs ends in 'é': **pasé** I spent; **hablé** I spoke; **me quedé** I stayed.

fue una experiencia bastante inolvidable   it was a fairly unforgettable experience. **Fue** is the preterite of both **ser** 'to be' and **ir** 'to go', so could mean either 's/he/it was' or 's/he/it went': **Clara fue a España** Claire went to Spain; **Natalia fue maestra** Natalie was a school-teacher.

yo empaqueté   I packed up; from **empaquetar** to pack up; **un paquete** a package or parcel.

luego ya contraté una compañía   then I hired a company (**contratar** to hire, contract). **Ya** means 'already' but here it is simply used as a filler.

me transportó todo, en conjunto   it transported everything for me, together. The 'ó' ending is the third person form of the '-ar' verb. **Llegó** she/he/it arrived; **habló** she/he spoke.

me pasó una cosa   something happened to me; **¿qué te pasó?** what happened to you?

tampoco lo olvidaré   I won't forget it either; **olvidar** to forget. **Olvidaré** is the future form and is dealt with in Unit 10; **lo olvidé** I forgot it.

me mancharon la alfombra   they stained my carpet (literally they stained the carpet to/for me); **manchar** to stain. The ending '-aron' corresponds to the third person plural: **me hablaron** they spoke to me.

me rompieron la televisión   they broke my television. The ending '-ieron' is used with an 'er' or 'ir' verb: **comieron chorizo y bebieron gaseosa** they ate sausage and drank lemonade.

les tuve que denunciar   I had to report them; **tuve que** (from **tener que** 'to have to') is irregular in the preterite tense.

les denuncié   I reported them; **denunciar** to denounce or report, to complain about.

pagué la mitad del coste del transporte   I paid half the cost of the transport. The ending here acquires a 'u' to keep the 'hard' sound of the 'g'. **Pagé** would be pronounced with the 'j' sound.

PRACTICE

1 Most of the verbs in that conversation were in the preterite (or past) tense and were verbs which end in '-**ar**'. So what do the following phrases mean?

a Me manché de chocolate.

_____

b Empaquetaron todas mis cosas.

_____

c ¡Fue terrible!

_____

d Rompí el vídeo.

_____

e Mis padres se mudaron a Francia en 1989.

_____

f Transportaron todos sus libros y ropa en coche.

_____

_____

g Olvidaron la bicicleta de mi hermano.

Answers p. 96

_____

2 Now listen to José Luis discussing his recent move and then answer the questions which follow.
You need the word **una mudanza** 'a move' and **desmontar** 'to take apart' or 'dismantle'.

a Where did José Luis move to?

_____

b Where did he move from?

_____

c When did he move?

_____

d How does he describe that year?

_____

e What did the removal company do?

_____

_____

f How efficient were they?

Answers p. 96

_____

3 Robbery in a jeweller's. Read an account of what happened in a jeweller's shop recently and then answer the questions which follow.

El pasado martes cinco delincuentes robaron 200.000 euros en joyas en una joyería de Madrid, situada en la calle de Goya. Dos personas entraron a la tienda quince minutos antes de la hora de cierre. Los dos individuos atacaron a la propietaria y a un cliente: después de gritar que era un atraco, la amenazaron con una pistola y abrieron la puerta a otros dos delincuentes que esperaban en la calle. En cuatro minutos, llenaron tres bolsas con las joyas y piedras preciosas expuestas en la vitrina. Antes de abandonar la joyería, los individuos dijeron a la propietaria que no avisara a la policía hasta pasados quince minutos. Salieron a la calle tranquilamente y se subieron a un coche azul aparcado delante de la tienda. Nadie se dio cuenta de lo que pasó, ni el portero del edificio.

VOCABULARY

una joyería	a jewellers' shop
el cierre	closing
un atraco	a hold-up
amenazar	to threaten
la bolsa	the bag
la piedra	stone
avisar	to warn, advise
darse cuenta de	to realise

a On what day of the week did the events take place? And at what time of day?

_____

_____

b What was the role of the five individuals?

_____

_____

c Where were the jewels?

_____

d What took four minutes?

_____

e What did the robbers say to the owner?

_____

f What was the colour of their car?

_____

g What was the reaction of the passers-by?

Answers p. 96

_____

4 Now Guillermo asks you about your recent move. You'll be using **me mudé, fue, rompieron, mancharon, denuncié** and **pagué**.

My luggage got lost!

Marga

¿Sabes lo que me pasó en mi último viaje a Inglaterra? Pues que me perdieron mi

equipaje. Fue una cosa un tanto extraña pero que realmente ocurrió. El problema llegó cuando llegué a Manchester y mi equipaje no aparecía por ningún sitio. Entonces, eh bueno, fui a reclamarlo naturalmente y me dijeron de que estaba en Amsterdam. Yo, es que me quedé realmente sorprendida, porque no entendía qué había ido a hacer mi equipaje a Amsterdam. Bueno, después de una serie de llamadas telefónicas, me dijeron que, al final, que estaba en Londres y entonces que mandarían un télex para reclamarlo. Y bueno, estuve tres días sin equipaje, pero al final llegó. Y fueron tres días realmente angustiosos, porque no tenía absolutamente nada que ponerme. Y es que, estaba con la misma ropa desde el día que había salido de casa y ¡fue algo un poco realmente asqueroso!

If it weren't there, the '**g**' would sound like '**j**'. (This is like **pagué** in Conversation 1.)

mi equipaje no aparecía por ningún sitio my luggage didn't appear in any place. **Aparecer**, 'to appear', is in another past tense called the imperfect which is explained in Unit 7.

fui a reclamarlo I went to claim it. **Reclamar** can also mean 'to complain'. **La hoja de reclamaciones** is the complaints form which restaurants, hotels etc. are obliged to give to clients who request it.

¿sabes lo que me pasó? do you know what happened to me?

el viaje the journey

me perdieron mi equipaje they lost my luggage (for me); **perder** to lose. The extra **me** at the start of the phrase emphasises that it was Marga's luggage they lost.

un tanto extraña a bit strange/odd. **Extraña** here agrees with **cosa** (thing).

realmente ocurrió it really happened; **ocurrir** to occur.

el problema llegó cuando llegué the problem arrived when I arrived. Notice the extra '**u**' in the spelling of the 'I (first person) form'.

me dijeron de que estaba en Amsterdam they told me it was in Amsterdam.

me quedé realmente sorprendida I was really surprised. **Quedarse** is a multi-use verb, which can often substitute for **estar**. Literally, it means 'to stay'; **¡estuve realmente sorprendida!** would be simpler.

no entendía qué había ido a hacer mi equipaje a Amsterdam I didn't understand what my luggage was doing in Amsterdam (literally, what my luggage had gone to do …).

llamadas telefónicas telephone calls; **gracias por la llamada** thanks for the call.

que mandarían un télex that they would send a telex. Words taken from other languages are usually masculine: **un fax, el modem, el disquete**.

fueron tres días realmente angustiosos they were three really dreadful days! **angustioso** distressing.

no tenía absolutamente nada que ponerme I had absolutely nothing to put on (myself). Look back at Unit 2 to refresh your memory about negatives.

estaba con la misma ropa I had the same clothes (on) (literally, I was with the same clothes). **Ropa** is usually singular in Spanish.

desde el día que había salido de casa from the day I had left home. Notice how you always need to use **de** after **salir: salgo de casa a las siete** I leave home at seven; **¿el tren sale de qué andén?** which platform does the train leave from?

¡fue algo un poco realmente asqueroso! It was really rather disgusting! Marga gets into a bit of a muddle here. She doesn't need to use both **poco** 'a bit' and **realmente** 'really'.

PRACTICE

5 Find the phrases in Conversation 2 on page 85 which correspond to the ones below.

a Do you know what happened?

_____

b They lost my luggage.

_____

c It really happened.

_____

d I went to reclaim it.

_____

e They said it was in London.

_____

f I was three days with no luggage.

_____

g It was really disgusting!

Answers p. 96

_____

6 If you send parcels by the Especial Express service with RENFE (the Spanish railway network), there's no chance of their getting lost. The service promises seven advantages: match the advantages (on the left), with the accompanying descriptions (on the right).

a	rapidez	**1**	Desde un paquete con impresos o una caja de flores.
b	alta frecuencia	**2**	Usted mismo puede facturar sus envíos en las estaciones y despachos centrales. ·
c	regularidad	**3**	Más de 100 trenes diarios, nocturnos y/o diarios.
d	comodidad	**4**	En menos de 24 horas transporta su mercancía a la estación de destino.
e	transporte de todo tipo de envíos	**5**	Seguridad de la mercancía y para usted y su empresa.
f	le esperamos hasta última hora	**6**	Sus envíos salen y llegan a destino puntualmente.
g	doble seguridad	**7**	Usted puede efectuar su envió hasta una hora antes de la salida del tren.

VOCABULARY

la rapidez	speed
el envío	mail
los impresos	printed matter
el despacho	office
la caja	box
la mercancía	merchandise

Answers p. 96

7 Listen to this short account of a haul of cocaine that was found on a flight from Colombia to New York. You will need the word **aduanero** 'customs officer'. Then answer the questions in English.

a What was the date mentioned? _____

b How much cocaine was found? _____

c Where had she come from? _____

d What was the flight number? _____

e What time did the girl go for her luggage? _____

f In which city had the luggage ended up? _____

Answers p. 96 **g** How old was the girl? _____

8 Now you discuss a problematic journey by air. You will be using the following words and phrases: **perdieron mi equipaje**; **llegué**; **estaba**; **¡fue asqueroso!**

Did you have a car accident?

Marga

Sí, fue en noviembre y fue en el cruce de una autopista. Yo estaba esperando a que se pusiera el semáforo en verde, entonces en el momento en que se puso en verde, yo me puse a, a pasar,

y bajaba un coche que se había pasado el semáforo en rojo. Entonces, bueno, me dio un golpe bastante fuerte, porque mi coche es pequeño, y entonces, no, tampoco es muy fuerte. Su coche es bastante grande, es un Peugeot 505, y tiene una defensa realmente grande. Entonces me cogió la aleta derecha delantera y parte del morro. Y ¡bueno! Creo que reaccioné bastante bien, ¿no? Porque no me puse nerviosa hasta que no me bajé del coche. Yo le quité el contacto, tiré del freno de mano, apagué la radio, me quité mis gafas y salí. Y en el momento que salí, ¡me puse a temblar! Y entonces el señor me dijo: pero bueno, ¿qué es que no me vio? ¿Por qué no frenó? Y le dije: pues no, no le vi, si le hubiera visto, hubiera frenado. Y dice, pues, lo siento mucho y tal, y yo, ya ya, ¡más lo siento yo!

bajaba un coche que se había pasado el semáforo en rojo a car was coming down that had jumped the lights (literally, a car which had passed the traffic light on red).

me dio un golpe bastante fuerte he gave me quite a hard knock

tampoco es muy fuerte it's not very strong either. As you know **tampoco** means 'neither': **a mí no me gustan las autopistas** I don't like motorways; **a mí tampoco** me neither, nor me.

una defensa a bumper

me cogió la aleta derecha delantera he caught my right front wing; **me cogió la aleta izquierda trasera** he caught the left back wing.

parte del morro part of the nose, front

creo que reaccioné bastante bien I think I reacted quite well

hasta que no me bajé del coche until I got out of the car. **Bajarse de** to get out: **me bajé del autobús** I got off the bus. Ignore the 'no' – it is redundant in this sentence.

yo le quité el contacto I switched off the

en el cruce de una autopista it was on the crossing with a motorway

yo estaba esperando con, a que se pusiera el semáforo en verde I was waiting for the lights to turn green. Marga rethinks what she is going to say, then opts for a subjunctive, because she is referring to a future event.

en el momento en que se puso en verde at the moment it went green. **Se puso** is from the verb **ponerse** to become: **me pongo muy moreno en el verano** I get very brown in the summer.

yo me puse a pasar I began to cross. **Ponerse a** means 'to begin to'. You could use **empezar** instead: **empecé a pasar**.

ignition (**le** – 'from it' or 'of it'). Another use of **quitar**: **me quité mis gafas** I took off my glasses; '**me quité las gafas**' is a more widely-used phrase.

tiré del freno de mano I put on the brake (literally, I pulled on the hand-brake).

apagué la radio I switched off the radio. Notice the extra '**u**' before the '**e**' in **apagué** (like **pagué** in Conversation 1 and **llegué** in Conversation 2).

pero bueno, ¿qué es que no me vio? what do you mean you didn't see me? (literally, but well, what is it that you didn't see me?)

Notice how Marga and the other car driver address each other as **usted**.

¿por qué no frenó? why didn't you brake?

pues no, no le vi well no, I didn't see you.

si le hubiera visto, hubiera frenado if I had seen you, I would have braked. **Hubiera** is another form of the subjunctive, which will be covered in Units 11 and 12.

y yo ya ya, ¡más lo siento yo! and I (said) OK, OK, I'm even sorrier than you! Strictly speaking, you should not apologise after an accident, in case of later insurance claims against you.

PRACTICE

9 Listen again to the recording and then number the events in the order in which they occurred.

Notice that all the verbs are in the preterite and all are in the '**yo** form'.

a   Me bajé del coche. _____

b   Estuve en un cruce. _____

c   Me quité las gafas. _____

d   Tiré del freno de mano. _____

e   Dije ¡Más lo siento yo! _____

f   Me puse a pasar. _____

g   Le quité el contacto. _____

h   Me puse a temblar. _____

i   Apagué la radio. _____

| Answers p. 96 |

10 Read this passage about how to react if you are involved in a traffic accident.

PROTECCIÓN CIUDADANA Y SEGURIDAD VITAL
Si está usted implicado en un accidente de carretera, debe:

i Detenerse y parar el motor, quitando el contacto.

ii Señalizar correctamente el vehículo o el obstáculo creado, para avisar a otros conductores. Si el accidente ha ocurrido de noche, iluminar el lugar.

iii Mover el vehículo accidentado al lugar donde cause menor obstáculo a la circulación.
(Esta operación NO se realiza si (a) hay heridos (b) el vehículo no interfiere en la circulación de la carretera.)

iv Mantener la calma en todo momento.

v En caso de incendio, usar el extintor de los vehículos implicados, o mantas, tierra o arena, pero NUNCA agua. Cerca del coche no se deben utilizar cerillas, ni fumar.

vi Ayudar a los heridos.

vii Avisar a las autoridades, informándoles del lugar del accidente cuando: **a** hay heridos; **b** es necesario restablecer la circulación por la carretera; **c** lo pide alguna de las personas implicadas en el accidente.

viii Quedarse en el lugar del accidente hasta que lleguen las autoridades.

Now find the Spanish equivalents of these English phrases and write them in the space provided.

a stop the engine _____

b indicate the vehicle in the correct manner _____

c to warn other drivers _____

d the vehicle does not impede road traffic _____
_____

e remain calm always _____

f in the event of fire _____

g help the injured _____

Answers p. 96 **h** remain at the site of the accident _____

11 Now for something completely different. Listen to Guillermo telling you all about the dance career of Joaquín Cortés who became an international hit in 1996. Then, in Spanish, fill in the biographical details in his CV below.

a Nació en _____ en el año _____

b En 1984 se incorporó al _____

c Allí bailó como solista en la obra titulada _____

d Abandonó la compañía en _____

e Empezó su carrera como _____

f En 1992, creó la compañía _____

g Creó la coreografía del vídeo de _____ de Mecano,
Answers p. 96 llamada _____

12 In this speaking exercise, you describe an accident in which you were involved. You will be using **ayer**, **el cruce**, **un golpe fuerte**, **no me puse nervioso/a** and **dije**.

me mudé el año pasado	I moved house last year
fue una experiencia inolvidable	it was an unforgettable experience
empaqueté todo	I packed up everything
contraté (a) una compañía	I contracted a company
me pasó una cosa	something happened to me
me mancharon la alfombra	they stained my carpet
rompieron la televisión	they broke the television
les denuncié	I complained about them
pagué la mitad	I paid half
¿sabes lo que me pasó?	do you know what happened?
realmente ocurrió	it really happened
llegué a Manchester	I arrived in Manchester
fui a (reclamarlo)	I went to (pick it up)
me quedé sorprendido/a	I was surprised
estuve sin equipaje	I was without luggage
al final llegó	finally it arrived
fueron tres días …	they were three days …
¡fue realmente asqueroso!	it was really disgusting!
fue en noviembre	it was in November
fue en el cruce de una autopista	it was on the crossing with a motorway
me puse a pasar	I began to pass
me dio un golpe fuerte	he gave me a strong blow
me cogió la aleta	he caught my wing
reaccioné bastante bien	I reacted quite well
no me puse nervioso/a	I didn't get nervous
me bajé del coche	I got out of the car
le quité el contacto	I switched off the ignition
tiré del freno de mano	I put on the handbrake
apagué la radio	I switched off the radio
me quité las (mis) gafas	I took off my glasses
salí	I got out/left
me puse a temblar	I began to tremble
el señor me dijo …	the man said to me …
¿no me vio?	didn't you see me?
¿por qué no frenó?	why didn't you brake?
yo le dije …	I said to him …
no le vi	I didn't see you
lo siento	I am sorry

The preterite tense

This past tense is used for completed actions in the past, e.g. I came, I saw, I conquered.

You may know the endings already, but here they are again in case you need to refresh your memory.

-ar verbs	-er and -ir verbs
esper é	perd í
esper aste	perd iste
esper ó	perd ió
esper amos	perd imos
esper asteis	perd isteis
esper aron	perd ieron

Stem-changing verbs ending in **-ir** change in the third person singular and plural – '**e**' changes to '**i**' and '**o**' changes to '**u**':

pedir (to ask for)	**sentir** (to feel)	**dormir** (to sleep)
el pidió	**ella sintió**	**el niño durmió**
ellos pidieron	**ellas sintieron**	**las niñas durmieron**

Some verbs have spelling changes. Look at these:

pagar	**entregar**	**sacar**
pagué I paid	**entregué** I handed over	**saqué** I took out

This is to keep the sound of the '**c**' and the '**g**' hard. (Try pronouncing these words without the '**u**' and you will see what happens!)

Ser and **ir** share the same forms in the preterite. So 'I was' and 'I went' are both **fui**.
fui, fuiste, fue   **fuimos, fuisteis, fueron**

You will need to learn these irregular verbs.
Dar to give: **di, diste, dio**   **dimos, disteis, dieron**
Ver to see: **vi, viste, vio**   **vimos, visteis, vieron**

A few verbs have their own set of endings which are attached to an irregular stem.

The most important are:
estar (**estuve** I was)	**hacer** (**hice** I did/made)
poder (**pude** I could)	**poner** (**puse** I put)
querer (**quise** I wanted to)	**saber** (**supe** I found out)
tener (**tuve** I had to)	**venir** (**vine** I came)

Note also: **dije** I said; **traje** I brought; **conduje** I drove

That's quite a lot to learn! You will find all the full forms in the back of the book. The more often you use them, the quicker you'll get to know them.

13   So how do you say the following things?

a   We went to the Café Rouge.   _____

b   I asked for a whisky.   _____

c   Carolina asked for a coca cola.   _____

d   My brother arrived.   _____

e   We talked.   _____

f   Then they went to the theatre.   _____

g   I saw a film.   _____

Answers p. 96

Personal pronouns

Here is a table with the personal pronouns. You will be familiar with them all, but this grid will help you keep track. Spanish grammar is rather woolly as regards **lo**, **la** and **le**, but if you follow the guidelines here, you won't go far wrong.

SUBJECT	OBJECT	AFTER A PREPOSITION (e.g. **a/por/para**)
yo	**me**	**mí**
tú	**te**	**ti**
él	**lo** (it, him) **le** (to him)	**él**
ella	**la** (it, her) **le** (to her)	**ella**
usted	**lo** (you, m.) **la** (you, f.) **le** (to you)	**usted**
nosotros	**nos**	**nosotros**
vosotros	**os**	**vosotros**
ellos	**los** (them, m.) **les** (to them)	**ellos**
ellas	**las** (them, f.) **les** (to them)	**ellas**
ustedes	**los** (you, m.) **las** (you, f.) **les** (to you)	**ustedes**

Here are some examples:

yo te veo	I see you
tú me ves	you see me
ella lo ve	she sees him/it
él la ve	he sees her/it
le damos un paquete	we give a parcel to her/to him
lo que me pasó	what happened to me
me dijeron	they told me
me cogió	he caught me
es para ti	it's for you
lo hizo por mí	he did it for me (on account of me)

Although the subject pronouns are given in some examples (**yo**, **tú** etc.) this is done only for you to see how they are used. Normally, they are used only for emphasis or contrast.

14 Try substituting a pronoun for the noun in italics.

a Perdí mi *equipaje.* _____

b Mandaron *el télex.* _____

c Puse *mi ropa.* _____

d Me quité *las gafas.* _____

e Apagué *la radio.* _____

f Quité *el contacto.* _____

g Cogió *la aleta derecha.* _____

Answers p. 96

15 Last year wasn't very good for you – explain why to Marisa. You'll be using **me mudé**, **fue**, **perdió**, **cajas**, **llegué**, and **reaccioné**.

16 Try retelling – out loud – the story which Marga told about her lost luggage.
If you are working with a partner, she/he will interject with questions and comments.
Here are some ideas:

Partner A	Partner B
Mi viaje a Manchester	¿Qué pasó después?
Mi equipaje	¿Y luego?
Desapareció	¡Pobre de ti!
Días angustiosos	¡Caramba!
Fue asqueroso	¡No me digas!
	¡Madre mía!

17 Try recreating the story of a traffic accident. There are some ideas below to help you. If you are working with a partner, each person can take a different scenario.

FECHA	DONDE	COCHE	PROBLEMA	REACCIÓN
3 de octubre	cruce con la calle Moreno	Opel Omega	cogió el morro	muy nervioso
19 de marzo	esquina con Avenida Mayor	Mercedes E 220	cogió la aleta derecha	bastante bien
24 de junio	autopista a Málaga	Ford Mondeo	cogió la aleta izquierda	me puse a temblar

EXERCISE 1

(a) I spilled chocolate down me (literally I stained myself with chocolate). **(b)** They packed all my things. **(c)** It was terrible! **(d)** I broke the video. **(e)** My parents moved to France in 1989. **(f)** They transported all their books and clothes by car. **(g)** They forget my brother's bicycle.

EXERCISE 2

(a) to León **(b)** from Ireland **(c)** last year **(d)** difficult **(e)** they packed his things and dismantled/took apart his furniture **(f)** reasonably so

EXERCISE 3

(a) Tuesday; fifteen minutes before closing time. **(b)** Two entered first and held up the owner and a client. Two more entered and helped fill the sacks. The last one was presumably the driver of the vehicle. **(c)** in the window **(d)** to fill the sacks **(e)** not to ring the police for a quarter of an hour **(f)** blue **(g)** No one noticed the events.

EXERCISE 5

(a) ¿Sabes lo que pasó? **(b)** Me perdieron mi equipaje. **(c)** Realmente ocurrió. **(d)** Fui a reclamarlo. **(e)** Dijeron que estaba en Londres. **(f)** Estuve tres días sin equipaje. **(g)** Fue realmente asqueroso.

EXERCISE 6

(a) 4 **(b)** 3 **(c)** 6 **(d)** 2 **(e)** 1 **(f)** 7 **(g)** 5

EXERCISE 7

(a) Friday, October 8th **(b)** 2 kilos **(c)** Bogotá **(d)** 992 **(e)** 6.00 pm **(f)** Los Angeles **(g)** 15

EXERCISE 9

(b) 1 **(f)** 2 **(g)** 3 **(d)** 4 **(i)** 5 **(c)** 6 **(a)** 7 **(h)** 8 **(e)** 9

EXERCISE 10

(a) parar el motor **(b)** señalar correctamente el vehículo **(c)** avisar a otros conductores **(d)** el vehículo no interfiere en la circulación de la carretera **(e)** mantener la calma en todo momento **(f)** en caso de incendio **(g)** ayudar a los heridos **(h)** quedarse en el lugar del accidente

EXERCISE 11

(a) Córdoba, 1969 **(b)** Ballet Nacional de España **(c)** Seis sonatas para la reina de España **(d)** 1990 **(e)** artista independiente **(f)** Joaquín Cortés Ballet Flamenco **(g)** una canción, 'Una rosa es una rosa'.

EXERCISE 13

(a) Fuimos al Café Rouge. **(b)** Yo pedí un whisky. **(c)** Carolina pidió una coca cola. **(d)** Llegó mi hermano. **(e)** Charlamos/hablamos. **(f)** Luego ellos fueron al teatro. **(g)** Yo vi una película.

EXERCISE 14

(a) Lo perdí. **(b)** Lo mandaron. **(c)** La puse. **(d)** Me las quité. **(e)** La apagué. **(f)** Lo quité. **(g)** La cogió.

7 HOW THINGS USED TO BE

Spanish spoken in Spain is quite fast – which may be why you don't understand the conversations or listening passages first time. If you are not familiar with certain words or structures it is difficult to sort out when one word begins and another ends. There are several ways to overcome problems with listening. You can try listening along with the transcript, until you are comfortable with the meaning. Then put the written version aside and listen again. Do you still understand each phrase? Or go back to an earlier unit and try listening to passages that you found difficult first time around. You will discover that, having worked on them, you now find them much easier to follow. Or try listening with a partner. You often find that he or she has understood parts that you've not caught – and vice versa. If you share this information, you can often piece together the whole passage. And never forget that the more you practise, the easier it becomes. So keep listening – in bed, in your car, while gardening – whenever.

Life before baby ...

Maite

Pues sí, mi vida antes, por ejemplo, en cuanto al trabajo, antes trabajaba unas treinta horas a la semana, y ahora trabajo solamente nueve horas a la semana. Y salía muchísimo, salía pues casi todos los fines de semana, y algunas veces durante la semana, también salía. No me preocupaba nada en realidad, no tenía una responsabilidad por la que trabajar, simplemente para pagar ¿no? la casa y ahora pues claro tengo una responsabilidad grande. Mm, no tenía que trabajar tanto en la casa y no tenía que hacer tantas comiditas y en fin tenía más tiempo libre. Eh, la verdad es que ahora no tengo ni un minuto para mí misma. Antes era más egoísta.

LISTEN FOR...	
trabajaba	I used to work
salía	I used to go out
no me preocupaba nada	nothing used to worry me

mi vida antes my former life, my life before; **mi vida después** my life afterwards.

en cuanto al trabajo as far as my work is concerned. Similarly, **en cuanto a mi hijo** as for my son.

trabajaba I used to work. This new tense, called the imperfect, describes how things used to be. There are only two sets of endings – one in '**-aba**' for '**-ar**' verbs and one in '**-ía**', for '**-ir**' and '**-er**' verbs. See page 108 for the full forms.

salía muchísimo I used to go out a lot; **salir** to go out. **Bebía muchísimo** I used to drink a lot.

algunas veces sometimes. **A veces** and **unas veces** mean the same thing.

no me preocupaba nada en realidad nothing really used to worry me; **preocuparse** to worry. Note that with this type of verb (a reflexive verb), **me** precedes the verb.

no tenía una responsabilidad por la que trabajar I didn't have any responsibility to work for (literally for which to work).

simplemente para pagar ¿no? la casa just to pay for the house (Maite means her mortgage!); **¿no?** Maite inserts this because she knows you will agree with her.

no tenía que trabajar tanto en la casa I used not to have to work so much at home; **tener que** to have to: **tenía que volver pronto a casa** I had to get home soon/early.

tantas comiditas so many little meals. **Una comida** a meal – add '**ito/a/os/as**' to mean 'little': **muchas cositas** lots of little things.

en fin in short

para mí misma for myself; **para sí mismo** for himself.

antes era más egoísta before, I used to be more selfish. (Remember that **egoísta** retains the '**-a**' ending in the masculine as well as in the feminine. There are only two irregular forms in the imperfect – **era**, 'I used to be' and **iba**, 'I used to go'.

1 Listen to the recording again and jot down the Spanish for the following English sentences. Don't look back!

a I used to work about thirty hours a week.

_____

b I used to go out a lot.

_____

c Nothing used to worry me.

_____

d I didn't have to work so much at home.

_____

e I had more free time.

_____

f I used to be more selfish.

Answers p. 112

_____

2 Listen to José Luis describing how life in Cea (his **pueblo** or 'village') has changed in the past twenty years. You will need the word **había** 'there used to be', which is the imperfect form of **hay** 'there is/are'; **una mercería** is a 'haberdashery' and **una fonda** is a 'modest hotel'.

Note seven differences between Cea as it was '**antes**' and how it is '**ahora**' – either in English or in Spanish if you prefer.

Cea hace veinte años ...
a
b
c
d
e
f
g

Answers p. 112

3 Read this short extract about how life used to be before Anabel started her university course. Then answer the questions which follow.

> **Bueno sí**, mi vida ha cambiado muchísimo desde que empecé la carrera. Antes, vivía en casa con mi familia, o sea, con mis padres y mis dos hermanos. Ahora, vivo en una residencia de estudiantes. Antes estaba en un colegio femenino donde conocía a todo el mundo – ahora no conozco a nadie – ¡somos trescientos alumnos en la clase de derecho romano! Antes comía muy bien – mi madre es vasca y cocina unos platos riquísimos. En cambio ahora o como en la cafetería de la universidad   donde la comida es pésima pero barata o me hago un sandwich y me lo como entre la clase de ciencia política y la de introducción a economía. Ahora lo que me gusta de mi nueva vida es que llevo lo que quiero – suelo llevar un jersey muy grande y unos tejanos. Antes tenía que llevar uniforme porque iba al convento. ¿Que si me gusta mi nueva vida? ¡Por supuesto que sí! Aunque echo mucho de menos a mi familia, me encanta ser independiente, más adulta y menos adolescente.

a Where does Anabel live now?

_____

b What sort of school did she use to go to?

_____

c There are three strands to Anabel's university course (**carrera**). Can you work them out?

_____

d What does she wear to class along with her jeans?

_____

e Why does Anabel like her new life?

_____

Answers p. 112

_____

4 You are retired (**estás jubilado/a**). Tell Guillermo what life was like when you used to have a job. You'll need: **trabajaba**, **me preocupaba**, **tenía que** and **egoísta**. You'll hear **descansado**, 'relaxed'.

Life in Barcelona

Maite

Y ¿cómo era tu vida en Barcelona antes?

Griselda

Pues era bastante diferente de lo

LISTEN FOR...

era bastante diferente	it was quite different
trabajaba a jornada completa	I worked full-time
tenía mucho trabajo	I had a lot of work

que es ahora. Básicamente porque trabajaba a jornada completa en una escuela y estaba enseñando como profesora de español, catalán y también daba clases de inglés como segunda lengua. Y como también estudiaba y también era completo, o sea, jornada completa de estudios entonces no tenía mucho tiempo para poder salir con los amigos o, especialmente durante la semana. Los fines de semana sí que salía con mis amigos pero durante la semana tenía mucho trabajo. Básicamente, preparaba exámenes, preparaba actividades, corregía y me levantaba siempre muy temprano, antes de las ocho y nunca me iba a la cama antes de la una.

¿cómo era tu vida ... antes? what was your life like before? (literally, how was your life before?) As you can see, **era** means 'it was' as well as 'she/he was' and 'I was'. The full forms are on page 108.

era bastante diferente de lo que es ahora it was rather different from what it is now (literally, from that which it is now).

trabajaba a jornada completa I used to work full-time (literally, a complete day). 'Part-time' is **a tiempo parcial** or **media jornada**.

en una escuela in a primary school. **Un colegio** is a (private) secondary school and **un instituto** a state secondary school.

estaba enseñando I was teaching. You can form a continuous tense in the past in much the same way as in the present – **estoy enseñando**, I am teaching. Look back to Unit 4 to refresh your memory.

daba clases de inglés como segunda lengua I used to give classes in English as a second language

estudiaba I was studying, I used to study

también era completo it was also full-time. Griselda means she was a full-time student as well as a full-time teacher. Since many courses are taught at night, this is perfectly possible.

preparaba exámenes I used to prepare/write exams; **un examen** an examination.

las actividades activities

corregía I used to correct, mark work (from **corregir**, 'to correct').

me levantaba siempre muy temprano I always used to get up very early; **levantarse** to get up.

nunca me iba a la cama I never went to bed. There are just two irregular verbs in the imperfect – **era** and **iba**. **Iba** can mean 'I she/he/it used to go'. It can even mean 'you used to go': **¿usted iba a un colegio de curas?** used you to go to a school run by priests?

5 The phrases in each column are opposites. Try matching them up.

a me iba a la cama	**1** me quedaba en casa, sola
b salía con mis amigos	**2** era igual
c trabajaba mucho	**3** me acostaba tarde
d me levantaba temprano	**4** me levantaba
e estaba enseñando	**5** me examinaba
f era diferente	**6** estaba aprendiendo
g preparaba exámenes	**7** descansaba mucho

Answers p. 112

6 Now read this passage in which a Spanish novelist writes about her life as a young girl.

Nuestra familia vivía parte del año en Barcelona y parte en París. Era un mundo muy cerrado al principio, pero se abrió cuando estalló la guerra civil. Tenía diez años y escribía cuentos y también teatro. Mi madre guardaba todo lo que escribía cuando era joven y lo ponía en un cajón en su dormitorio. ¡Yo no sabía! Sólo me enteré después. A los 16 años escribí una novela y sin hablar con nadie, fui a una editorial para mostrársela. Me dejaron pasar y yo vi al jefe. Era una persona muy correcta, muy simpática. Yo tenía un pánico tremendo porque era muy tímida cuando era joven. ¡Ahora ya no! El señor me pidió que escribiera el original a máquina y así lo hice. Después de unos días yo salía de mi casa y me encontré con él. Me dijo que le gustaba mucho mi libro y que lo iban a publicar. ¡Era imposible! ¡No me lo esperaba! Tenía que ir con mi padre a firmar el contrato porque era menor de edad. Y el jefe del editorial decía 'iPero si aún va con uniforme!'

Are these statements true or false?

	verdad	mentira
a The writer lived in a restricted world.	☐	☐
b She was unaffected by the war.	☐	☐
c She wrote short stories, plays and novels.	☐	☐
d Her novel was accepted straight away.	☐	☐
e Her mother kept her stories in a box in her bedroom.	☐	☐

f She is and always has been very shy. □ □

g Her father signed her contract for her. □ □

h Her footwear surprised the director of the publishing house. □ □

Answers p. 112

7 You've changed your job. Tell Marisa about your old one. You'll be using **trabajaba**, **era**, **daba**, **estudiaba** and **salía**.

A Catholic boarding school in the 70s

José Luis

Bueno, la vida en el internado era un poco difícil para un niño de diez, once años. Nos levantábamos pronto, por la mañana teníamos cuatro o cinco horas de clase, una pausa para la comida y después por la tarde otras dos o tres horas de clase. También teníamos horas de estudio después de terminar las clases y bastantes horas dedicadas a la oración, a cuestiones religiosas. También teníamos mucho deporte.

Maite

Pero ¿tenías tiempo para ver a tus padres? ¿Cuándo veías a tus padres?

José Luis

Solamente los veía tres veces al año, durante las vacaciones en Navidad, en Semana Santa y en las vacaciones de verano.

Maite

Pero ¿no les echabas de menos?

José Luis

Sí, mucho, pero la vida era así, no podías cambiarla, no podías cambiarla.

LISTEN FOR...	
nos levantábamos pronto	we used to get up early
teníamos cuatro horas de clase	we had four hours of class
los veía tres veces al año	I saw them three times a year

Many young people in Spain are educated in Catholic schools run by monks or nuns. If they live in the country like José Luis, they board.

en el internado   in the boarding school. **Un/a interno/a** is 'a boarder'; **era interno/a** I was a boarder.

nos levantábamos pronto   we used to get up early. In this conversation, other forms of the imperfect (past tense) occur. This is the 'we form' of an '-ar' verb: **nos acostábamos tarde** we used to go to bed late.

teníamos cuatro o cinco horas de clase we used to have four or five hours of classes. '**-íamos**' is the 'we form' of an '**-er**' or '**-ir**' verb: **antes, vivíamos en Barcelona** before, we used to live in Barcelona.

una pausa para la comida   a break for lunch. In phrases like these, **la comida** always refers to the midday meal, although it can mean a meal in general.

horas de estudio después de terminar las clases   study hours after the end of class. Remember to use an infinitive (**terminar, empezar**) after a preposition: **antes de empezar** before beginning.

bastantes horas dedicadas a la oración   quite a lot of hours dedicated to prayer

¿tenías tiempo para ver a tus padres? did you have time to see your parents? For the '**tú** form' of the imperfect, simply add '**-ías**' to the stem as in **¿cuando veías a tus padres?** when did you see your parents?

los veía tres veces al año I used to see them three times a year. Note that with **ver** 'to see', the ending is added to the stem '**ve-**'.

la Navidad Christmas. This is often used in the plural for the whole of the Christmas period – **las Navidades**.

Semana Santa Holy Week or Easter: **pasé Semana Santa en Roma** I spent Easter in Rome.

¿no les echabas de menos? didn't you (used to) miss them? **echar de menos** to miss. Simply add '**-abas**' to the stem for the '**tú**

form'. You may have noticed that José Luis said **los veía** 'I saw them' whereas Maite uses **les** for 'them' – **les echaba de menos**. Both are correct and reflect where each of the speakers is from. Maite is from Madrid and José Luis from the north.

la vida era así life was like that

no podías cambiarla you couldn't change it. Remember to put the pronoun (**la**, for **la vida**) on the end of infinitives: **no pude verla** I wasn't able to see her.

PRACTICE

8 That conversation included a number of verbs in the '**nosotros** form' of the imperfect tense. Match up the English and Spanish expressions.

a **Teníamos muchas horas de clase.**

b **Nos levantábamos temprano.**

c **No los veíamos muy a menudo.**

d **No podíamos cambiarla.**

e **Nos acostábamos a las nueve.**

f **Comíamos a la una.**

g **Hacíamos mucho deporte.**

1 We used to eat at one o'clock.

2 We had lots of hours of class.

3 We used to do lots of sport.

4 We used to go to bed at nine.

5 We used to get up early.

6 We couldn't change it.

7 We didn't see them often.

9 Listen to Marisa talking about her school days. You'll hear some new words: **una monja** a nun; **hija única** an only daughter; **la capilla** the chapel; **la misa** Mass. **Había** is the imperfect form of **hay** and means 'there was' or 'there were'.

a Where was Marisa at school?

_____

b How many girls were there at the school?

_____

c What sports did they play?

_____

d What time and day was Mass said?

_____

e Did Marisa go often?

_____

f What time did they start school?

_____

g Why did Marisa not see her parents very often?

Answers p. 112

_____

10 Here is an account of a woman, Maribel Fernández, who decided to leave her job as an editor to go self-employed.

> **Maribel** decidió vivir mejor. Era el año 1975 y trabajaba en la editorial GRAMA editando libros de texto. Eran los tiempos de la prehistoria cuando la máquina más sofisticada era la máquina de escribir. Maribel quería casarse y decidió que también quería tiempo libre. Así que primero se cambió a un empleo de mañana, y al año siguiente empezó a trabajar por su cuenta. Una doble sorpresa en aquellos tiempos cuando las mujeres sólo empezaban a incorporarse al mundo de trabajo y había muy pocos empresarios. Maribel buscó una socia, compró una máquina IBM, alquiló un local y creó dos puestos de trabajo. Todo iba muy bien hasta que llegó la crisis económica. Tenía que reducir personal y subcontratar, ser más flexible para sobrevivir. ¿Y ahora? Maribel sigue adelante: su empresa es más pequeña, pasa por épocas buenas y otras peores. Pero una cosa la tiene clara. Volvería a hacer lo mismo.

Would Maribel make the following remarks? If not, explain why – in English. You'll meet two new words: **arriesgarse** to take risks, **arrepentirse** to regret, repent

a Me gustaba mucho mi trabajo en la editorial y no quería dejarlo.

_____

_____

b No me gusta arriesgarme, soy muy prudente siempre.

_____

_____

c Soy independiente, original – un poco excéntrica quizá.

_____

d Me gusta trabajar en equipo.

_____

e Siempre trabajo en casa.

_____

f La crisis económica no me afectó.

_____

_____

g No me arrepiento de lo que hice.

_____

11 It's your turn now to talk about your school days. Guillermo will ask the questions. You will need **estaba**, **me gustaba**, **nos levantábamos**, **jugábamos** and **veíamos**. You'll also hear **¿qué hacíais?** what did you (plural) use to do?

KEY WORDS
AND PHRASES

¿cómo era tu vida antes?	what was your life like before?
trabajaba unas treinta horas	I used to work about 30 hours
salía muchísimo	I used to go out a lot
no me preocupaba nada	nothing worried me
no tenía que trabajar tanto	I didn't have to work so much
era más egoísta	I was more selfish
era diferente de lo que es ahora	it was different from what it is now
trabajaba a jornada completa	I used to work full-time
daba clases de inglés	I used to teach English
estudiaba	I used to study
no tenía mucho tiempo	I didn't have much time
tenía mucho trabajo	I had a lot of work
¿tenías tiempo?	did you have time?
teníamos ...	we had ...
cuatro horas de clase	four hours of classes
mucho deporte	a lot of sport
veía a mis padres	I used to see my parents
¿veías a tus padres?	did you see your parents?
¿no los echabas de menos?	didn't you miss them?
preparaba …	I prepared …
exámenes	for exams
actividades	activities
me levantaba muy temprano	I used to get up very early
nos levantábamos muy pronto	we used to get up very early
nunca me iba a la cama antes de la una	I never went to bed before one
en Navidad (es)	at Christmas
en Semana Santa	at Easter

Unit 7   How things used to be

GRAMMAR AND EXERCISES

The imperfect tense

Spanish has a second past tense which you need to learn. The imperfect tense (**el imperfecto**) is used in the following circumstances:

- To describe what you used to do (it is the equivalent of 'used to + verb' in English).
  Cuando vivía en Malasia, llovía todos los días.
  When I lived (used to live) in Malaysia, it rained (used to rain) every day.

- To translate 'I was -ing'.
  Lavaba el coche.   I was washing the car.
  Fregaba los platos.   He was doing the dishes.

- To describe things in the past which have no clear beginning or end.
  El cielo estaba gris y había grandes nubes.
  The sky was grey and there were great clouds.

How to form the imperfect:

There are only two sets of endings, one for '**-ar**' verbs and another for '**-er**' and '**-ir**' verbs.

hablar	volver	repetir
(yo) hablaba	volvía	repetía
(tú) hablabas	volvías	repetías
(el/ella/usted) hablaba	volvía	repetía
(nosotros) hablábamos	volvíamos	repetíamos
(vosotros) hablábais	volvíais	repetíais
(ellos/ellas/ustedes) hablaban	volvían	repetían

The verbs **ser** and **ir** are irregular:

ser	ir
era	iba
eras	ibas
era	iba
éramos	íbamos
erais	ibais
eran	iban

Ver adds the '**-ía**' endings to the stem **ve**: **veía** I/she/he used to see.

12 Read the following anecdote and underline each verb in the imperfect. Then jot down its infinitive and the meaning.

Yo estaba en la cocina preparando el desayuno cuando de pronto sonó el teléfono. Era mi hijo que llamaba de Nueva York, donde está trabajando para una agencia internacional.

Tranquilo, me dijo. Estoy perfectamente. Te llamo porque pienso volver a España la semana que viene y quería decirte que ime voy a casar!

No me lo podía creer. iMi hijo que sólo tenía veintitrés años y que pensaba viajar por el mundo entero! ¿Pero que podía decirle? Estaba tan contento. Hablaba de la cabina de un restaurante en donde estaban comiendo él y su novia. Por lo visto, comentaban cosas de su trabajo (los dos trabajan para la misma agencia) cuando de pronto le preguntó a ella si le apetecía casarse con él. Sí, así como suena. La chica dijo que sí, que cómo no, que qué buena idea y bueno, ya está – estarán en Madrid la semana que viene y casados en primavera.

_____

_____

_____

Answers p. 112

13 Can you translate the following sentences?

a   I used to live in Boston. _____

b   I went to school in Hartford. _____

c   It was a nice life. _____

d   I had two brothers. _____

e   And I liked playing with them. _____

f   I was very happy! _____

Answers p. 112

Estaba + -ando, -iendo

In Unit 4 you learned how to use the continuous tense in the present: **estoy haciendo una traducción** I am doing a translation. This emphasises that you are doing something at this moment. You can also use a continuous tense in the imperfect with the same sort of meaning:

Lavaba el coche	I was washing the car/I used to wash the car
Estaba lavando el coche (cuando ...)	I was washing the car (when ...)

This last form suggests that you were in the middle of doing something. But there is little difference between the two structures.

14 What were you doing when you met an old school friend? Translate the following sentences, using the continuous form.

a   I was having a drink in a bar. (**tomar**)

_____

b   I was studying in the library. (**estudiar**)

_____

c   I was watching a film. (**ver**)

_____

d   I was working in Paris. (**trabajar**)

_____

e   I was going back to work. (**volver**)

_____

f   I was driving my car. (**conducir**)

_____

Answers p. 112

Acababa de ...

In Unit 4 you learned that **acabo de** means 'I have just:'
Acabo de llegar de Berlín. I have just arrived from Berlin.
If you use the imperfect **acababa de**, it means 'I had just:'
Acababa de llegar de Berlín cuando se estalló una bomba en el aeropuerto.
I had just arrived from Berlin when a bomb went off in the airport.

15 What do these sentences mean?

a   Silvia acababa de volver de sus vacaciones en Lima cuando tuvo un accidente de coche bastante grave.

_____

b   Susana acababa de comprar el nuevo disco de Enrique Iglesias cuando Carlos le dijo que ya lo tenía.

_____

c   Acababan de mudarse de casa cuando murió el padre de Luisa.

_____

d   Acababa de escribir a mi hijo en Cuba cuando me llamó de La Habana.

_____

Answers p. 112

16 Now talk to Guillermo about your life in Gerona. You'll be using **vivía**, **había** and **tenía**.

17 Out loud, talk about how life used to be when you were ten years old. What did you use to do? Where did you use to live? How has your home town changed? Here are some ideas.

vivir con mis padres y mi hermano pequeño

jugar con mis amigos en el patio de recreo/en el parque

ir de vacaciones a la playa

me gustaba ...

regalarme dinero/juguetes (mis abuelos)

darme caramelos/tebeos (mis padres)

la vida era ...

mi pueblo era ...

había, no había ...

If you are working with a partner, ask **¿cómo era la vida antes?** and get them to reply using their own ideas or our suggestions.

If you like, you can contrast what things were like in the past with how they are now.

Antes vivía ..., ahora vivo ...

Antes Londres era ..., ahora es ...

Antes era fácil ..., ahora es difícil ...

Unit 7   How things used to be

EXERCISE 1

(a) Trabajaba unas treintá horas a la semana.
(b) Salía muchísimo. (c) No me preocupaba nada. (d) No tenía que trabajar tanto en la casa. (e) Tenía más tiempo libre. (f) Antes era más egoísta.

EXERCISE 2

Before Cea was (a) bigger (b) had more inhabitants (c) had more shops (d) there were three supermarkets (e) a haberdasher's (f) a small hotel (g) it was more prosperous
Cea era (a) más grande (b) tenía más habitantes (c) tenía más tiendas (d) había tres supermercados (e) una mercería (f) y una fonda (g) era más rica

EXERCISE 3

(a) in a hall of residence. (b) a girls' convent school (c) Social Sciences (some economics, politics and law). (d) a large sweater (e) she is more independent, more adult and less of an adolescent

EXERCISE 5

(a) 4 (b) 1 (c) 7 (d) 3 (e) 6 (f) 2 (g) 5

EXERCISE 6

(a), (c) and (e) are true; the rest are false

EXERCISE 8

(a) 2 (b) 5 (c) 7 (d) 6 (e) 4 (f) 1 (g) 3

EXERCISE 9

(a) In León, in northern Spain (b) 500 (c) tennis in summer, swimming in winter. (d) every day at 7.00 am (e) every day - it was compulsory (f) at 8.00 (g) they lived in Barcelona

EXERCISE 10

(a) No, she wanted to get married and have more free time. (b) No, otherwise she would not have left her steady job. (c) Yes, probably. (d) Yes, she found a partner (una socia). (e) No, she hired premises. (f) No, she had to make some of her employees redundant. (g) Yes.

EXERCISE 12

estar to be; ser to be; llamar to call; querer to want; poder to be able to; tener to have; pensar to think; hablar to speak; comentar to talk about; apetecer to feel like

EXERCISE 13

(a) Vivía en Boston. (b) Iba al colegio en Hartford. (c) Era una vida agradable. (d) Tenía dos hermanos. (e) Me gustaba jugar con ellos. (f) Era muy feliz.

EXERCISE 14

(a) Estaba tomando una bebida en un bar.
(b) Estaba estudiando en la biblioteca. (c) Estaba viendo una película. (d) Estaba trabajando en París. (e) Estaba volviendo al trabajo. (f) Estaba conduciendo mi coche.

EXERCISE 15

(a) Silvia had just come back from holiday in Lima when she had a fairly serious car accident.
(b) Susana had just bought the new Enrique Iglesias record when Carlos told her he already had it.
(c) They had just moved house when Luisa's father died. (d) I had just written to my son in Cuba when he called me from Havana.

8

SAYING WHAT YOU MEAN

POINTS TO REMEMBER

● describing events and things in the past: '**-ar**' verbs ending in '**-aba**' and '**-er**' and '**-ir**' verbs ending in '**-ía**'.
● saying: 'I had just ...', **acababa de ...**
● continuous tenses in the imperfect: **estaba llamando a mi novio cuando ...**

BEFORE YOU BEGIN

Many learners complain that they don't get enough speaking practice. This is probably true – so you need to make more opportunities for yourself. Don't just do the speaking exercises on your recording once: repeat them until you can do them without thinking. If you can speak without having to search for the words and their endings, you can then put some effort into content – into *what* you are going to say, not *how* you are going to say it. Once you are reasonably fluent, think about pronunciation and intonation. Did you sound convincing? Does a particular sound need working on? At odd moments in the day, try practising the key words and phrases out loud until you have got them off pat.

Unit 8   Saying what you mean

CONVERSATION 1

The worst meal you ever had

Gustavo   Sí, en un restaurante mejicano. La comida era de una apariencia muy atractiva pero imposible de saborear porque era muy picante.

LISTEN FOR...

saborear	to taste
picante	spicy
grasiento/a	greasy
sabía a vinagre	it tasted of vinegar
el pescado estaba atrasado	the fish was off

Marga   Fue en un restaurante en Oviedo y un camarero que me estaba sirviendo la sopa me la tiró por encima.

Andrés   En un restaurante me pusieron una paella que estaba muy fría y muy grasienta.

Carmen   Una vez me pusieron un gazpacho malísimo que estaba muy fuerte, sabía mucho a vinagre.

Rafa   Bueno, que yo recuerde, la comida peor que comí fue una vez en Inglaterra, donde pedí tortilla de patatas y lo que comía era todo lo más diferente a una tortilla de patatas.

Eduardo   Sí, pues mira, fuimos a comer en la zona de Luarca, a un restaurante y el pescado estaba atrasado, no se podía comer y aparte de todo, nos lo cobraron muy caro y no lo quisieron cambiar.

la comida era de una apariencia muy atractiva   the food looked very nice.

un camarero que me estaba sirviendo la sopa   a waiter who was serving me the soup. **Servir**, like **pedir**, changes the 'e' to an 'i' in the 3rd person preterite, and also in the present participle: **pidiendo** asking; **sirviendo** serving.

me la tiró por encima   he spilled it over me (literally, he threw it over me); **tirar** to throw or pull; **por encima** over.

me pusieron una paella   they served me a paella (literally, they put me ... from **poner** to put). Note the use of **poner** to put, instead of **servir**. You could say **me sirvieron una paella**.

un gazpacho   cold soup, a speciality of Andalucía.

saber means 'to know', **saber a**, 'to taste of': **sabe a ajo** it tastes of garlic.

que yo recuerde   as far as I remember. For the moment, just learn this as an idiom.

pedí tortilla de patatas   I ordered a potato (or Spanish) omelette. Remember the stem-change from 'e' to 'i' in the third person: **pidió una tortilla francesa** he asked for a plain omelette.

todo lo más diferente a   quite different from

aparte de todo, nos lo cobraron caro   apart from everything else, they charged us a lot for it; **cobrar** to charge. In a bar you could say: **¿me cobra?** will you charge me? (in other words, 'the bill please').

no lo quisieron cambiar   they refused to change it. Used as a negative in the preterite tense, **querer** (to want) means 'to refuse': **no quiso venir** he refused to come.

1 What was wrong with each dish? Listen to the opinions again and complete the grid – in Spanish. Choose the correct response from the box.

a pescado	
b comida mejicana	
c sopa	
d paella	
e gazpacho	

Answers p. 128

> fuerte   muy picante   atrasado   fría y grasienta
> se lo cobraron muy caro   se la tiró por encima
> sabía a vinagre

2 Who said what? Marga has been out and about in Oviedo doing a survey on bad restaurant meals. Listen to the recording and see if you can attribute the following remarks to the right people.

a Cuando fuimos a Cangas nos sirvieron una sopa casi fría y ¡con una mosca muerta!

b Yo estuve en México hace unos años y comí un pollo relleno con una salsa asquerosa.

c Fue en Alemania – no me gusta la comida alemana por ser demasiado grasienta.

d No he tenido malas experiencias. ¡La verdad es que a mí me gusta todo!

e Cuando estuve en Inglaterra me sirvieron una paella que parecía sopa.

1 Ricardo Salas: de Luarca
2 Jorge Cantero: de Ribadasella
3 Manolo González: de Gijón
4 Charo Giménez: de Ávila
5 Carolina Menéndez: de Oviedo

3 If some of these hygiene rules had been followed, there might not have been so many disastrous food experiences! Read the text and then complete the grids in English.

HIGIENE ALIMENTARIA

Cuando haces la compra, observa que:
1 Las carnes sean frescas, de buen aspecto y color.
2 Los pescados: ojos brillantes.
3 Frutas y verduras: es mejor comprarlas según la temporada.

Ya en la cocina y para evitar infecciones alimentarias (salmonela, botulismo), debes cuidar la higiene en la preparación de alimentos:

1 Tener las manos limpias, así como las superficies y cacharros de cocina.
2 Cocer bien los alimentos y consumirlos en menos de 2 horas. También puedes conservar por debajo de 10°C, pero recalentando bien, 70°C, antes de consumirlos.
3 Evitar contacto entre alimentos crudos y cocinados.
4 Frutas y verduras crudas: dejarlas en agua con lejía (2 gotas/el litro) durante 30 minutos y enjuagar abundantemente.

VOCABULARY

cuidar	to look after
los alimentos	food
cocer	to cook
recalentar	to reheat
crudo	raw
la lejía	bleach
enjuagar	to rinse

a What three principles should you follow when shopping to make sure that your purchases are healthy?

b What four rules should you keep when cooking food?

Answers p. 128

4 Now it's your turn to talk about a disappointing meal that you ate at a restaurant.

You'll be using: **fue** it was, **pedí** I ordered, **grasiento/a** greasy, **no se podía comer** it was inedible.

I have very high blood pressure

Paqui

¿Sabes que tengo un problema terrible con la tensión? Tengo la tensión muy alta. Hace ocho meses que me enteré. Fui al médico, porque me encontraba muy cansada, me encontraba agotada y me dolía mucho la cabeza. Entonces, fui al médico y me dijo que tenía la tensión alta. Entonces me recomendó que tenía que ponerme a tratamiento ¿no? Me dio unas pastillas y yo que no quería tomármelas, pero me recomendó, porque si no quería acabar con un derrame cerebral, me dijo que tenía que seguir el tratamiento.

LISTEN FOR...	
la tensión	blood pressure
me enteré	I found out
agotada	exhausted
me dio unas pastillas	he gave me some pills

tengo la tensión muy alta I have very high blood pressure

hace ocho meses que me enteré I found out eight months ago. Use **hace** to express the English 'ago': **hace dos meses** two months ago; **hace una semana** a week ago.

me enteré I found out (from **enterarse**, to find out).

me encontraba muy cansada I felt (found myself) very tired; **encontrar** to find and **encontrarse** to find oneself.

me dolía la cabeza my head ached (literally to me ached the head); **me duele la cabeza** I have a headache; **me dolía el estómago** I had stomach-ache; **me duele el estómago**, I have stomach-ache.

tenía que ponerme a tratamiento I had to follow a course of treatment (I had to put myself on a treatment).

y yo que no quería tomármelas and I who didn't want to take them. Adding **que** just makes the sentence more emphatic. And **tomármelas** is just **tomar** 'to take', with **me** and **las** tagged on the end. When you have an infinitive and pronouns you can attach these to the end of the infinitive. So either: **la voy a ver**, or **voy a verla**, is 'I'm going to see her'. You add an accent to **tomármelas** to keep the stress in the right place.

si no quería acabar con un derrame cerebral if I didn't want to end up with a stroke; **acabar** on its own means 'to finish' or 'to end up': **la película acaba bien** the film ends well (has a happy ending).

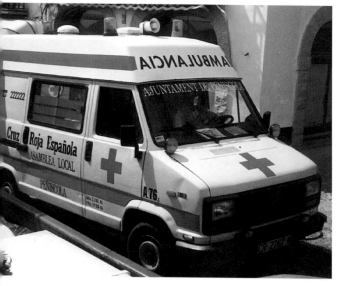

5 All the following phrases use the imperfect. Listen again to the recording and note down how Paqui expressed them in Spanish.

a I felt very tired. ————————————

b My head ached. ————————————

c I had high blood pressure. ————————————

d I had to follow a treatment. ————————————

Answers p. 128 **e** I did not want to take the pills. ————————————

6 Listen to this description of a bout of hepatitis that Marisa suffered from last year.

Then answer the questions in English. You will need **la gripe** flu, **los huesos** bones, **náuseas** sickness, and **cuello** neck.

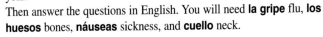

a How long did Marisa have to stay in bed?

————————————————————————

b Her symptoms were like those of another illness. Which one?

————————————————————————

c Which two parts of her body ached in particular?

————————————————————————

d Why could she not eat?

————————————————————————

e What three parts of her body went yellow?

————————————————————————

f What did Marisa take for the illness?

7

Remedios caseros – household remedies. You don't always have to go the doctor – especially if you have a minor upset. Read about what to do if you suffer from an upset stomach and/or sickness. Then complete the grid in English.

ACIDEZ DE ESTÓMAGO

El acidez ocurre si abusas del alcohol, tabaco, café o comida picante. También si comes demasiado rápido o no masticas bien. Se produce también en situaciones de estrés. Si no quieres utilizar antiácidos ni bicarbonato, lo mejor es tomar un vaso de leche tibia, una fruta o una porción de pan masticada lentamente.

VÓMITOS

Se sufre de vómitos por excesos en la comida, bebida, o tabaco. También por el dolor de cabeza. Cuando se sienten las primeras náuseas, es conveniente salir al aire fresco. Pon una compresa de agua fría en el cuello y mastica unos cubos de hielo o de leche condensada.

VOCABULARY

masticar	to chew
tibio	warm
conveniente	advisable
los cubos de hielo	ice cubes

		Acidez de estómago	Vómitos
a	Causas		
b	Remedios		

Answers p. 128

8

And now you talk about your health problems to Guillermo. You will hear **reponerse** 'to recover' or 'get better'.

A mosquito bite

Margarita	¿Me podría dar algo para esta picadura que me ... de un mosquito?
Farmacéutico	¿Cuándo la picaron?
Margarita	Esta mañana.
Farmacéutico	Esta mañana. ¿Tiene inflamación, no?
Margarita	Sí, un poquito.
Farmacéutico	¿Picores?
Margarita	También.
Farmacéutico	Le podemos dar unas pastillas o una pomada o ambas cosas.
Margarita	Bueno, pues, lo que usted vea que sea mejor.
Farmacéutico	Bueno yo le aconsejaría las pastillas, incluso la pomada, dos o tres días para que le quitase los picores momentáneamente.
Margarita	De acuerdo.
Farmacéutico	¿Anda bien del estómago?
Margarita	Bueno, regular.
Farmacéutico	Es que puede tomar las pastillas con infusión de manzanilla. Tres pastillas al día. La manzanilla ya sabe que le va muy bien para el estómago.
Margarita	Sí.
Farmacéutico	¿Algo más deseaba?
Margarita	Bueno, y para el dolor de cabeza, ¿qué me recomienda?
Farmacéutico	¿Qué? ¿Lleva muchos días con él?
Margarita	Pues, de dos a tres días.
Farmacéutico	¿Fiebre tiene?
Margarita	Pues no.
Farmacéutico	No tiene fiebre.
Margarita	No.
Farmacéutico	¿Digestiones? ¿Cómo las hace? ¿Bien?
Margarita	Bueno, hay veces que bien, otras veces regular.
Farmacéutico	Bueno, puede seguir con la manzanilla, a ver si le pasa con eso que es un problema de mala digestión.

LISTEN FOR...

esta picadura de mosquito	this mosquito bite
¿cuándo la picaron?	when were you bitten?
incluso la pomada	and the cream too
¿anda bien del estómago?	how's your stomach?

¿me podría dar algo para esta picadura que me ... de un mosquito? could you give me something for this bite which ... of a mosquito? Margarita changes her mind about what she wants to say; **una picadura** a bite, from **picar** to bite (of an insect).

¿picores? a rash, irritation? **Picor** is also from **picar**, and suggests something which itches.

unas pastillas, una pomada o ambas cosas some pills, a cream or both things; **ambos chicos** both boys.

lo que vea usted que sea mejor whatever you think (literally, see) is best; two present subjunctives here (**vea** from **ver**, and **sea** from **ser**) – this expresses uncertainty. The customer does not know what is best. Contrast with **esta pomada es mejor** this cream is best – a definite fact.

yo le aconsejaría las pastillas ... para que le quitase los picores momentáneamente I would recommend the tablets ... to take away the irritation for the time being; **aconsejar** to recommend; **quitase** is the imperfect subjunctive, after **para que** 'in order to ...'

¿anda bien del estómago? how is your stomach? (literally, does the stomach go well?). **¿anda bien del brazo?** how is your arm?

bueno, regular well, not too good; **¿cómo estás? regular** how are you? so-so.

infusión de manzanilla camomile tea; **manzanilla** is also a type of dry sherry.

¿algo más deseaba? were you wanting anything else? Use the imperfect to be a little more polite. The chemist could also have said **¿desea algo más?** do you want something else?

¿lleva muchos días con él? have you had it long? (literally, do you carry many days with it?).

¿digestiones, cómo las hace? how is your digestion?

a ver si le pasa con eso let's see if it goes away with that

PRACTICE

9 Does Margarita (in Conversation 3) have the symptoms that the chemist inquires about? Tick the appropriate box.

	sí	no	algunas veces
¿dolor de cabeza?	☐	☐	☐
¿inflamación?	☐	☐	☐
¿dolor de estómago?	☐	☐	☐
¿fiebre?	☐	☐	☐
¿malas digestiones?	☐	☐	☐
¿picores?	☐	☐	☐

Answers p. 128

10 Here are some health problems, typical of the summer months. Translate them. Use a separate piece of paper.

VOCABULARY

la abeja	bee
la avispa	wasp
el veneno	poison
peligroso	dangerous
prevenir	to prevent
aconsejar	to advise
evitar	to avoid
pelar	to peel
el corte de digestión	stomach cramp

LAS PICADURAS DE INSECTOS

El veneno de insectos como los mosquitos, abejas y avispas contiene numerosos compuestos tóxicos para el hombre pero sólo es peligroso en casos de agresión múltiple. Para prevenir las picaduras, conviene utilizar repelentes externos. Una vez que las tienes, se pueden utilizar pomadas a base de antibiótico y de corticoide.

LA ALIMENTACIÓN EN VERANO

Los especialistas nos hablan mucho del peligro que puede representar el agua durante el verano. Aconsejan beber agua mineral embotellada en los viajes al extranjero. 'Así se evita el gastroenteritis', dice Juan José Rodríguez Pérez, especialista en medicina familiar. 'También hay que evitar el consumo de helados, vegetales crudos y frutas no peladas, así como mariscos, mayonesa y derivados del huevo.'

LOS CORTES DE DIGESTIÓN

Conviene esperar al menos dos horas antes de volver a bañarse en el agua y hacerlo poco a poco, sobre todo en aguas muy frías. Por higiene, conviene ducharse antes y después del baño.

Answers p. 128

11

Now listen to some hints about what to do if you suffer from **deshidratación** 'dehydration' or **otitis** 'an ear infection' while on holiday.

Give three pieces of advice, in English, for avoiding **1** dehydration and **2** an ear infection in the summer. You'll hear **sudar** to sweat, and **el oído** the (inner) ear.

1
2

Answers p. 128

12

Now you go the chemist's because you have been stung by a wasp (**una picadura de avispa**). You'll be using: **una avispa**, a wasp, and **¿qué me recomienda?** what do you recommend?

KEY WORDS
AND PHRASES

era muy picante	it was very spicy
estaba ...	it was ...
muy fría	very cold
muy grasiento/a	very greasy
muy fuerte	very strong
sabía a ...	it tasted of ...
vinagre	vinegar
ajo	garlic
el pescado estaba atrasado	the fish was off
nos lo cobraron muy caro	they charged a lot for it
no lo quisieron cambiar	they wouldn't change it
tengo un problema terrible con la tensión	I have a terrible problem with my blood pressure
tengo la tensión muy alta	I have very high blood pressure
me encontraba ...	I was ...
muy cansada	very tired
agotada	exhausted
me dolía mucho la cabeza	my head ached terribly
me dio ...	he gave me ...
unas pastillas	some tablets
una pomada	a cream
manzanilla	camomile tea
un derrame cerebral	stroke
la inflamación	swelling
los picores	a rash
la fiebre	temperature
la mala digestión	indigestion

Using the imperfect and the preterite tenses together

First, look back at the dialogues and note when the preterite tense was used and when the imperfect was used. You will see that the preterite is used for completed actions which take place within a defined period of time (**me pusieron una paella**), and the imperfect for descriptions (**la paella estaba fría, atrasada**) or where no definite period of time is mentioned (**era diferente de lo que esperaba** 'it was different from what I expected').

13
So how do you say the following in Spanish?

a   The soup they served was cold. _____

b   I asked for a paella but it was greasy. _____

c   I ate the fish, but it was off. _____

d   They refused to change the vegetables (**la verdura**) which were

   not very attractive. _____

Answers p. 128

Positive commands with 'tú' and 'vosotros'.

Here's a quick recap on forming positive commands with **usted**. Begin with the first person singular of the present tense (**digo**): if the verb ends in '**-er**' or '**-ir**',   replace the '**o**' with '**a**' (sing.) or '**an**' (plural) – **diga(n)** say. If the verb ends in '**-ar**' (**bajar**), replace the '**o**' with '**e(n)**' (**baje usted, bajen ustedes**).
Now, you need to use different forms when telling people you address as **tú** (**vosotros** in the plural) what they should do.

Tú
- For most verbs, take the second person of the present tense and remove the final '**s**'.

hablas	you speak	**¡habla!**	speak!
respondes	you reply	**¡responde!**	reply!
pides	you ask	**¡pide!**	ask!

- There are eight common verbs with irregular forms.

¡di!	say!	**¡haz!**	do!
¡pon!	put!	**¡ten!**	have!
¡ve!	go!	**¡ven!**	come!
¡sal!	leave!	**¡sé!**	be!

Vosotros

- Start with the infinitive of any verb, subtract the final '**r**' and replace with '**d**'.

  ¡explicad!   explain!   **¡escoged!**   choose!

  ¡repetid!   repeat!

- Negative commands (when you tell people *not* to do something) are based on the subjunctive forms and are explained in Unit 11.

- One final point: if you use pronouns with a command, tack them on to the end to make longer forms like **dilo**, say it, or **dámelo** give me it. (Note the order of the pronouns in this last example).

Talking about illness

Use **tener** in specific expressions like:

tengo fiebre	I have a temperature
tengo dolor de garganta	I have a sore throat
tengo dolor de cabeza	I have a headache
tengo problemas de estómago/riñon	I have stomach/kidney problems
tengo la gripe	I have flu
tengo el dedo hinchado	I have a swollen finger
tengo diarrea	I have diarrhoea
tengo una insolación	I have sunstroke

Use **estar** in less specific expressions like:

no estoy bien (estoy mal)	I'm not well
estoy (un poco) resfriado/a	I have a (little) cold
estoy mareado/a	I'm feeling sick

Use **doler** (which is impersonal and works like **gustar**) in expressions like:

me duele el pie	my foot hurts
me duelen los ojos	my eyes hurt
me duelen los oídos	my ears hurt
me duele(n) mucho	it hurts a lot

Or use a verb:

toso mucho	I cough a lot (**toser** to cough)
¿como te sientes?	how do you feel?
me siento fatal	I feel awful! (**sentirse** to feel)

The doctor may tell you to do the following.

Toma:
aspirinas/vitamina C/jarabe para la tos/antibióticos/analgésicos cada cuatro horas, después de comer

Come:
poco/fruta y verdura

Bebe:
mucha agua/manzanilla

Evita:
el alcohol/la carne/comida grasienta

Quédate:
en cama unos días

Hazte:
un análisis (de sangre/de orina)

14   En la consulta del médico. You are a doctor. Tell your patient to:

a   drink lots of water

_____

b   take lots of exercise

_____

c   eat plenty of fruit and vegetables

_____

d   avoid fatty food

_____

e   go to the gym/swimming pool

_____

Y sobre todo ¡tómalo todo con calma!

Answers p. 128

15   Match the pictures with one of the phrases below.

a   Dile 'feliz cumpleaños'.
b   ¡Hazlo ahora mismo!
c   ¡Dámelo!

d   ¡Ven aquí!
e   ¡Salid de aquí, por Dios!
f   ¡Pon la mesa, Jordi!

Answers p. 128

16   Your turn to speak. In this exercise you talk to Guillermo about how awful you feel. You will be using **resfriado** a cold, **la gripe** the flu, **la fiebre** a temperature, **me duelen los ojos** my eyes ache and **un dolor de cabeza** a headache.

Unit 8   Saying what you mean

17 With the help of the information in the grid, try describing each meal out loud. If you are working with a partner, he or she can describe one meal and you the other.

VOCABULARY		MESÓN SANCHO PANZA	HOSTAL DON QUIJOTE
		la semana pasada	ayer
el mantel	tablecloth	sopa fría	pescado atrasado
sucio/a	dirty		
el ruido	noise	paella grasienta	verdura no muy fresca
limpio	clean		
maleducado	rude	personas que fumaban al lado	mucho ruido
		manteles sucios	no muy limpio
		muy caro	camareros muy maleducados

18 In this exercise, you are in the doctor's surgery (**en la consulta del médico**). These are your symptoms:

- **estás muy cansado**
- **tienes dolor de cabeza desde hace 24 horas**
- **vomitas todo lo que comes**

You can invent more if you wish. Tell the doctor about your problems.

If you are working with a partner, they can be the doctor. They can speak to you, using phrases like these:

- **¿qué le/te pasa?**
- **¿desde cuándo tiene/s ...**
- **lo que tiene/s que hacer es** (**descansar**, **tomar**, etc.)

EXERCISE 1

(a) pescado/atrasado, se lo cobraron caro
(b) comida mejicana/muy picante   **(c)** sopa/se la tiró por encima   **(d)** paella/fría y grasienta
(e) gazpacho/fuerte, sabía a vinagre

EXERCISE 2

(a) Ricardo Salas   **(b)** Manolo González   **(c)** Charo Jiménez   **(d)** Jorge Cantero   **(e)** Carolina Menéndez

EXERCISE 3

(a) Meat should be fresh and look good; fish should be bright eyed; buy fruit and vegetables in season.
(b) Hands, surfaces and cooking pots should be clean; cook ingredients well and consume within 2 hours or keep at temperatures below 10° and reheat at temperatures above 70°; keep raw and cooked ingredients separately; soak fruit and vegetables in water with a little bleach and rinse well.

EXERCISE 5

(a) Me encontraba muy cansada.   **(b)** Me dolía la cabeza.   **(c)** Tenía la tensión muy alta.   **(d)** Tenía que seguir el tratamiento.   **(e)** No quería tomarme las pastillas.

EXERCISE 6

(a) two months   **(b)** flu   **(c)** her head and bones
(d) she felt sick   **(e)** her face, neck and eyes
(f) tablets

EXERCISE 7

Acidity   **(a)** Causes: too much alcohol, tobacco, coffee and spicy food   **(b)** Remedies: a glass of warm milk, fruit or bread chewed slowly.
Sickness   **(a)** Causes: head aches, too much food, drink or tobacco   **(b)** Remedies: fresh air, a cold compress, sucking ice cubes or condensed milk

EXERCISE 9

Sí to everything except fiebre (no) and malas digestiones (algunas veces).

EXERCISE 10

Insect bites/stings. The poison of insects such as mosquitoes, bees and wasps contains a number of elements which are toxic to man but they are only dangerous if you have been bitten several times. To prevent bites, it is a good idea to use external insect repellents. Once you have them (the bites), you may use creams with an antibiotic and cortisone base.
Summer nutrition. Specialists talk a lot about the danger of water during the summer. They advise us to drink bottled mineral water on foreign visits. 'This is the way to avoid gastroenteritis', says Juan José Rodriguez Pérez, a specialist in family medicine. 'Also, you should avoid eating ice cream, raw vegetables and fruit which has not been peeled, as well as sea food, mayonnaise and egg derivatives.'
Stomach cramps. It is a good idea to wait for at least two hours before going into the water again and you should go in slowly, especially in very cold water. For reasons of hygiene, it is a good idea to take a shower before and after bathing.

EXERCISE 11

1 Drink plenty of liquid. Drink before and during exercising. Don't exercise too fiercely. Don't wear plastic-based clothes or shoes.
2 Take antibiotics. Take anti-inflammatory drugs. Keep the ears warm.

EXERCISE 13

(a) La sopa que sirvieron estaba fría.   **(b)** Pedí una paella pero estaba grasienta.   **(c)** Comí el pescado pero estaba atrasado   **(d)** No quisieron cambiar la verdura que no era (de una apariencia) muy atractiva.

EXERCISE 14

(a) bebe/a mucha agua   **(b)** toma/e mucho ejercicio   **(c)** come/a mucha fruta y verdura
(d) evita/e la comida grasienta   **(e)** ve/vaya al gimnasio/a la piscina

EXERCISE 15

(a) 1   **(b)** 5   **(c)** 2   **(d)** 3   **(e)** 6   **(f)** 4

9

MORE ABOUT THE PAST

WHAT YOU WILL LEARN

▶ how to talk about events in the recent past

▶ something about the federal regions in Spain

▶ more about putting forward your point of view

POINTS TO REMEMBER

● describing disastrous meals: **estaba frío, grasiento y atrasado**

● talking about your health: **tengo la tensión alta**, **dolor de cabeza**, **fiebre**, **malas digestiones**

● understanding the treatment: **toma/e aspirinas**, **vitamina C**; **descansa/e mucho**; **bebe/a mucha agua**

● using the preterite and the imperfect together: **no se podía comer pero lo cobraron muy caro**

BEFORE YOU BEGIN

Don't feel you have to stick to your book and cassette when you're learning Spanish. It can be quite motivating and morale-boosting to try out your knowledge in other areas. Why not buy a popular magazine or newspaper and see what you can make of it? The more lurid ones are usually a better bet than the very serious, as there are more pictures and large print to help you! The weekly magazine *¡Hola!* is a good choice. Its subject matter is the life of the rich and famous, so it uses the sort of everyday vocabulary which is useful for you to know. When you get tired of describing your own daily routine, house, garden or career, the appropriate vocabulary and structures will be reinforced when you read about how the other half live!

CONVERSATION 1

A difficult journey

Griselda

He tenido una mañana horrible hoy. Primero porque me he levantado tarde, tenía una cita a las doce, y he llegado tarde porque me he perdido. Pero lo primero que he hecho en casa ha sido ducharme, me he duchado, y después he mirado el mapa de carreteras y pensaba que no me costaría mucho tiempo llegar a donde tenía que llegar, pero no ha sido tan fácil. Primero, he salido de casa, (me) he conducido y después me he empezado a perder. Y he cogido muchas calles que no eran las que tenía que coger y al final he llegado bastante tarde.

LISTEN FOR...

he tenido una mañana horrible	I had a horrible morning
tenía una cita	I had an appointment
no ha sido tan fácil	it wasn't so easy

he tenido una mañana horrible hoy I've had a horrible morning today. Much as in English, Spanish uses the perfect tense ('have' + the past participle) when talking about the recent past: **he tenido un día terrible** I've had a terrible day.

me he levantado tarde I got up late. Look at page 140 in the grammar section for a full explanation of how to form this tense. You'll see that the pronoun (**me** in this case) precedes both parts of the verb: **se ha duchado** she/he has had a shower.

tenía una cita I had an appointment. This time, Griselda uses the imperfect because this isn't a definite action. Contrast **esta mañana he ido a una reunión** this morning I've been to a meeting.

he llegado tarde I arrived late. You have probably noticed that the ending of the past participle (the verb which often corresponds to the English ending in '-ed', has arriv-'ed') varies according to whether the original verb finishes in '-ar', '-er' or '-ir'. '-ar' verbs, like **llegar**, end in '-ado': **he hablado con el director** I've spoken with the director.

me he perdido I got lost. Verbs in '-er' (**perder**) and '-ir' (**vivir**) have past

participles which end in '-ido': **Lo he repetido muchas veces** I have repeated it over and over again.

lo primero que he hecho, ha sido ... the first (thing) I did was ... (literally the first that I have done has been ...) As usual, some verbs have irregular forms. Here are two examples: **he hecho** I have done/made; **ha sido** has been.

me he duchado I had a shower; **¿te has duchado?** have you had a shower?

he mirado el mapa de carreteras I looked at the road map. You could also say **el plano de la ciudad** the city map.

pensaba que no me costaría mucho trabajo llegar a donde tenía que llegar I thought it wouldn't be too difficult to get to where I had to go (literally, I thought it would not cost me much work to arrive where I had to arrive). Quite a mixture of verbs here! Again, **pensaba** and **tenía que** are in the imperfect because they are descriptions rather than actions. **Costaría** 'would cost' is another tense that you will be meeting in the next Unit.

he salido de casa I left home. Note how you must use **de** with **salir** 'to go out of': **hemos salido del cine a las once** we left the cinema at 11.00.

he conducido I drove

me he empezado a perder I began to get lost (to lose myself). Alternatively, you can add **me** to the infinitive: **he empezado a perderme**.

he cogido muchas calles que no eran las que tenía que coger I took a lot of streets which weren't those I had to take

PRACTICE

1 Listen to the recording again, if you have to, and number the events in the correct order.

a He mirado el plano de la ciudad. _____

b He conducido. _____

c He llegado a la cita bastante tarde. _____

d Me he duchado. _____

e Me he levantado tarde. _____

Answers p. 144 f Me he empezado a perder. _____

2 Now listen to what Guillermo and Marisa did this morning and jot down their activities in English, in the diaries below.

Guillermo	Marisa
8.00	
	11.00
8.05	
	1
8.30	
	2
1	
	3
2	
	4
3	
	5
2.00	

Answers p. 144

3 Javier has been on a business trip in England. Read this account of what he tells his wife about his first day and then decide whether the statements which follow are true or false.

Bueno hoy ha sido un día bastante atareado. He llegado tarde por un accidente que había en la carretera. He ido directamente a la empresa que está en pleno centro de la ciudad. No, no he tenido que ponerme el abrigo, ha hecho un tiempo precioso, ha brillado el sol casi todo el día. Incluso hemos comido fuera, en una terraza. Después hemos salido el señor Parker y yo a ver la nueva fábrica que están construyendo en las afueras. Hemos ido en coche hasta el hotel, me he quedado yo solo hasta las ocho y luego el señor Parker y su mujer han venido a recogerme para ir a cenar. Hemos cenado en un nuevo café-bar ... ha sido muy agradable, la verdad.

		verdad	mentira
a	Javier arrived late because he had an accident.	☐	☐
b	He visited the company, located near the city centre.	☐	☐
c	The weather has been very sunny.	☐	☐
d	They had lunch indoors, in a restaurant.	☐	☐
e	They went to see a new office building on the edge of town.	☐	☐
f	He and Mr Parker had a pre-dinner drink in the hotel.	☐	☐
g	The Parkers invited him home for a meal.	☐	☐

Answers p. 144

4 Now what did *you* do this morning? Answer Marisa's questions. You'll be using **no he tenido que, me he duchado, he salido, he desayunado** and **he llegado**.

Unit 9   More about the past

Federalism in Spain

Andrés	Las autonomías son una reacción espontánea a un fenómeno que ha ido sucediendo durante los últimos cuarenta años.

<table>
<tr><td colspan="2">LISTEN FOR...</td></tr>
<tr><td>las autonomías</td><td>the autonomous regions</td></tr>
<tr><td>cualquier gestión burocrática</td><td>any bureaucratic business</td></tr>
<tr><td>no han llegado a cumplir</td><td>they haven't managed to</td></tr>
<tr><td>su papel</td><td>fulfil their role</td></tr>
</table>

Carmen	Sí, y además también ha servido para agilizar toda la burocracia ¿no? Cualquier gestión burocrática es ahora mucho más rápida, porque hay cierta independencia de la administración del gobierno central.
Andrés	Pero el hecho de crear en cada autonomía unos parlamentos nuevos y unos gobiernos nuevos, ¿no ha aumentado o incrementado los costos al Estado?
Carmen	Sí, es posible, pero pienso que vale la pena, porque además también ha servido para revalorizar todas las costumbres populares y el folklore y todo eso.
Andrés	Pero sigo pensando que las autonomías en algunas regiones de España no han llegado a cumplir su papel. El papel que un pueblo está …
Carmen	Ah, te refieres al País Vasco ¿verdad?
Andrés	Sí, al País Vasco y a otras autonomías u otras regiones como Galicia y Cataluña.

las autonomías the autonomies. Andrés is referring to the 17 autonomous or federal regions of Spain. The three **autonomías históricas** to which he alludes later are the **País Vasco** (the Basque Country), **Galicia** and **Cataluña**, all of which were independent in the past and have their own distinct language and culture.

una reacción espontánea a spontaneous reaction

un fenómeno que ha ido sucediendo a phenomenon which has been occurring. You can use the perfect tense with a present participle ('**-iendo**', '**-ando**') to suggest continuity (been occurring rather than simply occurred).

además también ha servido para agilizar toda la burocracia besides, it has also served to speed up all the bureaucracy. The amount of red tape during the Franco years was notorious. It was partly due to excessive centralisation.

cualquier gestión burocrática any bureaucratic business. **Cualquiera** behaves likes **grande** and loses its final letter before a singular noun: **cualquier español** any Spaniard. **La gestión** can mean 'management', 'administration' etc.

el hecho de crear the (very) fact of creating. **Hecho** is the past participle of **hacer** to do or make. As a noun it can mean a 'fact' or 'deed'.

unos parlamentos nuevos some new parliaments. Remember that **unos** means 'some' – **me voy unos días** I'm going away for a few days. Each **autonomía** has its own regional parliament and administrative bodies. Similarly, **unos gobiernos nuevos** some new governments.

¿no ha aumentado o incrementado los costos al Estado? has it not increased the costs to the State? **Aumentar** and **incrementar** mean exactly the same.

pienso que vale la pena I think it's worth while. **No vale la pena** (it's not worth it) is a useful phrase.

para revalorizar todas las costumbres populares to revalue all the popular customs (traditions). **Popular** means 'of the people'. It is true that there has been a revival in local customs since the death of Franco; this is a semi-conscious way of proclaiming regional identity and, in some cases, a separation from the central State.

sigo pensando   I still think; **seguir** to go on, to continue. **Seguir** is one of the few verbs not followed by an infinitive (literally, I continue thinking).

no han llegado a cumplir su papel   they haven't yet managed to fulfil their role; **llegar a** means 'to manage to do

something': **no ha llegado a aprobar el examen** he hasn't managed to pass the exam; **cumplir** means 'to carry out', 'fulfil or honour an obligation': **Neni cumple años mañana** Neni's birthday is tomorrow (she fulfils/accomplishes years).

te refieres al País Vasco ¿verdad?   you mean the Basque country, don't you? **Referirse** is a useful verb: **me refiero a la chica rubia que ha venido a verme hoy** I mean/am talking about the blonde girl who has come to see me today.

PRACTICE

5   In Conversation 2 Andrés and Carmen both put forward arguments as to the pros and cons of regional government. In English, jot down the arguments for and against local autonomy, according to the two speakers.

En pro

1 _____

2 _____

En contra

1 _____

2 _____

Answers p. 144

6   Now listen to Guillermo telling us a little more about **autonomías**. Then answer the questions in English. You'll hear the word **tribunal**, 'court'.

a   How many **autonomías** are there?

_____

b   How many provinces were there under General Franco?

_____

c   With what country does Guillermo compare Spain?

_____

d   Which are the three **autonomías históricas?**

_____

e   Why do they have this name?

_____

f   What are the names of their languages?

_____

g   What do Cataluña and the País Vasco have that other **autonomías** don't?

Answers p. 144   _____

Unit 9   More about the past

7 Athough the Basque Country enjoys a good deal of independence, the members of the terrorist group ETA want still more **autonomía**. Listen to this passage about an attack on a bookshop (**una librería**) in Vitoria. You will need to know the words **librero** a book shop owner, **libertad** freedom, **odio** hate, **ciudadano** a citizen, and **apoyar** to support.

Link up the two halves of these sentences, all of which occur in the recording.

a	Una librería en Vitoria	1	no abandona su librería, sus libros y su casa.
b	La librería	2	porque 'los libros forman parte de la historia vasca'.
c	Los ciudadanos de Vitoria	3	fundada en el año '68 ...
d	Incluso han ofrecido libros a los terroristas	4	la han convertido en símbolo del odio de ETA a la libertad.
e	Los cócteles molotov	5	y los vascos en general, lo han apoyado.
f	Pero el propietario, Juan José Muñoz	6	ha sido objeto de ataques ...

Answers p. 144

8 Your turn to speak. You're still not too sure what an **autonomía** is, so Guillermo explains to you again. You'll be using **¿qué es? ¿cuáles son? ¿cuántas? ¿te refieres a?**

What has changed in Asturias?

Marga

¿Ha cambiado algo en Asturias desde que ésta tiene su propia autonomía?

Francisco

Creo sinceramente que ha cambiado bastante y

LISTEN FOR...	
ha cambiado bastante	it's changed quite a lot
ha mejorado la calidad y la cantidad	the quality and quantity have improved
hemos aumentado la red hotelera	we've increased the hotel network

además ha cambiado para bien. En general ha mejorado la calidad y la cantidad de los servicios prestados por la Administración pública al administrado, desde que ha tenido lugar el proceso autonómico, ya que la administración está más cerca del administrado, y permite conocer mejor y más directamente sus propios problemas y sus necesidades, aplicando las soluciones más exactas y correctas. En lo que se refiere a turismo, puedo opinar con pleno conocimiento de causa y la prueba de ello es que hemos mejorado las tareas de propaganda, de información y de atención al turista. Hemos aumentado la red hotelera y otras muchas actuaciones que la falta de tiempo me impide continuar.

¿ha cambiado algo en Asturias desde que ésta tiene su propia autonomía? has anything changed in Asturias since it has had its own self-government? The pronoun **ésta** 'this (one)' refers to **Asturias**.

para bien for the better; **para mal** for the worse

los servicios prestados por la Administración pública al administrado the services provided by the public Administration (Town/City Hall) to the citizen (literally, to the administered person); **prestar** means 'to lend'.

desde que ha tenido lugar el proceso autonómico since the autonomous process has taken place; **tener lugar** means 'to take place': **las conferencias tienen lugar en la sala X** the talks/lectures take place in room X. Alternatively, you can simply use '**son**' – **las conferencias son en la sala Y**. As a civil servant, **señor Francisco** speaks in a rather formal style.

sus propios problemas y sus necesidades its own problems and necessities; **esos pisos tienen garaje propio** those flats have their own garages.

en lo que se refiere a turismo as far as

tourism is concerned. Another use of **referirse**.

puedo opinar con pleno conocimiento de causa I can make a judgement with full knowledge of the facts; **pleno conocimiento de causa** is a set phrase.

la prueba de ello the proof of this; **ello** is a neuter form meaning 'this', 'that' etcetera: **ahora que estamos en ello** while we're at it.

hemos mejorado las tareas de propaganda we have improved the tasks of publicity; **mejorar** to improve. The word **propaganda** in Spanish does not have the negative connotation it has in English.

hemos aumentado la red hotelera we have increased the hotel network; **la red** means 'a chain' or 'network' or 'a power supply'; **la Red** is 'the Internet'.

otras muchas actuaciones many other activities. At the theatre **actuación** means a 'performance': **la actuación ha sido brillante** the performance was (has been) wonderful.

la falta de tiempo me impide continuar lack of time prevents me from continuing; **impedir** to prevent; **impedir** is a stem-changing verb like **pedir** 'to ask for'.

9 Guillermo's mother phones and wants to know what he's been doing since she last rang.

Listen to what he tells her. You'll need **pintar** 'to paint', and **fuerte** (here) 'shocking'. **Pedro Almodóvar** is a very popular Spanish film-director. Jot down in Spanish six things which Guillermo has done since he last spoke to his mother.

a _____

b _____

c _____

d _____

e _____

Answers p. 144   f _____

10 Read this postcard and then in English fill in the five major changes in Javi's life.

Hola Miguel

Te escribo desde Oviedo. ¡Cuánto tiempo, eh! No he tenido tiempo últimamente para ponerme en contacto porque he tenido unos exámenes importantísimos y he tenido que trabajar y estudiar mucho. Pero ahora estoy de vacaciones en Asturias y he pensado en ti y lo que estarás haciendo estos días. He tenido un año super atareado. Me he mudado de casa, he empezado a estudiar ingeniería en Zaragoza, he encontrado a una chica maravillosa y he salido muchas veces con ella a las montañas que, como sabes, no están lejos de aquí. ¡Ah! Y he aprobado mis exámenes, así que puedo seguir estudiando el año que viene. O sea que he tenido un año fantástico.

Pero sólo he hablado de mí mismo y de mis problemas y mis sueños. Y tú ¿qué has hecho? ¿qué piensas hacer? ¿qué planes tienes para el verano? ¿Por qué no me llamas uno de estos días y podemos salir de bares? Te podría presentar a Nuria ...
Hasta muy pronto
　　　　　　　Javi.

Cosas que he hecho este año

a
b
c
d
e

Answers p. 144

11 In this speaking exercise, Marisa corners you on the street to do a survey (**una encuesta**) on what people do before they leave for work in the morning. Reply to each question. You'll need **desayunar** 'to have breakfast', **lavarse el pelo** 'to wash your hair' and **¡qué raro!** 'how odd!'

Unit 9   More about the past

he tenido una mañana horrible	I've had a horrible morning
me he levantado tarde	I got up late
he llegado tarde	I arrived late
me he perdido	I got lost
me he duchado	I had a shower
he mirado el mapa	I looked at the map
no ha sido tan fácil	it wasn't so easy
he salido de casa	I left home
he conducido	I drove
he cogido muchas calles	I went down a lot of roads
una autonomía	an autonomous region
hay cierta independencia	there is a certain independence
la administración	administration
el gobierno central	central government
el parlamento	parliament
es posible	it's possible
vale la pena	it's worthwhile
las costumbres populares	popular customs
algunas regiones de España	some regions in Spain
te refieres al País Vasco ¿verdad?	you're referring to the Basque country, aren't you?
ha cambiado bastante	it has changed quite a lot
han mejorado la calidad y la cantidad	they have improved the quality and quantity
hemos mejorado	we have improved
hemos aumentado	we have increased
ha tenido lugar	has taken place
la información	information
la propaganda	publicity
ha cambiado ...	it has changed ...
para bien	for the better
para mal	for the worse
puedo opinar	I can give an opinion

GRAMMAR AND EXERCISES

The perfect tense

To form this tense, use the present tense of **haber** (to have) and add the past participle (in English, the equivalent to forms ending in '-ed', such as (has) walk'-ed', or '-en' such as (has) spok'-en' etc.

hablar	comer	vivir
he hablado	he comido	he vivido
has hablado	has comido	has vivido
ha hablado	ha comido	ha vivido
hemos hablado	hemos comido	hemos vivido
habéis hablado	habéis comido	habéis vivido
han hablado	han comido	han vivido

Unfortunately some of the past participles are irregular. Here is a list of the more common ones.

abrir	abierto	open(ed)	**He abierto la puerta.**	I have opened the door.
decir	dicho	said	**No ha dicho la verdad.**	He hasn't told the truth.
escribir	escrito	written	**No me ha escrito esta semana.**	She hasn't written to me this week.
hacer	hecho	done	**¡Dicho y hecho!**	No sooner said than done!
morir	muerto	died	**Ha muerto el presidente.**	The president has died.
poner	puesto	put	**He puesto mi abrigo nuevo.**	I've put on my new coat.
romper	roto	broken	**Ha roto con su novia.**	He's split up with his girlfriend.
ver	visto	seen	**¿Has visto mi diccionario?**	Have you seen my dictionary?

This tense is used to talk about the recent past, where in English we would use 'have' + past participle.

Asturias has changed a lot. **Asturias ha cambiado mucho.**

I have visited France. **He visitado Francia.**

Use this tense after words like:

hoy	**Hoy, he visto a Ana.**	Today, I saw Ana.
	Hoy, no he visto a Carolina.	I didn't see Caroline today.
esta semana	**Esta semana, he escrito una carta.**	This week, I wrote a letter.
este año	**Este año, he ido a Portugal.**	This year, I went to Portugal.
estas vacaciones	**Estas vacaciones, he vuelto a casa.**	These holidays, I went back home.
esta mañana	**Esta mañana, me he lavado el pelo.**	This morning I washed my hair.
todavía	**Todavía no ha llegado.**	He hasn't arrived yet.

Note that the nearest English equivalent does not always correspond to 'have + past participle'.

Just to refresh your memory about which past tense to use where:

- Use the perfect tense (**he salido, has tomado, ha comido** etc.) to translate the English 'I have' (gone out, drunk, eaten etc.) AND after expressions which suggest the recent past like **hoy** 'today', **esta mañana** 'this morning' and **todavía** 'still', 'yet'.

- Use the imperfect tense (**salía, tomabas, comía** etc.) to translate the English 'was doing', 'used to do' AND for descriptions in the past – **estaba oscuro** 'it was dark'.

- Use the preterite (**salí, tomaste, comió** etc.) to translate the English 'I went out', 'you drank', 'he ate' etc. – that is, for actions in the past which are over and done with.

12 You're telling a friend all the things you've done over the holidays. Choose the appropriate verb to complete each sentence.

Estas vacaciones:

a   He _____ a Asturias.

b   He _____ a la montaña más alta, el Naranjo de Bulnes.

c   He _____ los libros que compré en Madrid.

d   He _____ para el examen que tengo en septiembre.

e   He _____ de copas con unos amigos de por allí.

f   He _____ a mi familia en Gijón.

g   ¡No me he _____ muy temprano!

h   Me he _____ varias veces cuando hacía buen tiempo.

| ver | subir | estudiar | ir | levantar | bañar | leer | salir |

Answers p. 144

13 A late arrival. Now you tell Guillermo about why you arrived at an appointment rather later than expected. You will need the perfect tense of **perder, levantarse, tener, ducharse** and **poder**.

14 Read this short article which puts forward the reasons for and against the **despenalización del hachís** (the decriminalisation of cannabis). Read it through and then decide whether you are for or against. Using the phrases you learnt in Unit 4 (**yo creo que, opino que, pienso que** etc.) argue for your case out loud. If you are working with a partner, decide to take opposite views, using the opinions expressed in the article or any others you can think of. If you wish (and have time) you could then try arguing each other's case – or you could choose a different subject, giving yourself a few minutes to marshal your thoughts before you start.

Razones para el sí:

- Las drogas duras deben controlarse como los medicamentos y las blandas, como el tabaco y el alcohol.

- La ilegalidad beneficia a las mafias que acumulan cantidades enormes de dinero.

- Es la única forma de terminar con la delincuencia. El tráfico de hachís financia el de la cocaína.

- Considerar aceptable o no el consumo de una sustancia es sólo una cuestion cultural.

- El hachís conduce a otras drogas sólo porque es ilegal.

Razones para el no:

- El hachís es la entrada al consumo de otras drogas más peligrosas. Quien se droga con algo casi siempre quiere ir a más.

- Cuanto más facil es obtener una sustancia, más se consume y mayor es el riesgo de abusar.

- Si se quiere respetar la libertad individual, no es justo acudir después al dinero público para desintoxicarse.

- La legalización no termina con el verdadero problema de la drogadicción. Tenemos que ofrecer alternativas a la droga.

VOCABULARY	
drogas duras	hard drugs
drogas blandas	soft drugs
cuanto más ... más	the more ... the more
acudir a	to come, to turn to

EXERCISE 1
(e) 1 (d) 2 (a) 3 (b) 4 (f) 5 (c) 6

EXERCISE 2

Guillermo	Marisa
8.00 Went to the railway station	11.00 Got up
8.05 Caught the train	1 Had a bath
8.30 Arrived at the office	2 Had breakfast on the balcony
1 Spoke with the secretary	3 Read the newspaper
2 Dictated letters	4 Had another cup of coffee
3 Spoke with clients on the 'phone	5 Had an aperitif with a friend
2.00 Ate with the boss	

EXERCISE 3
They are all false except (c). (a) no, someone else had an accident (b) no, the company was in the centre of the city (d) no, they had it outside (e) it was a new factory (f) no, he was alone (g) no, they went out for a meal

EXERCISE 5
Pro – the administration has speeded up, more interest in local customs. Contra – more expensive and the autonomy has not always worked.

EXERCISE 6
(a) 17 (b) 50 (c) Germany (d) Cataluña, País Vasco and Galicia (e) they were independent states in the past (f) catalán, vasco and gallego (g) police force

EXERCISE 7
(a) 6 (b) 3 (c) 5 (d) 2 (e) 4 (f) 1

EXERCISE 9
(a) Ha tomado las pastillas. (b) Ha dormido muy bien. (c) Ha pintado la puerta de la cocina. (d) Ha jugado al squash. (e) Ha encontrado una chica. (f) Ha salido con ella al cine.

EXERCISE 10
(a) I've moved house. (b) I've started an engineering course. (c) I've met a fantastic girl. (d) I've been to the mountains a lot. (e) I've passed my exams.

EXERCISE 12
(a) salido (b) subido (c) leído (d) estudiado (e) ido (f) visto (g) levantado (h) bañado

WHAT YOU WILL LEARN

▶ how to talk about the future
▶ how to say ' I would ...'
▶ how to hire a car in Spain
▶ how to buy a radio-cassette
▶ how to make suppositions

POINTS TO REMEMBER

● talking about the recent past: **he podido, has sacado, ha comido**
● irregular past participles: **abierto, dicho, vuelto, escrito, hecho, muerto, visto**
● words which describe the political situation: **autonomía, independencia, gobierno, administración, parlamento**

BEFORE YOU BEGIN

When you are studying a reading passage or if you have picked up a Spanish magazine or newspaper, how do you cope with words you don't know or a structure you don't recognise? Firstly, it's a good idea to look at any accompanying photographs or pictures which will help you put the material in context. Look at the title of the piece or the by-lines. They often summarise the content of the text. Study the first and last paragraphs – the first paragraph tells you what the article will be about, and the last paragraph usually contains a brief summary or conclusion. Then read the rest of the article through, out loud if necessary, to get the drift. Once you have a general idea of the meaning, work through paragraphs, sentences and then individual words. Even if you don't know a particular word, you can often guess its meaning from its context: it helps to work out whether it is a noun or a verb. If it's an adjective, which noun does it go with? Use both grammatical *and* contextual clues. Note down any words or phrases which you find useful or interesting.

EL PAIS

DIARIO INDEPENDIENTE DE LA MAÑANA

EDICIÓN EUROPA
www.elpais.es

DOMINGO 5 DE ENERO DE 2003
Año XXVIII. Número 9.352

INFORMACION

Director: Francisco Esquivel   **ALICANTE**   AÑO 58-II EPOCA-NUMERO 4.921

What the future holds

Griselda

A ver, a ver ... Mm ... es muy interesante. A ver, la línea de la vida dice que tendrás una vida muy larga, muy, muy

LISTEN FOR...

tendrás una vida muy larga	you will have a very long life
terminará pronto	it will finish soon
encontrarás otro mejor	you will find a better one

larga y no hay ninguna interrupción, lo cual es bueno. La línea del trabajo ... mm ... ya no es tan buena. Creo que el trabajo actual terminará pronto, pero, pero, creo que en el futuro encontrarás otro mucho mejor. En cuanto a situación familiar, creo que aumentarás tu familia. Es probable que tengas más de un hijo y en la cuestión de amores, creo que vas a tener un romance muy pronto. ¿Parece bien?

María

¡Me parece estupendo!

In this conversation, Griselda is reading María's hand. **A ver, a ver** let's see, let's see. Simply repeat yourself if you wish to emphasise a statement: **pasa, pasa** do come in; **muy, muy larga** really long.

la línea de la vida the life-line

tendrás una vida muy larga you will have a very long life. **Tendrás** is the 'tú form' of **tener**, 'to have', in the future: **tendré** I will have; **tendrá** she/he/it will have. Unfortunately, **tener** is irregular! Most futures are formed by adding the endings (**é**, **ás, á, emos, éis, án**) to the infinitive. Turn to page 156 for a full explanation.

no hay ninguna interrupción there is no interruption, no break. **Ninguno/a** means 'no', 'none' or 'nobody' and is more emphatic than other negatives. It works like all other negatives (see page 28). It also loses its final 'o' before a masculine noun: **en ningún momento** at no time, **ningún problema** no problem.

lo cual es bueno which is good. **Lo cual** refers to the general idea which preceded it. It literally means 'that which'.

ya no es tan buena it's not so good. Here **ya** (already) suggests that, in comparison with the first prediction, this one is not so good.

el trabajo actual terminará pronto your present job will soon come to an end. Be careful with **actual** – it means 'now' or 'present': **actualmente** at the moment.

Terminaré pronto I will soon finish. This is the normal future form.

encontrarás otro mucho mejor you will find another, a much better one.

en cuanto a situación familiar as for your family situation

aumentarás tu familia you will increase your family; **aumentar** to increase.

es probable que tengas más de un hijo it is probable that you will have more than one child. After expressions of possibility or probability like **es posible** or **es probable**, Spanish uses the verb form known as the subjunctive.

en la cuestión de amores as for love(s), as far as love is concerned; **el amor** love.

¿Parece bien? does that sound good to you? **¡Me parece estupendo!** It sounds wonderful!

Unit 10 What I would like to do

PRACTICE

1 Here are the four areas in which Griselda gave her predictions in Conversation 1 on page 146. Under each heading, give a brief summary, in Spanish, of what Griselda said.

VIDA tendrás ...	FAMILIA
TRABAJO	AMOR

Answers p. 160

2 Here are three short news bulletins about forthcoming events in Latin America. Read them through. There is some vocabulary to help you.

a

QUITO, ECUADOR. El presidente de Ecuador anunció que el fin de semana empezará una gira por América Latina. Viajará a Estados Unidos, Brasil, Argentina y Perú. También afirmó que probablemente visitará Chile e intentará viajar a Colombia y Panamá también.

b

LIMA, PERÚ. El presidente peruano anunció que declarará ilegal la huelga que empezarán el martes los 500.000 funcionarios, si afecta los servicios de educación, transporte y justicia. Los funcionarios empezarán el miércoles al mediodía una huelga indefinida para reclamar aumentos salariales del 21,5 por ciento y para rechazar las privatizaciones de las empresas estatales de petróleos y de comunicaciones.

c

SAN SALVADOR. El presidente del Salvador dijo que, junto a sus colegas de Centroamérica, pedirá al presidente norteamericano, legalidad para los millones de inmigrantes de esa región que residen en Estados Unidos. El presidente hará una visita a Honduras en junio y se reunirá con los presidentes de la región. Hablarán de la inmigración, la inflación y el tráfico de drogas.

In the left hand column you will find several verbs taken from the text. Match them up with phrases in the right hand column with the same meaning.

a	hará una visita	1	hará un viaje
b	empezarán	2	discutirán
c	viajará	3	visitará
d	se reunirá	4	iniciarán
e	declarará	5	se encontrará con
f	hablarán	6	dirá que es

Answers p. 160

3 Now listen to this short news item which is similar to those you've just read. Listen for **unos niveles aceptables** which means 'acceptable levels'. Then complete the grid in English.

THE MEETING

Dates:	
Subjects:	
1	
2	
Delegates expected from:	
Venue:	

4 Now you tell Marisa about what her life is going to be like. You'll be using **tendrás** 'you will have', and **terminará** 'it will end'. You'll also need **la línea de la vida** and **largo/a**.

CONVERSATION 2

I want to hire a car

Yolanda ¡Hola, buenos días!

Sergio Buenos días, señorita, ¿qué deseaba por favor?

Yolanda Mire, es que me gustaría alquilar un coche. Voy a estar unos días aquí en Oviedo.

Sergio Bueno ¿días cuántos, más o menos?

Yolanda Como una semana. Me gustaría que fuera un coche pequeño.

Sergio Bueno, vamos a ver, tenemos una tarifa, tenemos varias tarifas de alquiler de coches, pero creo que el mejor, la mejor, la que tiene mejores condiciones es la de Europcar. Eh, tenemos un tipo de coche medio como puede ser un Ford Ka, un Ford Focus, un Renault Clio o un Renault Mégane.

Yolanda Bueno, yo creo que el Ford Ka estaría bien.

Sergio El Ford Ka estaría bien. Bueno, está normalmente, la tarifa del Ford Ka sería por semana (si lo alquila una semana, tiene derecho a kilometraje ilimitado) y esto le costaría doscientos diecisiete euros por siete días de alquiler de coche.

Yolanda Ah, pues muy bien, gracias.

Sergio De nada.

LISTEN FOR...

me gustaría alquilar un coche	I would like to hire a car
la tarifa de alquiler de coches	the car hire prices
kilometraje ilimitado	unlimited mileage

¿qué deseaba? what were you wanting? **¿qué desea?** is another alternative. You may also hear: **¿en qué puedo servirle?** how can I help you?

me gustaría alquilar un coche I would like to hire a car; **gustaría** is the conditional tense 'I would' – more about this on page 157. Remember that **alquilar** with an 'a' is a verb, and means 'to hire'. **Alquiler** with an 'e' is a noun and means '(car) hire'.

como una semana about a week

me gustaría que fuera un coche pequeño I would like it to be a small car, **fuera** (from **ser** 'to be') is a subjunctive and Yolanda uses it here because she is expressing a wish. It's enough just to be able to recognise the subjunctive at this point.

vamos a ver let's see – a similar expression to **a ver** which you met in Unit 9.

tenemos una tarifa we have a price list

al mejor, **la mejor** the best one. Sergio makes an error in gender at first, then corrects himself – **mejor** goes with **tarifa**.

la que tiene mejores condiciones the one that has the best terms. (**la** refers to **tarifa**)

un coche medio a medium-sized car

el Renault, **el Ford Ka**. Notice how for cars, you use use **el** because **el coche** is understood.

el Ford Ka estaría bien the Ford Ka would be good – again, the conditional tense, this time of **estar**.

el Ford Ka sería ... the Ford Ka would be ... This time **ser** rather than **estar** is used, because Sergio is referring to price: **¿cuánto sería?** how much would it be? **sería ... euros.**

tiene derecho a kilometraje ilimitado you have the right to unlimited mileage

esto le costaría ... this would cost you ...

5 These statements about Yolanda and the car hire are inaccurate. Read them through and then correct them.

a Yolanda va a estar dos días en Oviedo.

_____

b Yolanda quiere alquilar un coche grande.

_____

c El Ford Focus es un coche pequeño.

_____

d Yolanda se decide por el Renault Mégane.

_____

e La tarifa del Ford Ka es por día.

_____

f Le costaría treinta y un euros al día.

Answers p. 160

_____

6 Listen to a dialogue similar to Conversation 2 and then check the facilities which each car has on the grid below. You will need **permiso de conducir** 'driving licence' and **seguro** 'insurance'.

	clase económica	clase compacta
plazas		
aire acondicionado		
puertas		
seguro incluido		
kilometraje ilimitado		
precio al día		

Answers p. 160

7 But before you rent a car, you'll need your **carnet** or **permiso de conducir**, (your driving licence). Read this advert for a driving school, then answer, in English, the questions which follow.

Auto-Escuela P A R E D E S
CALLE DE FUENCARRAL, 41
Teléfono: 91 - 432 - 35 - 08

CARNET DE CONDUCIR B1
¡matricúlate ya!

2.100 euros

INCLUYE
- matrícula
- tramitación del permiso
- clases teóricas ilimitadas
- libros
- transporte al examen
- Placa L

25 clases de coche

- **10 de circulación de 45 minutos**
- **15 de maniobras de 35 minutos**

El alumno practicará en circuito cerrado al tráfico. Así, podrá estar solo al volante más pronto.

Las clases prácticas se realizarán con coches nuevos PEUGEOT y GOLF equipados con aire acondicionado y dirección asistida.

HORARIO
de 9.00 a 20.00

CLASE TEÓRICA
de 15.00 a 16.00

a How many theory classes can you have?

b How long are the 'manoeuvre' classes?

c Who takes the pupil to the driving test?

d Who buys the L plate?

e What two features do the school cars have?

f What is the advantage of practising on a private circuit?

Answers p. 160

8 Now you try hiring a car. You'll be using **me gustaría alquilar**, **sería** and **estaría bien**.

Which would you recommend?

Yolanda	Mira, me gustaría comprarme un casete.
Joven	¿Más o menos tienes una idea de cómo lo querías?
Yolanda	No. Quería que fuera un precio módico pero no tengo ninguna idea en especial.
Joven	Vamos a ver. Tienes el clásico radiocasete monogram que parte de los cincuenta euros, o casetes estereofónicos a partir de cien euros, o aparatos copiadores de cintas que andarían sobre los doscientos euros.
Yolanda	Eh bueno … ¿cuál me recomendarías tú?
Joven	Si eres una persona que copias cintas o te gusta copiar canciones para los amigos, quizás te venga bien el mejor radiocasete copiador.
Yolanda	Sí. ¿Tienes algún modelo más de este tipo?
Joven	Pues, de este tipo ahora mismo en las existencias, no, pero se podría pedir uno, ¿eh?
Yolanda	Mm. Así que dices que son cien euros, ¿no? más o menos.
Joven	No, doscientos euros el copiador y cien euros el estéreo normal.

LISTEN FOR...

me gustaría comprarme	I would like to buy a
un casete	cassette recorder
¿cuál me recomendarías tú?	which would you recommend me?

me gustaría comprarme un casete I would like to buy myself a cassette (literally, it would please me to …). **Casete** can be either masculine or feminine. If it is feminine, it means the 'cassette tape' itself. The recorder is **el casete** (m.).

¿más o menos tienes una idea de cómo lo querías? do you have some idea of what you want? (literally, more or less do you have an idea of how you were wanting it?). Notice how the young man adresses Yolanda as **tú**, although he doesn't know her. This is common among young people.

quería que fuera un precio módico I would like (literally, I was wanting) it to be a reasonable price; **fuera** is a subjunctive form of **ser** (more on this in Unit 12).

que parte de los cincuenta euros from 50 euros (**partir de** "to start from')

a partir de cien from 100; **a partir de** from: **a partir de ahora** from now on.

aparatos copiadores de cintas tape copying machines

que andarían sobre los doscientos euros which would be about 200 euros – (literally, which would go on/around 200 euros.)

¿cuál me recomendarías tú? which would you recommend? Use **cuál** when offering a choice: **¿cuál quieres?** which one do you want? **Recomendarías** is another example of the conditional tense (See Grammar section in this unit.)

las cintas tapes. You can also use **una casete**.

las canciones songs; **una canción** a song.

quizás te venga bien el mejor radiocasete copiador perhaps you'd be better off with the best radiocassette that copies. **Venga** is a subjunctive form of **venir**. The assistant uses this form after **quizás** (perhaps) because he is suggesting a possibility. More on this in Unit 11.

en las existencias in stock

pero se podría pedir uno but we (one) could order one

¿así que dices que son cien euros? so you say that they are 100 euros? **¿así que te vas?** so you are going?

9 Listen to the dialogue again and say whether these statements are true or false.

		verdad	mentira
a	Yolanda quiere comprar un casete de un precio razonable.	☐	☐
b	Los radiocasetes en mono cuestan a partir de los cincuenta euros.	☐	☐
c	Los radiocasetes estereofónicos parten de cien euros.	☐	☐
d	El joven cree que un casete copiador le vendría bien a Yolanda.	☐	☐
e	Hay modelos de todos los tipos en las existencias.	☐	☐

Answers p. 160

10 Now listen to Marisa talking about a new computer (**un nuevo ordenador**) which she would like to have at home. Then answer the following questions in English. You'll need **correo electrónico** 'e-mail' and **un juego** 'a game'.

a Where does Marisa already have a computer?

b How could her children use the Internet?

c What three things would she and her husband use it for?

d Who does Marisa write to via electronic mail?

e Who would her children write to?

Answers p. 160

f What three other things would they use it for?

11 Label each item in Spanish, using the vocabulary below. Some of the words are new to you, so you will need to use different strategies for working them out. Start by labelling the items you already know. Then read the other words out loud and try to guess what they might mean. You might be able to work out others by a process of elimination. As a final resort, use the vocabulary list at the back of the book.

> disco duro   platina   cinta   carrete   diapositiva   flash
> objetivo   ratón   pantalla   elepé   disco compacto
> impresora   teclado   disco

12 Now you speak to Guillermo about a new piece of electronic equipment that you would like to buy. You'll be using **me gustaría comprar** and **¿cuál me recomendaría usted?**

KEY WORDS
AND PHRASES

a ver	let's see
muy interesante	very interesting
tendrás una vida muy larga	you will have a very long life
el trabajo actual terminará pronto	your present job will soon finish
en cuanto a …	as for …
no es tan bueno/a	it's not so good
la línea	line
largo/a	long
el futuro	the future
me gustaría alquilar un coche	I'd like to hire a car
me gustaría que fuera un coche pequeño	I'd like it to be a small car
un coche medio	a medium-sized car
la tarifa que tiene mejores condiciones	the list with the best terms
el Ford Ka estaría bien	the Ford Ka would be good
tiene derecho a kilometraje ilimitado	you have the right to unlimited mileage
me gustaría comprarme un casete	I would like to buy myself a cassette recorder
¿cuál me recomendarías tú?	which would you recommend?
¿tienes algún modelo más?	do you have any other models?
no tengo ninguna idea	I have no idea
un precio módico	a reasonable price
un casete	a cassette recorder
un ordenador	a computer
un estéreo	a stereo
el correo electrónico	electronic mail (email)
un aparato	a machine
una cinta (una casete)	a tape
más o menos	more or less
a partir de (cincuenta euros)	from (50 euros)
las existencias	stocks
copiar	to copy
una canción	a song

GRAMMAR AND EXERCISES

The future tense

Here is how the future tense goes:

yo tomar -é	I will take
tu tomar -ás	you will take
él tomar -á	he will take
ella tomar -á	she will take
Vd. tomar -á	you will take
nosotros tomar -emos	we will take
vosotros tomar -éis	you will take
ellos tomar -án	they will take (masculine)
ellas tomar -án	they will take (feminine)
Vds. tomar -án	you will take (**usted** plural)

■ There is only one set of endings for all verbs: **yo hablaré**, **comeré**, **viviré**.

■ Reflexive pronouns keep the same position: **me ducharé** I will have a shower.

■ There are a few irregular stems – here are the most frequent:
yo querré I will want, **yo podré** I will be able to, **yo pondré** I will put, **yo saldré** I will leave, **yo sabré** I will know/find out, **yo diré** I will say/tell, **yo haré** I will do/make, **yo tendré** I will have, **yo vendré** I will come.
Lo haré mañana I'll do it tomorrow. **Vendré en coche** I'll come by car.

13 Read this account of an interview that Pablo has in Madrid. Put all the verbs in brackets into the 'yo form' of the future tense – except where **nosotros** is indicated.

> Mañana (ir) a Madrid. (Coger) el tren de las nueve y media y (estar) en Madrid a las tres. (Tomar) un taxi al apartamento de un amigo y al llegar allí, lo (llamar). (Ducharse), (cambiarse) de ropa y supongo que (salir, nosotros) a cenar. Luego (ir, nosotros) de copas o quizás al cine. El día siguiente, tengo la entrevista con R.S.I., así que (levantarse) pronto para estar allí a tiempo. (Volver) a casa por la tarde y (llegar) bastante tarde, me imagino.

Answers p. 160

Unit 10   What I would like to do

14 Using the future. Think of three things you intend to do this summer and jot them down in the space provided, e.g. **Este verano iré a Colombia a practicar el español.** You'll find three models in the answers.

Este verano ...

a _____

b _____

c _____

The conditional tense (expressing 'would')

The conditional starts with the same stem as the future (regular or irregular) and adds the imperfect endings with '**-ía**' to the end. So:

yo tomar -ía	I would take
tú tomar -ías	you would take
él tomar -ía	he would take
nosotros tomar -íamos	we would take
vosotros tomar -íais	you would take
ellos tomar -ían	they would take

And:

yo querría	I would like
yo pondría	I would put
yo sabría	I would know
yo diría	I would say

and so on ...

15 The eternal question of what you would do if you were to win the lottery – **si te tocara la lotería**. Use the ideas below to write six sentences. Remember to use the conditional. Sentence **a** is an example. There are possible answers on page 160.

Si me tocara la lotería ...

a Comprar un Porsche porque _Compraría un Porsche porque es un coche muy rápido._

b Comprar una casa en _____.

c Visitar a mi familia en _____.

d Ir de vacaciones a _____.

e Abrir una cuenta de ahorros en _____.

f Dar muchos regalos a _____.

g Hacer una fiesta para _____.

158

16 Now *you* say what you would do if you won the lottery. Guillermo will guide you on the recording. You'll be using the conditional tense with verbs like **haría**, **sería**, **iría** and **daría**.

17 Look at these predictions for some of the star signs and predict (out loud) what will happen to people with those star signs and what they might be doing in ten years' time. If you are working with a partner, predict his or her future too, by using the ideas here or by turning back to Griselda's comments in the first Conversation.

Aries 21 marzo al 20 abril

Favorable. Simplifica tu trabajo porque necesitarás colaboración de tus compañeros. Salud: muy bien. Dinero: bien. Trabajo: muy bien. Amor: muy bien. Suerte: bien.

Géminis 21 mayo al 21 junio

Regular. Aceptarás una invitación sentimental que no dará buen resultado. Verás que te resulta complicado relacionarte con la persona que amas. Salud, dinero, trabajo, amor: todos regular. Suerte: mal.

Cáncer 22 junio al 22 julio

Normal. Tendrás un poco de melancolía. En el trabajo, tendrás más satisfacción. Salud y trabajo: bien. Dinero: muy bien. Amor: regular. Suerte: bien.

Escorpio 24 octubre al 22 noviembre

Muy favorable. Magnífica perspectiva en tus actividades profesionales, lo cual mejorará tu vida privada y amorosa. Utilizarás más tu inteligencia que tu esfuerzo físico. Salud, amor y suerte: muy bien. Dinero y trabajo: excelente.

Acuario 21 enero al 18 febrero

Favorable. Tu situación económica mejorará este mes. Buscarás a nuevos amigos. Tendrás que ser prudente en cuestión de amores. Salud, dinero, amor y suerte: bien. Trabajo: muy bien.

Piscis 19 febrero al 20 marzo

Excelente. En el trabajo podrás eliminar una pequeña injusticia. Lo deberás a la claridad de tus ideas. Excelentes posibilidades en el amor. Salud, dinero y amor: excelente. Suerte: muy bien.

ANSWERS

EXERCISE 1

VIDA: tendrás una vida muy larga y no hay ninguna interrupción. **TRABAJO:** pronto tendrás un trabajo mejor. **FAMILIA:** tendrás más de un hijo. **AMOR:** tendrás un nuevo romance.

EXERCISE 2

(b) 3   **(b)** 4   **(c)** 1   **(d)** 5   **(e)** 6   **(f)** 2

EXERCISE 3

12 and 13 March/price of coffee and a possible strike/Central America, Mexico, Colombia and Ecuador/Copán in Honduras.

EXERCISE 5

(a) una semana   **(b)** un coche pequeño
(c) un coche medio   **(d)** el Ford Ka
(e) por semana   **(f)** por semana

EXERCISE 6

	clase económica	clase compacta
plazas	5	5
aire acondicionado	no	sí
puertas	3	5
seguro incluido	sí	sí
kilometraje ilimitado	sí	sí
precio al día	31€	38€

EXERCISE 7

(a) as many as you like   **(b)** 35 minutes
(c) the school   **(d)** the school   **(e)** air conditioning and power steering   **(f)** you can start driving alone earlier

EXERCISE 9

(a), **(b)** and **(d)** are true, the others are false.

EXERCISE 10

(b) at the office   **(b)** for their school work
(c) finding out train timetables, booking hotel rooms and renting cars   **(d)** to her sister in Colombia
(e) to their cousins and friends in the U.S
(f) for language learning, learning to type and for games

EXERCISE 11

(a) carrete (film, spool)   **(b)** objetivo (lens)
(c) flash   **(d)** diapositiva (slide)   **(e)** impresora (printer)   **(f)** teclado (keyboard)   **(g)** disco duro (hard disk)   **(h)** ratón (mouse)   **(i)** pantalla (screen)   **(j)** elepé (LP)   **(k)** platina (deck)
(l) cinta or casete (tape, cassette)   **(m)** disco compacto (CD)   **(n)** disco (record)

EXERCISE 13

iré, cogeré, estaré, tomaré, llamaré, me ducharé, me cambiaré, saldremos, iremos, me levantaré, volveré, llegaré

EXERCISE 14

(a) Trabajaré en Francia por dos o tres meses.
(b) Visitaré a mi familia en Boston.   **(c)** Viajaré a la costa con mi hermana.

EXERCISE 15

(b) Compraría una casa en Venezuela.   **(c)** Visitaría a mi familia en las Bahamas.   **(d)** Iría de vacaciones a Colombia.   **(e)** Abriría una cuenta de ahorros en el Banco de Vizcaya.   **(f)** Daría muchos regalos a mis amigos y a mis parientes.   **(g)** Haría una fiesta para mis compañeros de clase.

11 | TALKING ON THE TELEPHONE

- ▶ how to use appropriate telephone language
- ▶ how to recognise the subjunctive
- ▶ how to use commands with **usted**

POINTS TO REMEMBER

- ● the future tense (I will …): **tendré, seré, terminaré, encontraré, aumentaré** etc.
- ● the conditional (I would …): **me gustaría, estaría, sería, costaría** etc.
- ● hiring a car: **me gustaría alquilar un coche, un coche medio, la tarifa**
- ● buying electronic goods: **un casete, un ordenador, un estéreo**

BEFORE YOU BEGIN

In this unit you are introduced to the subjunctive – an alternative set of verb forms. The subjunctive has mostly disappeared in English apart from in phrases such as 'if I were (rich)' or 'long live (the king/queen)', but it is still alive and well in Spanish and is used very frequently in everyday conversation as well as in more formal styles. It is not complicated to master – you will easily become familiar with it. The activities you are asked to complete in these units are more of a consciousness-raising exercise than anything else – that is, to make you aware of the forms rather than to produce them actively. So why bother with the subjunctive in the first place? Simply because it is used very frequently and sooner or later you are going to wonder why verbs don't follow the patterns you have already learnt. Indeed, it has cropped up many times in earlier units.

Maite leaves an urgent message

Contestador automático

Hola. Éste es el tres cero dos quince diecinueve. Puede dejar su recado después que termine la señal.

Maite

Hola, soy Maite. Mira, que simplemente quiero decir que vuelvas a casa en cuanto puedas. ¿Vale? Es urgente.

LISTEN FOR...

puede dejar su recado	you can leave your message
la señal	the tone
en cuanto puedas	as soon as you can

contestador automático   answer phone; **contestar** to reply. **El cajero automático** is the automatic cash dispenser at a bank.

el tres cero dos quince diecinueve   In Spanish, telephone numbers can either be said separately or in pairs. In this example, the first three numbers are given as separate digits and the last ones in pairs.

su recado   your message

después que termine la señal   after the end of the tone (literally, after the signal ends). **Termine** is the first example of the subjunctive. The subjunctive is required after time expressions when referring to the future: **después que vuelva** after I (will) get back.

soy Maite   it's Maite. Note how Spanish rephrases this to say 'I am …': **soy Juan** it's me, Juan; but if someone else relays the message they say: **es Carlos** it's Carlos (on the phone).

quiero ... que vuelvas a casa   I want you to come home. Again, **vuelvas** is the subjunctive form. It is used because Maite is telling someone else what to do (literally, I want that you should come home).

en cuanto puedas   as soon as you can. Again, **puedas** is subjunctive – after **en cuanto**, it means 'as soon as you can'. Maite is again

referring to a future action. In all these examples – **puedas, vuelvas, termine** – the only difference in form is that 'a' substitutes for 'e' and 'e' for 'a' (**puedas** not **puedes**, **vuelvas** not **vuelve** and **termine** not **termina**). So making a mistake may not even be noticed.

PRACTICE

1

Link up phrases from both columns to make complete sentences.

a Soy
b Éste es
c Quería decir
d Es

e ¿Puedes volver a casa

1 en cuanto llegues a la estación?
2 la directora de la Agencia EmeTres.
3 muy importante.
4 el veintidós, cuarenta y seis, cincuenta y cuatro.
5 que compres un pollo para la cena.

Answers p. 176

2

Match these five telephone expressions with the appropriate illustration.

a Hola, soy Cristina.

1

b ¿Puedo dejar un recado?

2

c Lo siento. Se ha equivocado de número.

3

d ¿Se puede poner Miguel?

4

e Llamaba para decirte que el coche está en el garaje.

5

Answers p. 176

3

Listen to this telephone conversation about an evening out and then answer, in English, the questions which follow. You'll hear the word **la cartelera** the entertainments page.

a What had Marisa thought of doing that evening?

b Why does Guillermo want to go out?

c Which film does Guillermo suggest first

1 *Shine*
2 *La guerra de las galaxias* (*Star Wars*)
3 *El paciente inglés* (*The English Patient*)

d Why does Marisa not want to see that film?

_____

e Why does Guillermo not want to see *El paciente inglés*?

_____

f What does Guillermo suggest then?

_____

_____

g Marisa does not agree to one of his suggestions. Which one?

_____

h What does she suggest?

_____

Answers p. 176

4 Now it's your turn to ring Guillermo. You'll be using: **soy (Marisa) ¿está Guillermo?**, **llamaba para decirte**, and **¿quieres venir a verme?**

José Luis isn´t in

Maite

Hola, soy Maite. ¿Está José Luis?

Voz

Un momento por favor. Mire, no, no está en este momento. ¿Quiere dejar un recado?

Maite

No, déjelo. ¿A qué hora estará?

Voz

Calculo que sobre las once o así. ¿Quiere que le diga, que le llame cuando, cuando vuelva?

Maite

No, está bien. Le volveré a llamar mañana cuando tenga un momento libre. Eh, no, bueno, sí, dígale que ha llamado Maite y que me quedaré en casa hasta que me llame ¿vale?

Voz

De acuerdo.

LISTEN FOR...	
¿quiere que le diga que le llame?	do you want me to tell him to call?
le volveré a llamar mañana	I will ring again tomorrow

¿está José Luis? is José Luis there? Notice how Spanish uses **estar** to mean 'to be present'.

voz (f.) a voice; **las voces** voices

¿quiere dejar un recado? do you want to leave a message? **dejar** to leave.

no, déjelo no, leave it. This is an example of the formal command with **usted**. More about this on page 174. Notice how, with a command, you put the pronoun, **lo** (it) on the end of the verb: **llámala** call her.

sobre las once o así around eleven or thereabouts

¿quiere que le diga que le llame cuando vuelva? (three subjunctives in one sentence!) do you want me to tell him to call when he comes in? (literally, do you want that I should tell him that he should call you when he comes?) The subjunctive is also used after expressions such as 'to wish' or 'to want', 'to hope' and so on. **Vuelva** is also a subjunctive form because Maite is referring to a future event.

le volveré a llamar I will call him again; **volver a** + an infinitive means to do something again: **nunca lo volveré a hacer** I will never do it again.

cuando tenga un momento libre when I have a moment free. Again, a subjunctive form after **cuando**, because Maite is referring to future time.

eh no, bueno, sí ... Maite changes her mind and decides to leave a message after all.

dígale tell him; **dígame** is the phrase used when you first pick up the phone, and is equivalent to 'hello'.

que me quedaré en casa hasta que me llame that I will stay at home until he calls (me); again, **hasta que** refers to an event in the future, so **llame** instead of **llama**.

5 If possible, without looking back at the conversation, decide whether these statements are true or not. If they aren't, correct them.

a   Ha llamado María.

_____

b   José Luis está en casa pero está ocupado.

_____

c   José Luis volverá a las diez o así.

_____

d   La chica le llamará más tarde, por la noche.

_____

e   La chica se quedará en casa hasta que la llame José Luis.

Answers p. 176

_____

6 Listen to the conversation on your recording and then answer, in English, the questions which follow.

a   What four things does Carlos want callers to record?

_____

_____

b   When does Guillermo call (three points of information)?

_____

c   Why does Guillermo not leave his phone number?

_____

d   What relation is Juan to Guillermo?

_____

e   What does he study?

_____

f   When is Guillermo and his party going out?

_____

g   What does he ask Carlos to do, if he gets back home before 10?

Answers p. 176

_____

7 Here are some messages from the VIDA SOCIAL column of a local newspaper. Read them through and then complete the grid in English.

Carla Montaner González: te deseamos toda tu familia un día muy feliz y que en tus 23 años, obtengas el permiso de conducir. Te lo mereces. Eso sí, tienes que estudiar mucho. Muchísimas felicidades

Angeles Guerrero Gómez: feliz cumpleaños. Espero que tengas un buen día. Un beso de tu marido que te quiere.

Vanesa Escudero Sanz: muchas felicidades, preciosa, en este tu primer cumpleaños, de parte de tus tíos, tías, y abuelos. ¡Que sigas siendo tan maravillosa!

Pepa: muchísimas felicidades y que pases un día maravilloso de parte de todas tus amigas de la oficina.

Ana: ¡18 años! ¡Muchas felicidades y que pases un día maravilloso y sobre todo no se te olvide invitarnos! Tus primas, Raquel y Natalia.

Paz León: muchísimas felicidades en el día de tu cumpleaños. Esperamos que cumplas muchos más. Te escribimos esto para que veas lo mucho que te queremos, Mercedes y Montse.

VOCABULARY	
cumplir años	to have a birthday
siendo (from **ser**)	'being'

	De ...	Deseando que ...	Edad
Carla			
Angeles			
Vanesa			
Pepa			
Ana			
Paz			

Answers p. 176

8 This time you don't get the person you wanted. You'll be using **¿está ...?**, **la llamaré mañana** (I'll call her tomorrow) and **cuando tenga un momento libre**.

CONVERSATION 3

🎧 A good luck call

José Luis	Bueno, ¡que te vaya muy bien en Madrid con tu nuevo trabajo! Espero verte pronto. En cuanto llegues, llámame a casa. De todas formas es posible que te vea la semana próxima porque tengo que ir a Madrid para una reunión.

¡que te vaya muy bien!	good luck!
te recogeré el correo	I'll pick up your mail
te lo mandaré	I'll send it to you

....

José Luis No creo que haya ningún problema. Pasaré por tu piso para ver si todo está en orden , te recogeré el correo y te lo mandaré en cuanto pueda.

....

José Luis Sí, ya lo sé. Y dile a Carlos que venga por aquí uno de estos días a vernos.

....

José Luis No, prefiero que nos quedemos aquí todos hasta junio y luego nos vayamos todos a Alicante a ver a los primos.

....

José Luis No, creo que no podamos estar tanto tiempo fuera. Acuérdate que yo tengo que trabajar.

....

José Luis Bueno, sí. Es posible que vayamos a finales de agosto, por un fin de semana, por ejemplo.

....

José Luis: Bueno, nada, mira, me tengo que ir. Ya te llamaré en agosto. ¿De acuerdo? Adiós entonces.

¡que te vaya muy bien con tu nuevo trabajo! good luck with your new job; **vaya** (from **ir** 'to go') is another example of the subjunctive. The literal translation is 'that all may go very well for you'. As you see, the form is completely irregular. José Luis is expressing a wish, hence the subjunctive.

de todas formas in any case

es posible que te vea I may see you (literally, it's possible that I may see you). This time the subjunctive is used because the verb occurs after an expression of possibility: **quizá te vea** perhaps I'll see you.

no creo que haya ningún problema I don't think there is any problem; **haya** is the subjunctive form of **hay** (there is/there are) and is used after an expression of doubt (**no creo que**).

te recogeré el correo I'll pick up your post; **recoger** to pick up.

y dile a Carlos que venga por aquí and tell Carlos to come (around) here. This is a command (tell him to come) so the subjunctive form is used (**venga**).

no, prefiero que nos quedemos aquí todos todas no, I prefer that we all stay here; **quedarse** to stay. The subjunctive occurs

---

because José Luis uses an expression of preference. This is why the next verb (**que nos vayamos** 'that we all go') is subjunctive too.

no, creo que no podamos estar tanto tiempo fuera   I don't think that we can spend so much time away. Another expression of doubt which leads José Luis to use the subjunctive.

acuérdate   remember (from **acordarse** 'to remember'); **yo me acuerdo cuando ...** I remember when ...

bueno, nada, mira, me tengo que ir ...   well then, look, I've got to go. A series of filler words which bring the conversation to a close.

PRACTICE

9   From what you know about José Luis's conversation, is he likely to have made the following remarks?

a   Algunas veces voy de viaje de negocios.
b   Cuando voy a Madrid, es para divertirme.
c   Yo te quiero ayudar como pueda.
d   Tenemos familia en Alicante.
e   Yo suelo tener dos meses de vacaciones en verano.
f   Me escapo un fin de semana de vez en cuando.

Answers p. 176

10   Here is a message that María received by e-mail. Read it through and then answer, in English, the questions which follow.

Hola María,
****

Espero que no estés muy ocupada y que tu familia te deje respirar.

Te quería preguntar si no te importa que dé tu nombre como referencia en mi CV. Tú eres la única persona que puede opinar sobre mi trabajo de profesora de español aquí en Barcelona. He solicitado trabajo en una academia de idiomas para los cursos de verano. Si te llega alguna carta de la academia, pidiendo referencias, te agradecería si pudieras contestarla.

No quiero darte más dolores de cabeza de los que ya puedas tener, pero espero que no te importe.

Hasta pronto
****

Yolanda
****

a What are the two things which Yolanda hopes for in the first sentence?

_____

b What favour does she ask María?

_____

c Why does she ask María in particular?

_____

d Where does Yolanda hope to work in summer?

_____

e What does she not want to give María?

Answers p. 176

_____

11

In this conversation Marisa receives a good luck call. You'll be using **recoger mi correo, si todo está en orden** and **quizás** (perhaps). Now listen to some other useful expressions which are used on the telephone:

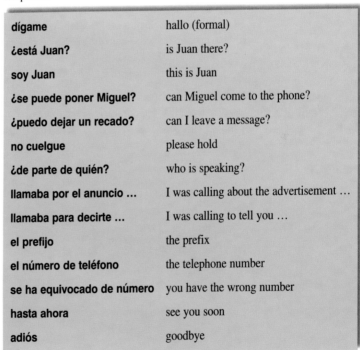

dígame	hallo (formal)
¿está Juan?	is Juan there?
soy Juan	this is Juan
¿se puede poner Miguel?	can Miguel come to the phone?
¿puedo dejar un recado?	can I leave a message?
no cuelgue	please hold
¿de parte de quién?	who is speaking?
llamaba por el anuncio ...	I was calling about the advertisement ...
llamaba para decirte ...	I was calling to tell you ...
el prefijo	the prefix
el número de teléfono	the telephone number
se ha equivocado de número	you have the wrong number
hasta ahora	see you soon
adiós	goodbye

KEY WORDS
AND PHRASES

éste es el tres cero dos, quince diecinueve	this is 302 1519
puede dejar un recado	you can leave a message
¿quiere dejar un recado?	do you want to leave a message?
después que termine la señal	after the tone
déjelo	leave it
dígame	hallo (formal, on telephone)
hola, soy ...	hallo, it's ...
¿está ...?	is ... there?
no está en este momento	she/he's not here at the moment
¿a qué hora estará?	what time will he be in?
se ha equivocado de número	you've got the wrong number
mira/e	look
nada (at the end of a conversation)	nothing more (to say)
es urgente	it's urgent
le volveré a llamar mañana	I'll ring again tomorrow
dígale que ha llamado ...	tell him/her that ... called
¡qué te/le vaya muy bien!	good luck!
espero verte pronto	I hope to see you soon
no creo que haya ningún problema	I don't think there's a problem
pasaré por tu piso	I'll drop in at your flat
te recogeré el correo	I'll pick up your post
te lo mandaré en cuanto pueda	I'll send it to you as soon as I can
ya te llamaré en agosto	I'll call you in August
acuérdate ...	remember ...
es posible que vayamos ...	it's possible that we may go ...

The subjunctive

The subjunctive is an alternative set of verb forms. In this unit, you will learn to recognise the present tense only. Look at these forms and decide how they differ from the ones you already know.

hablar	comer	vivir
habl -e	com -a	viv -a
habl -es	com -as	viv -as
habl -e	com -a	viv -a
habl -emos	com -amos	viv -amos
habl -éis	com -áis	viv -áis
habl -en	com -an	viv -an

So the new ending is the opposite of the one you already know – 'a' becomes 'e' (**habla** to **hable**) and 'e' becomes 'a' (**come** to **coma**). Note the 'yo form' – **hable, coma** and **viva.**

- Stem-changing verbs keep the stem change in the subjunctive. So, **yo piense, yo vuelva, yo pida, yo prefiera.** (There are one or two other minor changes here that you will find in the verb tables.)

- Verbs which have an irregular first person (**yo**) keep this in the subjunctive. So, **yo diga, yo haga, yo ponga, yo traiga, yo tenga, yo venga.** This form also goes right through the tense (**digamos, hagas, pongáis, tengan** etc.).

- You may need to change the spelling a little, now that you have swapped the 'a' and 'e' endings, so that you keep the same sound:
  yo coja (from **coger**), **yo saque** (from **sacar**).

- Four common verbs have completely irregular forms right through the tense. Here are the 'yo forms':
  yo sea (from **ser**), **yo vaya** (from **ir**), **yo sepa** (from **saber**), **haya** (from **haber**)

13 Try and work out the subjunctive forms for the following verbs. Look them up in the verb table if you have a problem.

a él (ser) _____

b ellos (comprar) _____

c ella (decir) _____

d Vd. (oír) _____

e tú (tener) _____

f yo (conducir) _____

g él (dormir) _____

h nosotros (beber) _____

i tú (decir) _____

j ella (ir) _____

k ellos (saber) _____

l yo (traer) _____

Answers p. 176

So, when do you use the subjunctive?

This is a complex area but there are a few clear-cut cases. Let's look at these first.

- Usually, you need a two-part sentence with one subject in the first half and another, a different one, in the second. The two parts are joined by **que**. Look at these sentences:

	1	2
I want you to come.	**(Yo) quiero**	**que (tú) vengas.**
I want to come.	**Quiero venir.** (No subjunctive as the subject is the same – **yo**.)	

The first verb (here, **quiero**) also has to fall into a certain category of meaning – in this case, those verbs which express wanting, liking, persuading, and emotions.

Some common verbs which work like this are: **decir, preferir, pedir, querer, esperar, sentir**.

Siento que no puedas venir.	I am sorry you can't come.
Prefiero que no vaya.	I prefer him not to go.
Quiero que estudien esta lección para la próxima clase.	I want you to study this lesson for the next class.
Espero que estés bien.	I hope you're well.

- Another category of verbs are those which suggest uncertainty, doubt, disbelief or possibility. Here are some of the more common ones:

Dudo que venga a tiempo (dudar).	I doubt he'll come in time.
No es cierto que estén en España.	It's not true that they're in Spain. *But*
Es cierto que están en España.	It's true that they're in Spain.
No creo que sea así.	I don't think it's like that. *But*
Creo que es así.	I think it's like that.
Es posible/probable que vaya.	It's possible/probable he might go.

- After certain expressions like **para que** (in order to), **antes de que** (before), **a menos que** (unless), **aunque** (even though, even if).

  Aunque venga pronto, no saldré con él.   Even if he comes early, I won't go out with him.

- After expressions which refer to future events :

En cuanto vuelva, llamaré a mi marido.	As soon as I get back, I will call my husband.
Cuando llegue a casa, me cambiaré.	When I get home, I'll change (clothes).
Quédate aquí hasta que venga mamá.	Stay here until mum comes back.

14   First underline the subjunctive form in these sentences and then try translating them.

a   En un examen, haz primero las preguntas que sabes. Luego las que no crees que sepas muy bien.

_____

_____

b   Para que hagas bien un examen, tienes que prepararte con mucho tiempo antes.

_____

c   Antes que se me olvide, ¿puedes echar esta carta al correo?

_____

d Prefiero que llames mañana, a eso de las seis.

e Cuando vaya a España en el verano, estaré con mis primos en Málaga.

f Busco un piso que tenga calefacción central.

g Puede ser que le escriba mañana.

h No creo que tenga muchos problemas con aprobar el examen de conducir.

i Es posible que salgamos todos a cenar mañana.

j No es cierto que se vayan a casar.

VOCABULARY	
aprobar	to pass
suspender	to fail

Answers p. 176

Formal commands (Imperatives with 'usted')

■ Now that you know the subjunctive you can tell people what they must or must not do by using the appropriate form of the present subjunctive. So to give directions to someone you call '**usted**', you might say:
Mire, vaya todo recto y luego gire a la derecha. No tome la primera calle, sino la segunda. Cruce la plaza y doble la esquina.

■ As you can see, these forms are all third person of the subjunctive. To tell someone *not* to do something, simply place '**no**' in front of the verb: **no corra(s) tan deprisa** don't run so fast.

■ The only special imperative forms are those used with **tú** and **vosotros** (see Unit 8). All the others (including negative commands with **tú/vosotros**) are variations of the subjunctive.

15 This passage tells you what to do when going for a job interview. Match up the Spanish phrase with its English translation. Then work out the infinitive of each verb.

a	**Estreche la mano del entrevistador con firmeza.**	**1**	Prepare your interview in advance.
b	**No fume durante la entrevista.**	**2**	Write a brief letter afterwards.
c	**Mantenga una actitud relajada y natural.**	**3**	Shake the interviewer's hand firmly.
d	**Mire directamente a los ojos del entrevistador.**	**4**	Don't wear too much make-up.
e	**Sonría de vez en cuando.**	**5**	Maintain a relaxed and natural attitude.
f	**Prepare la entrevista con antelación.**	**6**	Smile from time to time.
g	**Redacte una breve carta después.**	**7**	Don't smoke during the interview.
h	**No lleve demasiado maquillaje.**	**8**	Look straight at the interviewer.
i	**No interrumpa al entrevistador.**	**9**	Don't interrupt the interviewer.

Answers p. 176

AND FINALLY...

16 Your turn to speak. In this exercise you are arranging to go to a party at Marisa's house. You'll be using **¿cuándo es?** And **¿qué número de autobús es?**

17 Below you have Juan's side of a conversation. Fill in Marta's replies with whatever you feel appropriate. Then read the full conversation out loud. If you are working with a partner, she/he can take the other role. There are possible answers on page 176.

Juan	Marta
Hola, te llamaba para invitarte a una fiesta.	_____
	_____
Es una fiesta de cumpleaños.	_____
	_____
Mi hermana.	_____
	_____
Mira, ¿puedes traer algo de beber o de comer?	_____
	_____
No sé, una pizza o quizá una tortilla.	_____
	_____
Es el fin de semana, el sábado.	_____
	_____
A partir de las diez en casa de José.	_____
	_____
En la calle Romero, número 12, cerca del colegio Santa Teresa.	_____
	_____
Puedes ir o en autobús o en metro.	_____
	_____
Bueno, nada. Me tengo que ir. Hasta el sábado ¿vale?	_____
	_____

EXERCISE 1

(a) 2   (b) 4   (c) 5   (d) 3   (e) 1

EXERCISE 2

(a) 3   (b) 5   (c) 2   (d) 1   (e) 4

EXERCISE 3

(a) Reading a new novel.   (b) He has a friend from Valencia staying who wants to go out.   (c) Star Wars   (d) She does not like science fiction.   (e) He has seen it already.   (f) That she comes round and they look at the entertainment page.   (g) To their eating before the film.   (h) That they eat after.

EXERCISE 5

(a) No, ha llamado Maite.   (b) No está José Luis.   (c) Volverá a las once o así.   (d) No, ella le llamará al día siguiente.   (e) Verdad.

EXERCISE 6

(a) Their name and the day and time they ring. Also their phone number.   (b) Tuesday, 13th,   6.00 pm   (c) Carlos already has it.   (d) They are cousins.   (e) Medicine.   (f) At ten that   evening.   (g) To go round to his house before   10.00 pm.

EXERCISE 7

	De …	Deseando que …	Edad
Carla	the family	she gets her driving licence	23
Angeles	her husband	she has a good day	
Vanesa	uncles, aunts, grandparents	goes on being marvellous	1
Pepa	friends	she has a wonderful day	
Ana	cousins	she invites her cousins	18
Paz	Mercedes and Montse	she has more birthdays	

EXERCISE 9

(a), (c), (d), (f) are likely to have been said;   (b) and (e) are unlikely.

EXERCISE 10

(a) That María is not too busy and that her family is giving her some peace (literally, allowing her to breathe).   (b) If she can give her name as a referee.   (c) María is the only person who can have an opinion about her work as a teacher.   (d) In a private language school.   (e) Any more headaches.

EXERCISE 13

(a) sea   (b) compren   (c) diga   (d) oiga   (e) tengas   (f) conduzca   (g) duerma   (h) bebamos   (i) digas   (j) vaya   (k) sepan   (l) traiga

EXERCISE 14

(a) In an exam, do (haz, hacer) the questions you know first. Then the ones you think you don't know (sepas, saber) very well.   (b) So that you can do (hagas, hacer) an exam well, you have to prepare a long time in advance.   (c) Before I forget (olvide, olvidar) can you post this letter?   (d) I prefer you to call (llames, llamar) tomorrow, at about six.   (e) When I go to (vaya, ir) Spain, I will stay with my cousins in Málaga.   (f) I am looking for a flat (tenga, tener) with central heating.   (g) I might write (escriba, escribir) to him tomorrow.   (h) I don't think he will have (tenga, tener) many problems passing his driving test.   (i) It is possible that we'll all go out (salgamos, salir) tomorrow to eat.   (j) It is not true that they are going (vayan, ir) to get married.

EXERCISE 15

(a) 3 (estrechar)   (b) 7 (fumar)   (c) 5 (mantener)   (d) 8 (mirar)   (e) 6 (sonreír)   (f) 1 (preparar)   (g) 2 (redactar)   (h) 4 (Llevar)   (i) 9 (interrumpir)

EXERCISE 17

¿Una fiesta? ¡Qué bien! ¿Qué tipo de fiesta es? Y ¿quién cumple años? Sí, ¿qué quieres? Por supuesto. Ah, y ¿cuándo es, la fiesta? Sí, ¿a qué hora? Y ¿dónde vive José? Y ¿cómo se va allí? Muy bien … Sí, vale, hasta el sábado entonces.

12 IF ONLY...

POINTS TO REMEMBER

● telephone talk: **dígame** hallo, **¿está Juan?** is Juan there? **soy Juan** it's (me) Juan
● **¿de parte de quién?** who is speaking?
● filler words: **mira/e** look, **nada** well, that's all
● present subjunctive: **¡qué te vaya muy bien!** good luck! **no creo que haya ningún problema** I don't think there's a problem, **te lo mandaré en cuanto pueda** I'll send it as soon as I can

BEFORE YOU BEGIN

So you've made it to the last unit – congratulations! You have learned a lot of Spanish and should now be able to express yourself and understand Spanish in a range of situations. Unfortunately, you can't stop here. It's very easy to forget a language unless you maintain it. Here are some ways of making sure that you don't forget what you've learned. If you don't already have satellite television, why not invest in a system which can get Spanish stations? This doesn't have to be more expensive than the usual systems – you just need your satellite to be pointing in the right direction. Next time you go to a Spanish-speaking country, check out the newspaper kiosks and find a magazine or newspaper that you could subscribe to. Try and meet Spanish speakers – either native speakers or students like yourself. Meet with them regularly and practise as much as you can. And of course, the more you can visit a Spanish-speaking country, the better. Good luck with your Spanish – and enjoy yourself! **¡Que te diviertas!**

Unit 12 If only …   177

CONVERSATION 1

My ideal house

Maite

Sí, bueno, mi casa ideal, me gustaría que tuviera pues, por lo menos, cinco habitaciones, no está mal, y también me gustaría que tuviera un jardín grande, que hubiera una piscina también, mediana, y que bueno, que las habitaciones y la casa en general fuera espaciosa y eso sí, luminosa, que fuera luminosa con mucha luz y que tuviera la oportunidad de invitar a mucha gente. Y así sería mi casa ... Ah, bueno, también que estuviera situada quizá en el campo para estar en contacto con los animales etcétera, y ... pero que no estuviera muy lejos de la ciudad.

LISTEN FOR...

me gustaría que tuviera ...	I would like it to have ...
espaciosa	spacious
luminosa	light

sí, bueno ... yes, well ... Take note of these filler words – they are useful for rounding out your conversation and making you sound more authentic.

me gustaría que tuviera I would like it to have; **tuviera** is the imperfect subjunctive of **tener**. You learned in Unit 11 that the subjunctive mood is required after **me gusta** + a verb. After **me gustaría que** (the conditional of **gustar**) you need to use the imperfect subjunctive. Don't worry about learning all the whys and wherefores. You will find that the same verbs keep cropping up in similar contexts and that they soon become familiar.

por lo menos at least

que hubiera una piscina también that there should be a swimming pool too; **hubiera** is the imperfect subjunctive of **hay** 'there is, there are': **que hubiera una pista de tenis** that there should be a tennis court; the '**hubiera** form' is used after **me gustaría** 'I would like there to be'.

mediana middle-sized

(me gustaría que) la casa fuera espaciosa (I would like) the house to be spacious; **fuera** is the imperfect subjunctive of **ser** 'to be'.

que fuera luminosa, con mucha luz that it be light, with a lot of light; **la luz** light, **las luces** lights. Remember that you can use **la luz** to mean 'the electricity'.

así sería mi casa that's what my house would be like

que estuviera situada en el campo that it should be situated in the countryside; **estuviera** is another imperfect subjunctive, this time from **estar**.

que no estuviera lejos de la ciudad that it shouldn't be far from the city. Remember that **estar** rather than **ser** is used, because Maite is talking about place – *where* her house is.

12 If only ...

1 On the grid below check off the features which Maite's ideal house should possess. You may need to listen to the recording again.

cincuenta habitaciones	
un jardín pequeño	
que fuera espaciosa	
una piscina grande	
en el campo	
cerca de la ciudad	
que tuviera mucha luz	
que tuviera espacio para invitar a muchas personas	

Answers p. 192

2 Listen to Guillermo talking about his ideal home, which is quite different from Maite's. As you listen, note down, in English, five differences between Guillermo's and Maite's descriptions.

a _____

b _____

c _____

d _____

Answers p. 192   e _____

3 Isabel tells you about *her* ideal house. Read her description and then answer the questions in English.

Bueno, a mí me gustaría vivir en una casa en el campo, una casa vieja pero modernizada, claro, con calefacción central y todas las comodidades de una casa nueva. Me gustaría también que fuera luminosa y espaciosa con unas ventanas grandísimas que dieran a un jardín enorme. ¡Me haría falta un jardinero! Me gustaría poder andar del salón directamente al jardín en donde podría tomar el té a las cuatro con unas amigas. Y sería siempre verano, y yo me pondría un vestido de algodón estampado y un sombrero de paja. Me gustaría que hubiera también una cocina grande en donde podríamos hacer pasteles, mis hijos y yo. Y en el invierno (me he cambiado de aviso, también habría invierno) nos sentaríamos allí, toda la familia, cerca de la estufa, a charlar y a tomar café. También me gustaría que hubiera una mesa de billar para que vinieran los amigos de mis hijos a jugar y una piscina para las amigas de mi hija. Así la casa estaría llena siempre de jóvenes y habría un ambiente juvenil.

Pero mi dormitorio estaría apartado y tranquilo y yo podría escaparme a leer en paz cuando quisiera. ¡Qué sueño!

a What is special about the windows in Isabel's ideal home?

_____

b Where would she be in summer? What would she do?

_____

c And in winter?

_____

d What would she wear in summer?

_____

e Why would she like a billiard table and a swimming pool?

_____

f Where would she escape to? What would she do there?

Answers p. 192

_____

 4 Now you talk about your ideal house.
You'll need: **agosto** 'August',
luminoso and **espacioso**.

12 If only ...

My ideal woman

Maite
Y ¿cómo sería tu mujer ideal?

LISTEN FOR...

que intentara buscar un trabajo	that she should try to find a job
por sí misma	for herself

José Luis
Bueno, es complicado pensar en una mujer ideal, pero, pero bueno, lo intentaré. Mi mujer ideal, me gustaría que tuviera un cierto atractivo físico, que fuera inteligente, que tuviera algo de dinero o un poco de dinero, que intentara buscar un trabajo por sí misma, que fuera, volviendo al aspecto físico, que fuera alta, más bien. En cuanto a la nacionalidad no tengo ninguna preferencia. Cualquier nacionalidad entra dentro de mis planes y yo creo que esto es todo lo que te puedo decir sobre la mujer ideal.

¿cómo sería tu mujer ideal? what would your ideal woman/wife be like? Remember **¿cómo es ...?** what is ... like? **¿cómo es tu piso?** what is your flat like?

pensar en una mujer ideal to think about an ideal woman; **pienso en ella** I am thinking about her. But **pensar de** to think of: **¿qué piensas del nuevo jefe?** what do you think about the new boss?

lo intentaré I will try (to do) it

un cierto atractivo físico a certain physical attraction. You could say (more simply): que **fuera atractiva** that she be attractive.

que tuviera algo de dinero that she should have some money; **algo** something.

que intentara buscar un trabajo por sí misma that she should try to find a job of/on her own. José Luis means that she should be independent; **trabajar por sí mismo** to work for oneself.

volviendo al aspecto físico going back to her physical characteristics

que fuera alta, más bien that she should be on the tall side; **más bien** rather.

en cuanto a la nacionalidad as for her nationality. **En cuanto a** is a useful phrase: **en cuanto a su aspecto físico, a su inteligencia, a su trabajo.**

cualquier nacionalidad entra dentro de mis planes any nationality forms part of my plans (would be acceptable).

PRACTICE

5 Read these statements about José Luis's ideal woman and decide whether he might have said them or not.

VOCABULARY	
la belleza	beauty
menudo/a	petite/slight

sí   no

a La belleza no me importa. ☐ ☐

b Me gustaría casarme con una española. ☐ ☐

c Yo tengo un buen salario, así que prefiero que mi mujer no trabaje fuera de casa. ☐ ☐

d El dinero para mí es bastante importante. ☐ ☐

e Prefiero que una mujer sea menos inteligente que yo. ☐ ☐

Answers p. 192

f Me gustan las mujeres menudas. ☐ ☐

6 Listen to Griselda's description of her ideal man and then tick off the seven qualities that she mentions.

Me gustaría que fuera:

simpático ☐

alto ☐

moreno ☐

hablador ☐

cariñoso ☐

Me gustaría que le gustara:

cocinar ☐

limpiar ☐

planchar ☐

Me gustaría que tuviera:

un ideal en la vida ☐

un trabajo que le gustara ☐

Answers p. 192

mucho dinero ☐

12 If only …

7 Here's an interview with a young man called Alfonso Mellado about his ideal reading material. You'll note that there are a mixture of tenses. Read it through and then complete the grid in English. Remember the word **tebeo** means 'comic'.

¿Cuándo empezó a coleccionar libros?
Cuando empecé a vivir solo.

¿Y cuántos libros tiene usted ahora?
Yo diría que unos dos mil o así.

¿Qué tipo de lectura prefiere?
Leo muchas novelas y algo de poesía
... me gustaría que hubiera más
poetas contemporáneos ...

¿Quién es su autor preferido?
No tengo un solo autor preferido.
Por ejemplo me encantan las novelas
policíacas. También me interesan los
novelistas suramericanos como
García Márquez y Carlos Fuentes.

¿Qué leía cuando era joven?
Leía más bien los tebeos. Los tebeos
de entonces eran fantásticos.

¿Que tipo de novela no leería nunca?
No me atraen los grandes
'bestsellers', tipo John Grisham. No

diría que no tuvieran calidad, sólo
que no me interesan. No entro
dentro de esa cultura americana.

Seguro que tendrá un lugar preferido para leer.
Sí, ¡el baño! Nadie me molesta
cuando estoy. Si alguien me llama
por teléfono, no me pongo. También,
los fines de semana, me gusta leer
tumbado en la cama.

¿Ha pensado escribir una novela?
No, nunca. No podría. No me
gustaría que la gente me criticara ni
que el público no me comprara el
libro.

¿Cuáles son los próximos libros que va a leer?
No tengo ni idea. Soy un lector
anárquico e impulsivo. Muchos libros
que compro ni los leo.

How many books	
Preferred reading	
What he read when young	
Favourite author	
Favourite place to read	

Answers p. 192

8 Now Marisa talks about her new flat-mate. You'll be using important adjectives such as **nuevo/a**, **simpático/a**, **inteligente**, **alto/a** and **guapo/a**.

What would you do if ...?

María	¿Qué harías si ganaras el gordo de Navidad?
Maite	Me compraría mi casa ideal.
Griselda	Yo me iría a dar la vuelta al mundo.
José Luis	Yo les daría un poco de dinero a los pobres.
María	¿Qué dirías a tus vecinos si hicieran mucho ruido por la noche?
Maite	Les diría que estuvieran más callados.
Griselda	Yo probablemente iría a verlos y me quejaría.
José Luis	Yo me uniría a la fiesta.
María	¿Qué harías si encontraras la agenda personal de un amigo?
José Luis	Se la devolvería.
Maite	Yo leería algo.
Griselda	Yo le llamaría y diría 'te la has olvidado'.

¿qué harías si ganaras el gordo de Navidad? what would you do if you won the Christmas lottery? In sentences like 'What would you do if ...? the first verb 'would' is always conditional (here, **harías**). The second (introduced by **si**, 'if') is imperfect subjunctive (here, **ganaras**). In this conversation, all the verbs are second person (**tú**) and the subjunctive ending is '**-as**'. **El gordo de Navidad** is the Christmas jackpot.

yo me iría a dar la vuelta al mundo I would go off on a world cruise; **dar la vuelta** to go around. Notice that the second and third people to reply use **yo**, 'I' – which is usually omitted. This is because they are contrasting their replies with someone else's. I would do (**haría**), but I would go (**yo iría**). Griselda also says **me iría** rather than **iría**. Using the extra pronoun (**me**, **te**, etc.) emphasises and strengthens the verb: 'I am going off or away', rather than 'I am going'.

yo les daría un poco de dinero a los pobres I would give a bit of money to the poor. The extra **les** 'to them', is optional.

¿qué dirías a tus vecinos si hicieran mucho ruido? what would you say to your neighbours if they made a lot of noise? A new imperfect subjunctive for you: **hiciera**, from **hacer**.

les diría que estuvieran más callados I would tell them to be quieter; **callado(s)** quiet. The imperfect subjunctive is used again here because Maite is using a verb of command or persuasion: **decir a ... que ...** to tell ... to do ...

iría a verlos I would go to see them; **los** 'them' is added to the end of the infinitive. See Grammar section in this unit.

me quejaría I would complain; **quejarse** to complain; **una queja** a complaint.

yo me uniría a la fiesta I would join the party! **unirse a** to join.

la agenda personal the personal diary. You can also use the word **el diario**.

se la devolvería I would return it to him; **se** means 'to him/to her'. Usually you would use **le** but it is not correct to use **le** and **la** or **lo** immediately following each other, so **se** is substituted: **se lo doy** I give it to him.

diría 'te la has olvidado' I would say 'you have forgotten it'; **olvidarse** to forget.

PRACTICE

9 Read through these phrases and make your choice about what *you* would do. Then invent another possibility (**d**). You might use words like **viajar**, **ahorrar**, **gritar**, **enfadarse**, **esconder**, **reírse** etc.

¿Qué harías si te tocara el gordo de navidad?

a   Iría de vacaciones. □

b   Me compraría un coche maravilloso. □

c   Les compraría una casa a mis padres. □

d   _____

¿Qué dirías a tus vecinos si hicieran mucho ruido?

a   No haría nada. Lo aguantaría. □

b   Los llamaría por teléfono. □

c   Llamaría a la puerta. □

d   _____

¿Qué harías si encontraras el diario de un amigo?

a   Se lo devolvería. □

b   Leería un poco. □

c   Lo dejaría en donde lo encontré. □

d   _____

10 What would you do if …? Listen to some more moral dilemmas and then fill in the grid below. You'll hear **un semáforo rojo** a red (traffic) light, **un vendedor ambulante** a door-to-door sales person, **se siente atraído** feels attracted to, and **dudas** doubts.

a	yes	no	it depends
Griselda			
Maite			
José Luis			

b	yes	no	it depends
Maite			
José Luis			
Griselda			

c	yes	no	it depends
Maite			
José Luis			
Griselda			

d	yes	no	it depends
Griselda			
Maite			
José Luis			

11 Read this extract about superstitions and then answer, in English, the questions which follow. You don't need to understand every word to answer the questions.

El color amarillo: Antes, era un color sagrado pero ahora tiene aspectos negativos. Ya en el siglo XII en el arte y la literatura, el amarillo representa la falsedad y la traición. También es el color con que se representa a Judas. Es considerado un color agresivo, el color del desorden y de la locura. En toda Europa, aparece en la ropa de los payasos y los locos.

El número 13: El origen de esta superstición parece estar en la narración de la Ultima Cena en la Biblia en la que estaban reunidos Jesús y sus 12 apóstoles. Uno de ellos era Judas Iscariote que luego le traicionó a Cristo.

El viernes y el martes: El viernes es un día malo en Estados Unidos y el Reino Unido porque es el día en que murió Cristo. En España, sin embargo, el día de mala suerte es el martes, sobre todo si es 13 también.

Se dice que es por una terrible derrota que sufrió un martes Jaime I el Conquistador, en Játiva.

El gato negro: Los gatos negros son compañeros de las brujas que se convierten en uno de estos animales para entrar en las casas y hacer enfermar a personas o animales. Pero esta superstición no es general, ya que en algunos pueblos en el norte de España, el gato negro trae buena suerte y riqueza.

Derramar la sal: La sal viene del mar que escapa al dominio de los seres humanos. Por eso es un elemento fuera de su lugar. La sal es también el símbolo de la amistad y si se derrama, la amistad se rompe. La palabra salario viene de la paga que se les daba a los soldados para que compraran la sal, un producto caro.

a Which three superstitions have biblical connections?

_____

b Which two colours are considered unlucky? _____

c Which superstition changes its meaning in different regions of Spain?

_____

d To which superstition does the following proverb apply? **El martes, ni te cases, ni te embarques**. _____

Answers p. 192

e What happens if you spill salt? _____

12 So what would you do if you won the lottery? Reply to Guillermo's questions. You'll be using the conditional tense, so all your verbs will end in '**-ía**' – **haría**, **iría**, **compraría** and so on.

12 If only ...

KEY WORDS
AND PHRASES

mi casa ideal	my ideal house
mi hombre/mujer ideal	my ideal man/woman
me gustaría ...	I would like ...
que tuviera ...	it to have ...
que hubiera ...	there to be ...
que fuera ...	it to be ...
que estuviera situada ...	it to be situated ...
espacioso/a	spacious
luminoso/a	luminous (full of light)
con mucha luz	with lots of light
me gustaría que intentara	I would like (her) to try
un atractivo físico	a physical attractiveness
es complicado	it's complicated
lo intentaré	I will try
en cuanto a ...	as for ...
la nacionalidad	the nationality
el aspecto físico	the physical aspect
el gordo de Navidad	the Christmas lottery prize
¿qué harías si ...?	what would you do if ...?
me compraría mi casa ideal	I would buy my ideal house
me iría a dar la vuelta al mundo	I would go round the world
les daría un poco de dinero a los pobres	I would give a bit of money to the poor
les diría que estuvieran más callados	I would tell them to be more quiet
yo iría a verlos	I would go and see them
me quejaría	I would complain
me uniría a la fiesta	I would join the party
tendría la tentación de ...	I would be tempted to ...
la leería	I would read it
yo se la daría	I would give it to him
yo miraría	I would look
se la devolvería	I would give it back
yo le llamaría	I would call him

Imperfect subjunctive

Besides the present subjunctive (Unit 11), there is another tense, the imperfect subjunctive, which you should also be able to recognise.

In order to form this tense, start from the third person plural of the preterite tense, subtract the endings and add the following ones:

hablar (hablaron)	comer (comieron)	vivir (vivieron)
habla -ra	comie -ra	vivie -ra
habla -ras	comie -ra	vivier -as
habla -ra	comie -ras	vivie -ra
hablá -ramos	comié -ramos	vivié -ramos
habla -rais	comie -rais	vivie -rais
habla -ran	comie -ran	vivie -ran

There is an alternative set of endings in 'se' (hablase, comiese, viviese etc.). This form means exactly the same, but is not used so frequently.

You use this tense in all the situations in which you would use the present – that is, after verbs of emotion, doubt, negative expressions and so on. What determines whether you should use one or the other is the tense of the main verb. So: present, future, perfect and imperative tenses are followed by the present subjunctive:

Pido	que me compre leche.	I ask him to buy me milk.
Pediré	que me compre leche.	I will ask him to buy me milk.
He pedido	que me compre leche.	I have asked him to buy me milk.
Pide	que me compre leche.	Ask him to buy me milk.

And imperfect, preterite and conditionals are followed by the imperfect subjunctive:

Pedía	que me comprara leche.	I asked him to buy me milk.
Pedí	que me comprara leche.	I asked him to buy me milk.
Pediría	que me comprara leche.	I would ask him to buy me milk.

13 Here are some common verbs in this tense. Match them up with their English equivalent.

a Si yo quisiera ...   1 If I were ...
b Si yo fuera ...   2 If I left ...
c Si yo tuviera ...   3 If there were ...
d Si hubiera ...   4 If I wanted ...
e Si yo dejara ...   5 If I had ...

Answers p. 192

More about personal pronouns

In Unit 6 you learned about personal pronouns (**yo**, **lo**, **la**, **le** etc.) and where to place them. Go back to the unit if you need to refresh your memory.   Here are a few more guidelines on how to use pronouns.

- They usually precede the verb – except with a positive command, where they go after.
  ¡hazlo ahora! do it now! But **¡no lo hagas!** don't do it!

- With infinitives and present participles they may precede *or* go after the verb:
La voy a ver.	I'm going to see her.
Voy a verla.	I'm going to see her.
Te estoy hablando.	I'm talking to you.
Estoy hablándote.	I'm talking to you.
  (Note how the '**a**' acquires an accent to keep the stress on the same syllable.)

- If you use a direct pronoun (**lo**, **la**, **los**, **las**) and an indirect pronoun ('to him', 'to me' etc.) the indirect pronoun always comes first:
Te lo doy.	I give it to you. (**el diccionario, el dinero** etc.)
¿Me la das?	Will you give it to me? (**la carta, la bolsa** etc.)

Se lo ...

- As noted in Conversation 3, in Spanish two pronouns beginning with 'l' do not come together.
  Le/les is therefore replaced by **se** in this combination:
Se lo dio.	He gave it to her/to him/to them
Se lo dijo.	He said it to her/him/them.

- As you can see, there is plenty of room for confusion! If you want to make things absolutely clear, add **a él/a ella/a Vd/a ellos/a ellas/a Vds**:
Se lo dio a ella.	He gave it to her.
Se lo dijo a ellas.	He said it to them (the girls/women).

Le(s) and Lo(s)

- Either of these forms can be used for 'him' or 'them' (people). You will hear both, depending on which part of Spain or Latin America you are visiting. *But* if you are referring to a masculine thing/s – you *must* use **lo/s**. Similarly if you are saying '*to* him/her/it/them' you *must* use **le/s**.
Le/lo veo.	I see him.
Lo veo.	I see him/it.
Le doy el diario.	I give (to) him the diary/newspaper.

14 Try translating these sentences.

a Fue a buscarlo. _____

b Le/lo encontré en la cafetería. _____

c ¿Saliste con él? _____

d ¿Viste a Eduardo? _____

e Sí, le/lo vi. _____

f ¡Caramba! ¡Lo dejé en el bar! _____

g Lo voy a lavar ahora. _____

h Se la mandé ayer. _____

i Me lo voy a poner esta tarde. _____

j Los fueron a visitar. _____

Now check to see if you are right. Using your translation, try to re-translate each sentence back into Spanish.

Answers p. 192

15 Now add the appropriate pronoun in the gap.

a Ayer vi a Sara. _____ vi en la biblioteca. (I saw her in the library).

b Mañana voy a dar mi trabajo a mi tutor. _____ _____ voy a dar. (I am going to give him it).

c Esta mañana he escrito el tema para la clase de historia. _____ he escrito. (I have written it).

d Ayer perdí la clase de español. _____ perdí. (I missed it).

e Voy a alquilar el piso en la calle Montés. Voy a alquilar _____ (I'm going to rent it).

f Todavía no he lavado mi ropa. No _____ he lavado. (I haven't washed it).

g He olvidado la cartera en casa. _____ he olvidado. (I have forgotten it).

h Llamé a mis padres el viernes. _____ llamé. (I called them).

i Encontré a una chica estupenda en la discoteca. _____ encontré. (I met her).

j Ahora te presto el disco. _____ _____ presto. (I'll lend you it).

Answers p. 192

AND FINALLY...

16 As this is the last spoken exercise in the book, it ranges a little more widely than usual. Guillermo has come to meet you off the aeroplane in Madrid. You'll be using **estuvimos esperando**, **está lloviendo** and **dejar las maletas**.

17 You've just arrived in Madrid. Here are some cue cards with ideas as to what you might do on your first evening. If you are working on your own, go through them one by one and say what you are going to do, when and with whom. If you have a partner, each of you chooses a different card.

Discuss: **a** which sort of restaurant you wish to go to
b what you will do afterwards
c who you will be going with
d how you are going to get home afterwards

Use full sentences and say why you have chosen these options.
You may need to fight your corner!

> un restaurante francés
> ir a ver una comedia
> ir con tus primos
> volver en autobús

> un restaurante chino
> ir a ver una ópera
> ir con amigos
> volver a casa en taxi

> un restaurante italiano
> ir a ver una película romántica
> salir con la familia
> volver a casa en metro

> un restaurante español
> ir al teatro a ver una obra clásica
> ir con tu esposo/a
> volver a casa a pie

18 And lastly, why not try this general knowledge quiz? If you know the answers, say them out loud, using full sentences. If you are working with a partner, ask three questions and then swap roles for the next three.

a ¿Cuál es el periódico más leído de España?
b ¿Quién escribió Don Quijote?
c ¿De qué nacionalidad es Alain Juppé?
d ¿Cuál es la capital de Ecuador?
e ¿Dónde se tuvieron lugar los juegos olímpicos de 1992?
f ¿En qué autonomía está Oviedo?
g ¿Quién era Eva Perón?
h ¿Quién jugó el papel de Eva Perón en la película Evita?
i ¿De qué color es la bandera española?
j ¿Cómo se llaman los actores de Breakthrough Spanish 2?
k ¿Cuál es el día que trae mala suerte en España?
l ¿En qué ciudad está el Museo del Prado?
m ¿Quién es Joaquín Cortés?
n ¿En qué ciudad tiene lugar Romeo y Julieta de Shakespeare?
o ¿En qué ciudad murió la princesa Diana?

Answers p. 192

Unit 12 If only ...

EXERCISE 1

cincuenta habitaciones	✗
un jardín pequeño	✗
que fuera espaciosa	✔
una piscina grande	✗
en el campo	✔
cerca de la ciudad	✔
que tuviera mucha luz	✔
que tuviera espacio para invitar a muchas personas	✔

EXERCISE 2

(a) Guillermo wants to live in the city centre. **(b)** He wants a one room studio apartment. **(c)** He doesn't want a garden. **(d)** He would like a balcony. **(e)** He doesn't want a swimming pool.

EXERCISE 3

(a) They would be large and give directly on to the garden. **(b)** She would be in the garden having tea. **(c)** She would be in the kitchen next to the stove. **(d)** She would wear a printed cotton dress and a straw hat. **(e)** She would like them so that her children's friends would visit. **(f)** She would go to her bedroom to read in peace.

EXERCISE 5

(a) no **(b)** no **(c)** no **(d)** sí **(e)** no **(f)** no

EXERCISE 6

Me gustaría que fuera: simpático ✔, hablador ✔, cariñoso ✔
Me gustaría que le gustara: cocinar ✔, planchar ✔
Me gustaría que tuviera: un ideal en la vida ✔, un trabajo que le gustara ✔

EXERCISE 7

Number of books	about 2000
Preferred reading	novels and poetry
What he read when he was young	comics
Favourite author	No one in particular, but he likes detective stories and South American authors like García Márquez and Carlos Fuentes.
Favourite place to read	the bathroom and lying on his bed

EXERCISE 10

(a) All say yes. **(b)** Maite, yes; José Luis and Griselda, it depends. **(c)** Maite no; José Luis and Griselda yes. **(d)** All say yes.

EXERCISE 11

(a) unlucky yellow, unlucky days and number 13 **(b)** yellow and sometimes black **(c)** the black cat **(d)** to unlucky Tuesday **(e)** you lose a friend

EXERCISE 13

(a) 4 **(b)** 1 **(c)** 5 **(d)** 3 **(e)** 2

EXERCISE 14

(a) He went to find him/it. **(b)** I found him/it in the café. **(c)** Did you go out with him? **(d)** Did you see Edward? **(e)** Yes, I saw him/it. **(f)** Heavens! I left it in the bar! **(g)** I am going to wash him/it now. **(h)** I sent it to him/her/them yesterday. **(i)** I am going to wear it this evening. **(j)** They went to visit them.

EXERCISE 15

(a) La **(b)** Se lo **(c)** Lo **(d)** La **(e)** alquilarlo **(f)** la **(g)** La **(h)** Los/les **(i)** La **(j)** Te lo

EXERCISE 18

(a) *El País* **(b)** Miguel Cervantes **(c)** francés **(d)** Quito **(e)** Barcelona **(f)** Asturias **(g)** la mujer del general Perón, dictador de Argentina **(h)** Madonna **(i)** amarillo y rojo **(j)** Guillermo, Marisa and Carlos **(k)** martes, 13 **(l)** Madrid **(m)** es un bailarín español **(n)** Verona **(o)** París

VERB LIST

This section is divided into four parts: first, regular verb tables where you will find all the forms of the three types **-ar**, **-er** and **-ir**. Then comes a section on stem-changing verbs, followed by another on verbs which have special spelling changes. Finally, there is an alphabetical list of the more common irregular verbs and verbs which have special meanings or take certain prepositions.

Stem-changing verbs which occur in this list have their changes marked in brackets. We'll only indicate the irregularities in the verb – other forms will be as normal. Derivative verbs won't be included because they behave just like their 'parent': for example, **convenir** to agree, behaves like **venir** to come and won't be listed separately.

Abbreviations:

inf. = infinitive	pp. = past participle
rc. = radical changing	pr. subj. = present subjunctive
pret. = preterite tense	fut. = future tense
imp. subj. = imperfect subjunctive	fam. command = familiar command
pres. = present tense	for. command = formal command

Regular verbs

	-ar	-er	-ir
infinitive	**hablar** to speak	**aprender** to learn	**vivir** to live
present participle	**hablando** speaking	**aprediendo** learning	**viviendo** living
present	I speak, am speaking do speak **hablo** **hablas** **habla** **hablamos** **habláis** **hablan**	I learn, am learning do learn **aprendo** **aprendes** **aprende** **aprendemos** **aprendéis** **aprenden**	I live, am living, do live **vivo** **vives** **vive** **vivimos** **vivís** **viven**
imperfect	I was speaking, used to speak, spoke **hablaba** **hablabas** **hablaba** **hablábamos** **hablabais** **hablaban**	I was learning, used to learn, learned **aprendía** **apendías** **aprendía** **aprendíamos** **aprendíais** **aprendían**	I was living, used to live, lived **vivía** **vivías** **vivía** **vivíamos** **vivíais** **vivían**

	-ar	-er	-ir
preterite	I spoke, did speak	I learned, did learn	I lived, did live
	hablé	**aprendí**	**viví**
	hablaste	**aprendiste**	**viviste**
	habló	**aprendió**	**vivió**
	hablamos	**aprendimos**	**vivimos**
	hablasteis	**aprendisteis**	**vivisteis**
	hablaron	**aprendieron**	**vivieron**
future	I shall speak, I will speak	I shall learn, I will learn	I shall live, I will live
	hablaré	**aprenderé**	**viviré**
	hablarás	**aprenderás**	**vivirás**
	hablará	**aprenderá**	**vivirá**
	hablaremos	**aprenderemos**	**viviremos**
	hablaréis	**aprenderéis**	**viviréis**
	hablarán	**aprenderán**	**vivirán**
conditional	I would speak, I should speak	I would learn, I should learn	I would live, I should live
	hablaría	**aprendería**	**viviría**
	hablarías	**aprenderías**	**vivirías**
	hablaría	**aprendería**	**viviría**
	hablaríamos	**aprenderíamos**	**viviríamos**
	hablaríais	**aprenderíais**	**viviríais**
	hablarían	**aprenderían**	**vivirían**
perfect	I have spoken	I have learned	I have lived
	he hablado	**he aprendido**	**he vivido**
	has hablado	**has aprendido**	**has vivido**
	ha hablado	**ha aprendido**	**ha vivido**
	hemos hablado	**hemos aprendido**	**hemos vivido**
	habéis hablado	**habéis aprendido**	**habéis vivido**
	han hablado	**han aprendido**	**han vivido**
pluperfect	I had spoken	I had learned	I had lived
	había hablado	**había aprendido**	**había vivido**
	habías hablado	**habías aprendido**	**habías vivido**
	había hablado	**había aprendido**	**había vivido**
	habíamos hablado	**habíamos aprendido**	**habíamos vivido**
	habíais hablado	**habíais aprendido**	**habíais vivido**
	habían hablado	**habían aprendido**	**habían vivido**
familiar commands (positive)	speak	learn	live
	habla	**aprende**	**vive**
	hablad	**aprended**	**vivid**
familiar commands (negative)	don't speak	don't learn	don't live
	no hables	**no aprendas**	**no vivas**
	no habléis	**no aprendáis**	**no viváis**

	-ar	-er	-ir
formal commands	speak	learn	live
	hable	**aprenda**	**viva**
	hablen	**aprendan**	**vivan**
present subjunctive	I *(may)* speak	I *(may)* learn	I *(may)* live
	hable	**aprenda**	**viva**
	hables	**aprendas**	**vivas**
	hable	**aprenda**	**viva**
	hablemos	**aprendamos**	**vivamos**
	habléis	**aprendáis**	**viváis**
	hablen	**aprendan**	**vivan**
imperfect subjunctive (**-ra** form)	I *(might)* speak	I *(might)* learn	I *(might)* live
	hablara	**aprendiera**	**viviera**
	hablaras	**aprendieras**	**vivieras**
	hablara	**aprendiera**	**viviera**
	habláramos	**aprendiéramos**	**viviéramos**
	hablarais	**aprendierais**	**vivierais**
	hablaran	**aprendieran**	**vivieran**
imperfect subjunctive (**-se** form)	I *(might)* speak	I *(might)* learn	I *(might)* live
	hablase	**aprendiese**	**viviese**
	hablases	**aprendieses**	**vivieses**
	hablase	**aprendiese**	**viviese**
	hablásemos	**aprendiésemos**	**viviésemos**
	hablaseis	**aprendieseis**	**vivieseis**
	hablasen	**aprendiesen**	**viviesen**

Stem-changing verbs

1. **-ar** and **-er** verbs: **o** ▷ **ue**
    contar(ue) to count
    present **cuento, cuentas, cuenta: contamos, contáis, cuentan**
    present subjunctive **cuente, cuentes, cuente: contemos, contéis, cuenten**
    formal commands **cuente, cuenten**

2. **-ar** and **-er** verbs: **e** ▷ **ie**
    perder (ie) to lose
    present **pierdo, pierdes, pierde: perdemos, perdéis, pierden**
    present subjunctive **pierda, pierdas, pierda: perdamos, perdáis, pierdan**
    formal commands **pierda, pierdan**

3. **-ir** verbs: **e** ▷ **i**
    pedir (i, i) to ask for
    NB: Where there are two changes, the first is for the present, the second for
    the preterite and present participle.
    present participle **pidiendo**
    present **pido, pides, pide: pedimos, pedís, piden**
    preterite **pedí, pediste, pidió: pedimos, pedisteis, pidieron**
    present subjunctive **pida, pidas, pida: pidamos, pidáis, pidan**
    imperfect subjunctive **pidiera (-se), pidieras, pidiera: pidiéramos,
    pidierais, pidieran**
    formal commands **pida, pidan**

4. **-ir** verbs: **o** ▷ **ue, o** ▷ **u**
    dormir (ue, u) to sleep
    present participle **durmiendo**
    present **duermo, duermes, duerme: dormimos, dormís, duermen**
    present subjunctive **duerma, duermas, duerma: durmamos, durmáis,
    duerman**
    imperfect subjunctive **durmiera (-se), durmieras, durmiera: durmiéramos,
    durmierais, durmieran**
    formal commands **duerma, duerman**

5. **-ir** verbs: **e** ▷ **ie, e** ▷ **i**
    sentir (ie, i) to feel sorry, to regret, to feel
    present participle **sintiendo**
    present **siento, sientes, siente: sentimos, sentís, sienten**
    preterite **sentí, sentiste, sintió: sentimos, sentisteis, sintieron**
    present subjunctive **sienta, sientas, sienta: sintamos, sintáis, sientan**
    imperfect subjunctive **sintiera (-se), sintieras, sintiera: sintiéramos,
    sintierais, sintieran**
    formal commands **sienta, sientan**

Spelling changing verbs

1   Verbs ending in **-gar**:
pagar   to pay for
preterite **pagué, pagaste, pagó: pagamos, pagasteis, pagaron**
present subjunctive **pague, pagues, pague: paguemos, paguéis, paguen**
formal commands **pague, paguen**

Other verbs like **pagar** are **jugar** to play and **llegar** to arrive.

2   Verbs ending in **-car**:
explicar   to explain
preterite **expliqué, explicaste, explicó: explicamos, explicasteis, explicaron**
present subjunctive **explique, expliques, explique: expliquemos, expliquéis, expliquen**
formal commands **explique, expliquen**

Other verbs like **explicar** are **tocar** to touch, **equivocarse** to make a mistake, **sacar** to take out, **secar** to dry and **marcar** to dial.

3   Verbs ending in **-ger** or **-gir**:
coger   to take hold of (things)
present **cojo, coges, coge: cogemos, cogéis, cogen**
present subjunctive **coja, cojas, coja: cojamos, cojáis, cojan**
formal commands **coja, cojan**

Other verbs like **coger** are **dirigirse** to go towards, **escoger** to choose and **recoger** to pick up.

4   Verbs ending in **-zar**:
cruzar   to cross
preterite **crucé, cruzaste, cruzó: cruzamos, cruzasteis, cruzaron**
present subjunctive **cruce, cruces, cruce: crucemos, crucéis, crucen**
formal commands **cruce, crucen**

Other verbs like **cruzar** are **aterrizar** to land, **comenzar** to begin, **empezar** to begin and **organizar** to organise.

5   **-er** and **-ir** verbs with stem endings in **a**, **e** and **o**:
leer   to read
present participle **leyendo**
past participle **leído**
preterite **leí, leíste, leyó: leímos, leísteis, leyeron**
past subjunctive **leyera (-se), leyeras, leyera: leyéramos, leyerais, leyeran**
Other verbs like **leer** are **caer** to fall, **creer** to believe, **oír** to hear and **traer** to bring.

6   Verbs ending in **-cer** or **-cir** preceded by a vowel:
conocer   to know
present **conozco, conoces, conoce: conocemos, conocéis, conocen**
present subjunctive **conozca, conozcas, conozca: conozcamos, conozcáis, conozcan**
formal commands **conozca, conozcan**

Other verbs like **conocer** are **aparecer** to appear, **nacer** to be born, **ofrecer** to offer, **parecer** to seem, **pertenecer** to belong to and **reconocer** to recognise.

Irregular verbs, verbs with special meanings, verbs + prepositions

abrir	to open **he abierto** (perfect)
acabar de	+ inf. to have just. Use this verb in the present tense: **acabo de llegar** I've just arrived, or in the imperfect: **acababa de llegar** I had just arrived.
acordarse de	to remember (rc; **ue**)
acostarse	to go to bed (rc: **ue**)
alegrarse de	to be happy to
andar	to walk **anduve** etc. (pret.) **anduviera** etc. (imp. subj.)
aprender a	to learn how to
apretar	to tighten (rc: **ie**)
asistir a	to be present at
atender	to attend, pay attention, look after (rc: **ie**)
atravesar	to cross (rc: **ie**)
ayudar a	to help someone to
conducir	to drive **conduzco, conduces** etc. (pres.), **conduje** etc. (pret.), **conduzca** (for. command)
contar	to count (rc: **ue**)
costar	to cost (rc: **ue**)
cubrir	to cover **cubierto** (pp.)
dar	to give **doy, das** etc. (pres.), **di, diste, dio** etc. (pret.), **dé, des, dé** etc. (pr. subj.)
decidirse a	to decide to
decir	to say **digo, dices, dice, decimos, decís, dicen** (pres.), **dije, dijiste, dijo, dijimos, dijisteis, dijeron** (pret.), **diré, dirás** etc. (fut.), **he dicho** (perf.), **di, decid** (fam. command)
despertarse	to wake up (rc: **ie**)
doler	to be painful (rc: **ue**) **me duele el pie** my foot hurts
dormir	to sleep (rc: **ue**)
dormirse	to fall asleep
empezar a	to begin to (rc: **ie**)
encantar	to enchant **me encanta** I like it very much
encender	to light, switch on (rc: **ie**)
encontrar	to find (rc: **ue**)
enseñar a	to teach
entender	to understand (rc: **ie**)
escribir	to write **escrito** (pp.)
estar	to be **estoy, estás** etc. (pres.), **estuve, estuviste** etc. (pret.)
faltar	to be missing **falta Juan** John's missing
freír	to fry **frito** (pp.) **huevos fritos** fried eggs
haber	to have (auxiliary) **he, has, ha, hemos, habéis, han** (pres.), **hube** etc. (pret.), **he, habe** (fam. command), **hay** there is/are, **había** there was/were
hacer	to do/make **hago, haces** etc. (pres.), **hice, hiciste, hizo, hicimos, hicisteis, hicieron** (pret.), **haré, harás** etc. (fut.), **hecho** (pp.), **haz, haced** (fam. command)
importar	to matter **no importa** it doesn't matter
interesar	to interest **no me interesa** I'm not interested
invitar a	to invite
ir	to go **voy, vas, va, vamos, vais, van** (pre.), **fui, fuiste, fue, fuimos, fuisteis, fueron** (pret.), **iba, ibas** etc (imp.), **vaya, vayas** etc. (pr. subj.), **ve, id** (fam. command), **he ido** etc. (perf.)
irse	to go off, to go away

llover	to rain (rc: **ue**) **está lloviendo** it's raining
morir	to die (rc: **ue**) **muerto** (pp.)
mostrar	to show (rc: **ue**)
mover	to move (rc: **ue**)
nevar	to show (rc: **ie**) **está nevando** it's snowing
oler	to smell (rc: **ue**) **huelo, hueles** etc. (pres.), **huele a cebolla** it smells of onions, **huela, huelas, huela, olamos, oláis, huelan** (pr. subj.)
olvidarse de	to forget to
pensar	to think (rc: **ie**) **pensar en** to think about
perder	to lose (rc: **ie**)
persuadir a	to persuade
poder	to be able (rc: **ue**) **podré** etc. (fut.), **pude** etc. (pret.)
poner	to put **pongo, pones** etc. (pres.), **pondré** etc. (fut.), **puesto** (pp.), **puse, pusiste** etc. (pret.), **pon, poned** (fam. command)
ponerse	to put on **me pongo el abrigo** I put on my coat
"	to become **se puso pálida** she went (became)pale
preferir	to prefer (rc: **ie**)
probar	to try (rc: **ue**)
quedar	to stay, be left **no me queda dinero** I've no money left
querer	to want (rc: **ie**) **querré** etc. (fut.), **quise** etc. (pret.)
quitarse	to take off **se quitó los zapatos** he/she took off his/her shoes
romper	to break **roto** (pp.)
saber	to know **sé, sabes** etc. (pres.), **sabré** etc. (fut.), **supe** etc. (pret.), **sepa** etc. (pr. subj.)
saber a	to taste of
salir	to go out **salgo, sales** etc. (pres.), **saldré** etc. (fut.), **sal, salid** (fam. command)
sentarse	to sit down (rc: **ie**)
sentir	to feel (rc: **ie**) **lo siento** I am sorry
ser	to be **soy, eres, es, somos, sois, son** (pres.), **sea, seas, sea** etc. (pr. subj.), **fui, fuiste, fue, fuimos, fuisteis, fueron** (pret.), **era, eras, era, éramos, erais, eran** (imp.), **sé, sed** (fam. command)
servir	to serve (rc: **ie**)
servirse	to help oneself **!sírvase!** help yourself!
soler	to be accustomed to (rc: **ue**) **suelo venir a España todos los años** I usually come to Spain each year
sonar	to ring (rc: **ue**)
sonar a	to sound like
tener	to have (rc: **ie**) **tengo, tienes** etc. (pres.), **tendré, tendrás** etc. (fut.), **tuve, tuviste** etc. (pret.), **ten, tened** (fam. command)
tener que	+ inf. to have to
traer	to bring **traigo, traes** etc. (pres.), **traje, trajiste** etc. (pret.), **traído** (pp.)
tratar de	to try to
tratarse de	to be about **en la película se trata de la guerra civil** the film is about the civil war
valer	to be worth **¿cuánto vale?** how much is it? **vale** OK **val, valed** (fam. command)
venir	to come (rc: **ie**) **vengo, vienes** etc. (pres.), **vendré** (fut.), **vine, viniste** etc. (pret.), **ven, venid** (fam. command)
ver	to see **veo, ves, ve** etc. (pres.), **veía, veías** etc. (imp.), **visto** (pp.)
volver	to go back (rc: **ue**), **vuelto** (pp.)
volver a	+ inf. to do something again

VOCABULARY

key to abbreviations used

n noun
v verb
adj adjective
adv adverb
prep preposition
m masculine
f feminine
sing singular
pl plural
irreg irregular

A

abandonar to leave, to desert
abeja (*f.*) bee
abierto/a open
abonar to pay
abrigo (*m.*) coat
abrir to open
absolutamente absolutely
abuelos (*m.pl.*) grandparents
abusar to abuse
acabar to finish, to end up
acabar de to have just done something
accidente (*m.*) accident
aceite (*m.*) oil
aceptar to accept
acercar to bring closer, to pass
acidez de estómago (*f.*) an upset stomach
aconsejar to advise, to recommend
acordarse to remember
actitud (*f.*) attitude
actividades (*f.pl.*) activities
acto (*m.*) act
actuación (*f.*) activity, performance
actual now, present
actualmente at the moment
acudir a to come, to turn to
acuerdo (*m.*) agreement; **de acuerdo** all right
acumular to accumulate, to gain
además moreover
aditamentos (*m.pl.*) accessories, equipment

administración (*f.*) administration
Administración Pública (*f.*) public administration
aduanero (*m.*) customs officer
afectar to affect
aficionado/a *adj* keen; *n* (*m.*) fan
afirmar to state, to declare
afortunadamente fortunately
afueras (*f.pl.*) outskirts
agenda (*f.*) diary
agente de viajes (*m./f.*) travel agent
agilizar to speed up
agosto (*m.*) August
agotado/a exhausted
agradable agreeable, pleasant
agradecer to thank
agresión (*f.*) aggression
agua mineral embotellada (*f.*) bottled mineral water
agua (*f.*) water
aguantar to bear, to put up with
aguardiente (*m.*) rum, spirit
ahora now; **ahora mismo** right now
aire acondicionado (*m.*) air conditioning
ajedrez (*m.*) chess
ajo (*m.*) garlic
ajustado/a tight
alejar to move away
alemán, alemana *n*, *adj* German
Alemania (*f.*) Germany
aleta (*f.*) wing of a car
alfombra (*f.*) carpet

algo something
algodón (*m.*) cotton
alguien somebody, someone
algun/alguno/a any, some
alimentario/a *adj* food
alimentos (*m.pl.*) food
allí there
alquilar to hire
alquiler (*m.*) (car) hire
alrededor de around
alto/a tall, high, loud; **de alto** high
alumno/a (m./f.) pupil, student
amabilidad (*f.*) friendliness
amarillo/a yellow
ambiente (*m.*) atmosphere
ambos/as both
amenazar to threaten
amigo/a (*m./f.*) friend
amistad (*f.*) friendship
amor (*m.*) love
amplio/a wide, large
amueblado/a furnished
análisis de orina (*m.*) urine test
análisis de sangre (*m.*) blood test
anárquico/a anarchic
de ancho wide
andar to walk
angustioso/a distressing
antelación (*f.*) advance
antena parabólica (*f.*) satellite dish
anteriormente previously
antes (de que) before, former
antiácidos (*m.pl.*) antacids
antiguo/a old, classic
anunciar to announce, to advertise
añadirse to add
año(*m.*) year; **el año pasado** last year
aparato (*m.*) machine
aparecer to appear
apagar to turn off, to put out
apariencia (*f.*) appearance
apartar to move away, to set aside
apellido (*m.*) surname
apetecer to want to, to feel like
aplicado/a hard-working
apoyar to support
aprender to learn
aprobar to approve of, to pass (an exam)
aquel, aquella, aquellos/as *adj* that (one), those
aquí here
arena (*f.*) sand
armario (*m.*) cupboard, wardrobe, closet
arrepentirse to regret, to repent
arriesgarse to take risks
arroz (*m.*) rice

arte contemporáneo (*m.*) contemporary art
artículo (*m.*) article
artístico/a artistic
ascensor (*m.*) lift, elevator
así like this, like that
asistir to assist
aspirina (*f.*) aspirin
asqueroso/a disgusting
atareado/a busy
atender to serve
ático (*m.*) attic
atraco (*m.*) hold-up
atractivo/a attractive
atrasado/a off (food), slow, late (people)
atrasarse to be late
atributo (*m.*) attribute
aumentar to increase
aumento (*m.*) increase
aunque although, even though
autobús (*m.*) bus
autonomías (*f.pl.*) autonomous regions
autopista (*f.*) motorway
autoridades (*f.pl.*) authorities
avisar to warn, to advise
avispa (*f.*) wasp
ayuda (*f.*) help
ayudar to help
azafata (*f.*) (air) hostess
azafrán (*m.*) saffron
azúcar (*m.*) sugar

B

bailar to dance
bailarín (*m.*) dancer
baile (*m.*) dance
bajar to go/come down, to take down
bajarse de to get out, to get off (a bus etc.)
baloncesto (*m.*) basketball
banco (*m.*) bank
bandera (*f.*) flag
bañarse to have a bath
barato/a cheap
barrio (*m.*) neighbourhood
bastante enough, quite
bater to beat
beber to drink
bebida (*f.*) drink
belleza (*f.*) beauty
beneficiar to benefit
beso (*m.*) kiss
bicicleta (*f.*) bicycle
bien well
billar (*m.*) billiards
biografía (*f.*) biography
boca (*f.*) mouth

bolsa (*f.*)   bag
brazo (*m.*)   arm
brillante   shining
brillar   to shine
bruja (*f.*)   witch
bueno/a   good
burocracia (*f.*)   bureaucracy
buscar   to look (for)

C

cabeza (*f.*)   head
cacharro (*m.*)   pot, thing
cada   each, every
cafetera (*f.*)   coffee machine
caja (*f.*)   box
cajero automático (*m.*)   automatic cash dispenser
cajón (*m.*)   drawer
calamares (*m.pl.*)   squid
calculadora (*f.*)   calculator
calefacción central (*f.*)   central heating
calentar   to heat
calidad (*f.*)   quality
callado/a   quiet
calle (*f.*)   street
calma (*f.*)   calm
cama (*f.*)   bed
cámara (*f.*)   camera
camarero/a (m./f.)   waiter/waitress
cambiar   to change, to exchange
cambio (*m.*)   bureau de change
caminar   to walk
camino (*m.*)   path
campo (*m.*)   countryside, land, field
canción (*f.*)   song
cansado/a   tired
cansar   to tire, grow tired
cantidad (*f.*)   quantity; **gran cantidad de**   a lot of
caña (*f.*)   draught beer (peninsular Spanish)
capilla (*f.*)   chapel
cara (*f.*)   face
cariñoso/a   affectionate, warm
carne (*f.*)   meat
carnet de conducir (*m.*)   driving licence
caro/a   expensive
carrera (*f.*)   university course
carrete (*m.*)   roll of film
carretera (*f.*)   road
carro (*m.*)   cart, (Latin American) car
carta (*f.*)   letter
cartelera (*f.*)   entertainments page
cartera (*f.*)   wallet, briefcase
en casa   at home
casado/a   married

casarse   to get married
casete (*f.*)   cassette tape, (*m.*) tape recorder
causa (*f.*)   cause
cebolla (*f.*)   onion
celebrar   to celebrate
cenar   to dine; **cenar fuera**   to dine out
censura (*f.*)   censure, censorship
cerca de   nearby, close
cerilla (*f.*)   match
cerrado/a   closed, shut
cerrar(se) to shut, to close
cerveza (*f.*)   beer
charlar   to chat, talk
cheques de viaje(ro) (*m.pl.*)   travellers' cheques
chico/a (*f./m.*)   boy/girl
chorizo (*m.*)   sausage
cielo (*m.*)   sky
ciencia (*f.*)   science
cierto/a   true, certain
cigarrillo (*m.*)   cigarette
cima (*f.*)   top
cine (*m.*)   cinema
cinta (*f.*)   cassette tape
circuito (*m.*)   track, circuit
circulación (*f.*)   traffic
ciruela (*f.*)   plum
cita (*f.*)   appointment
ciudad (*f.*)   city, town
ciudadano/a (*m./f.*)   citizen
claridad (*f.*)   light, brightness
claro   of course
cliente/a (*m./f.*)   customer
cobrar   to charge
cocaína (*f.*)   cocaine
cocer   to cook
coche (*m.*)   car
cocina (*f.*)   kitchen, cooking
cocinado/a   cooked
código postal (*m.*)   post code
coger   to catch
cola (*f.*)   queue
colaboración (*f.*)   collaboration
coleccionar   to collect
colega (*m./f.*)   colleague, friend
colegio (*m.*)   (private) secondary school
coles de Bruselas (*m.pl.*)   Brussels sprouts
coliflor (*f.*)   cauliflower
colocar   to put or place
colombiano/a *n, adj*   Colombian
colorado/a   red
comedor (*m.*)   dining room, canteen
comida (*f.*)   food
comodidad (*f.*)   convenience, comfort
compañero/a (*m./f.*)   colleague
compañía (*f.*)   company

comparsa (*f.*) procession
compra (*f.*) purchase, shopping
comprar to buy
compuesto/a dressed up; composed of
comunicación (*f.*) communication, connection
con with
con antelación in advance
concretamente specifically
concurso (*m.*) competition
condición (*f.*) condition
conducir to drive, to lead
conductor (*m.*) driver
conferencia (*f.*) talk, lecture
en conjunto together
conocer a to know, to be acquainted with;
  to meet
conocimientos (*m.pl.*) knowledge
conserje (*m.*) caretaker, receptionist
conservar to preserve, to remain
considerar to consider
constantemente constantly, non-stop
construir to build
consulta del médico (*f.*) doctor's surgery
consumar to commit, to carry out
consumo (*m.*) consumption
contacto (*m.*) contact
contar to count, to tell; **contar con** to rely
  on
contestador automático (*m.*) answer phone
contestar to answer, to reply
contratar to hire, to contract
controlar to control
conveniente advisable
conversar to talk
convertir to convert, to turn
copa (*f.*) glass
copiar to copy
coreografía (*f.*) choreography
coronilla (*f.*) crown of the head; **estoy hasta
  la coronilla** I'm fed up
correcto/a correct
corregir to correct
correo (*m.*) post, mail; **correo electrónico**
  e-mail
cortar to cut
corte de digestión (*m.*) stomach cramp
corticoide (*m.*) corticosteroid
cosa (*f.*) thing
cosecha (*f.*) cereal/harvest
costa (*f.*) coast
costar to cost, to be hard to do
costo, coste (*m.*) cost
costumbre (*f.*) custom
crear to create
creer to believe, to think
cruce (*m.*) crossing

crudo/a raw
cruz (*f.*) cross
cuadrado/a square
cualquier/a any
cuando when
cuanto más ... más the more ... the more;
  en cuanto a ... as far as ... is concerned;
  en cuanto puedas as soon as you can
cuarenta forty
cuarto/a fourth
cuarto (*m.*) room, bedroom; **cuarto de
  baño** (*m.*) bathroom
cuatro four
cubos de hielo (*m.pl.*) ice cubes
cubrir to cover
cuello (*m.*) neck
cuenta (*f.*) cheque, bill
cuenta de ahorros (*f.*) savings account
cuenta corriente (*f.*) current account
por su cuenta free-lance
cuento (*m.*) story
cuestión (*f.*) question; **en la cuestión de ...**
  as far as ... is concerned
cuidado (*m.*) care
cuidar to look after
cultura (*f.*) culture
cumplido/a polite
cumplir to fulfil
cumplir años to have a birthday
cura (*m.*) curé, priest
curso (*m.*) year, course

D

dado que given that
dar *irreg* to give
dar la vuelta to go around
darse cuenta to realise
debajo underneath
deber *n* (*m.*) duty; *v* to owe
débil weak
decir to say, to tell
declarar to declare, to state
decorar to decorate
dedo (*m.*) finger, toe; **dedo gordo** thumb,
  big toe
defenderse to protect oneself
defensa (*f.*) bumper, defence
degustar to taste
dejar to leave
delante in front
deletrear to spell
delgado/a slim
delincuencia (*f.*) delinquency
demasiado too much, too many
demostrar to prove, to demonstrate

dentro (de) inside, in
denunciar to denounce, to report, to complain about
depender to depend on; **depende de** it depends on
deporte (*m*.) sport
derecha (*f*.) right
derivación (*f*.) derivation, consequence
derramar to spill
derrame cerebral (*m*.) brain haemorrhage, stroke
derrotar to beat, to overcome
desafortunadamente unfortunately
desagradable disagreeable
desaparecer to disappear
desayunar to have breakfast
descansado/a relaxed
descansar to rest
desde from, since
desear to desire, to wish
desempleado/a unemployed
desfile (*m*.) procession
deshidratación (*f*.) dehydration
desintoxicarse to undergo detoxification
desmontar to take apart
desorden (*m*.) mess
despacho (*m*.) office
despacio slowly
despenalización (*f*.) decriminalisation
desplazarse to move around, to travel, to go
después after, afterwards
destino (*m*.) destination, fate
desventaja (*f*.) disadvantage
devolver to return
diapositiva (*f*.) slide, transparency
diario *n* (*m*.) diary, newspaper; *adj.* daily
diarrea (*f*.) diarrhoea
diferente different
dígame hello (formal, on the telephone)
dinero (*m*.) money
dirección (*f*.) address
directamente directly
director(a) (*m./f.*) manager
disco duro (*m*.) hard disk
disco (*m*.) record
disco compacto (*m*.) CD
discoteca (*f*.) disco
discutir to discuss
disfraz (*m*.) costume, disguise
disfrutar to enjoy
disponer de to dispose of, to have
disponible available
dispuesto/a ready, willing
disquete (*m*.) diskette
distancia focal (*f*.) focal distance
divertir to amuse

divisas (*f.pl.*) foreign currency;
  en divisas foreign exchange
divulgar to spread, to broadcast
DNI (*m*.) national identity card
doce twelve, twelfth
doler to hurt; **me duele el estómago** I have stomach-ache
dolor de cabeza (*m*.) headache
dominio (*m*.) control, command
dorarse to go golden brown
dormir to sleep
dormitorio (*m*.) bedroom
drogadicción (*f*.) drug addiction
drogas blandas (*f.pl.*) soft drugs
drogas duras (*f.pl.*) hard drugs
ducha (*f*.) shower
ducharse to have a shower
dudar to doubt
durante during

E

echar to throw
echar de menos to miss
económico/a economic, economical
edad (*f*.) age
edificio (*m*.) building
educación (*f*.) education
efectivamente really
efectivo (*m*.) cash
efectuar to do, to undertake, to carry out
egoísta selfish
ejemplo example
ejercicio (*m*.) exercise
él he
elaboración (*f*.) production, working
elepé (*m*.) LP
eliminar to remove, to dispose of
ella she
ellas (*f. pl.*) they
ellos (*m. f.*) they
embarcar to embark
emigrar to emigrate
emisora (*f*.) radio station
emitir to broadcast
emocionante moving, exciting
empanada (*f*.) type of pie or pasty stuffed with fish or pork
empaquetar to pack up
empezar to begin (to)
empleado/a (*m./ f.*) employee
empleo (*m*.) job
empotrado/a fitted
empresa (*f*.) firm
empresario (*m*.) business man
encantado/a delighted

encantar to charm, to delight; **me encanta** I love (it)

encanto (*m.*) charm

encima over

encontrar to find

encontrarse to find oneself, to feel

enfadarse to get cross

enfermarse to fall ill

enfermo/a ill, sick

enjuagar to rinse

ensalada (*f.*) salad

ensayar to practise

en seguida at once, straight away

enseñanza (*f.*) teaching, education

enseñar to teach, to show

entender to understand

enterarse to find out

enterar to inform, to notify

entierro (*m.*) burial, funeral

entonces then

entrada (*f.*) entrance

entrar to enter, come in

entregar to hand over

entrevista (*f.*) interview

entrevistador (*m.*) interviewer

envío (*m.*) mail

equipaje (*m.*) luggage

equipo de sonido (*m.*) sound system

equipo (*m.*) team, equipment

equivocarse to make a mistake, to be wrong

ermita (*f.*) hermitage, shrine

escaparse to escape

escoger to choose

esconder to hide

escribir to write

escuchar to listen to

escuela (*f.*) primary school

esfuerzo (*m.*) effort

espabilado/a alert

espacio (*m.*) space, room

espacioso/a spacious

español(a) Spanish

español (*m.*) Spanish language

especialista (*m./ f.*) specialist

esperar to wait (for), to expect, to hope (for)

espontáneo/a spontaneous

esquiar to ski

esquina (*f.*) corner

estación (*f.*) station

estado (*m.*) condition, status, state

Estados Unidos (*m.pl.*) United States

estadounidense American

estampado/a *adj* printed; *n* (*m.*) pattern

estante (*m.*) shelf

estar *irreg* to be

estatal *adj* state

estéreo (*m.*) stereo

estimulante *adj* stimulating; *n* (*m.*) stimulant

estipulado/a set, stipulated

estómago (*m.*) stomach

estrechar to narrow, to strengthen (links)

estudiante (*m./f.*) student

estudiar to study

estudio (*m.*) study

estufa (*f.*) heater, stove

estupendo/a wonderful

evitar to avoid

examen (*m.*) exam, test

excéntrico/a eccentric

exento/a exempt

(en) existencias (*f.pl.*) (in) stock

experiencia (*f.*) experience

extintor (*m.*) fire extinguisher

extranjero/a *adj* foreign; *n* (*m./ f.*) foreigner

extraño/a strange, odd

F

fábrica (*f.*) factory

fabricar to make, to produce

fácil easy

facilidad (*f.*) ease

factor clave (*m.*) key factor

facturar to dispatch

faenas de la casa (*f.pl.*) housework

falsedad (*f.*) lie, falsehood

falta de lack of

falta (*f.*) mistake, lack

familia (*f.*) family

familiar *adj* family

fanático/a fanatic

fantástico/a fantastic

fe (*f.*) faith

fecha (*f.*) date

feliz happy; **feliz cumpleaños** happy birthday

fenómeno (*m.*) phenomenon

feria (*f.*) fair, market

festejar to celebrate

ficha (*f.*) form

fiebre (*f.*) temperature

fiesta (*f.*) party, holiday

fijo/a fixed, permanent

fin (*m.*) end; **en fin** in short; **a finales de** at the end of

fin de semana (*m.*) weekend

física (*f.*) physics

físico/a physical

florido/a flowery

fluidez (*f.*) fluency

fonda (*f.*) (small) hotel

forma (*f.*)   way (to do something)
formado por   formed by
formar   to form, to make up
formulario (*m.*)   form
francés, **francesa** *n*, *adj*   French
frecuencia (*f.*)   frequency
fregar   to wash up
freír *irreg*   to fry
freno (**de mano**) (*m.*)   (hand) brake
frío/a   cold
fruta (*f.*)   fruit
fue (see **ser**, **ir**)
fuera   out, outside
fuerte   strong, fierce, shocking
fumar   to smoke
funcionamiento (*m.*)   operation
funcionario/a (*m./ f.*)   government worker
fútbol (*m.*)   football
futuro (*m.*)   future

G

gafas (*f.pl.*)   glasses
galleta (*f.*)   biscuit, cookie
gama (*f.*)   selection
gambas (*f.pl.*)   prawns
ganar   to win
garaje (*m.*)   garage
garganta (*f.*)   throat
gaseosa (*f.*)   lemonade
gastos de comunidad (*m.pl.*)   community charges
gato (*m.*)   cat
gazpacho (*m.*)   cold soup
generalmente   generally
gente (*f.*)   people
gestión (*f.*)   business, management, administration
gesto (*m.*)   gesture
giro (*m.*)   tour
gobierno (*m.*)   government
golf (*m.*)   golf
golpe (*m.*)   blow, hit
golpear   to hammer, knock
gordo/a *adj*   fat; *n* (*m.*)   lottery
gracia (*f.*)   charm, wit
gramática (*f.*)   grammar
grande   big, large
grasiento/a   greasy
gratis   free
griego/a *n*, *adj*   Greek
gripe (*f.*)   flu
gritar   to shout
grupo (*m.*)   group
guapísimo/a   very handsome, very beautiful
guapo/a   handsome, beautiful

guardar (**la**) **cola**   to queue up
guerra (*f.*)   war
guía (*m./f.*)   guide; (*f.*)   guidebook, handbook
guía de usuario (*f.*)   users' guide
gustar   to like
gusto (*m.*)   taste, pleasure

H

habitación (*f.*)   bedroom
hablador/a   talkative, chatty
hablar   to speak, to talk
hace   (+ expression of time) ago
hacer *irreg*   to do/make
hachís (*m.*)   cannabis
hacia   towards
hacia abajo   downwards
hacia arriba   upwards
harina (*f.*)   flour
hasta   until, till, up to
hecho (*m.*)   fact
herida (*f.*)   wound
hermano/a (*m./ f.*)   brother/sister
higiene (*f.*)   hygiene
hijo (*m.*)   child, son
hinchado/a   swollen
hoja de reclamaciones (*f.*)   complaints form
hombre (*m.*)   man
hondo/a   deep
hora (*f.*)   hour
horario (*m.*)   timetable, opening hours
hoy   today
huelga (*f.*)   strike
huesos (*m.pl.*)   bones
huevo (*m.*)   egg; **cocido**   hard-boiled, **frito**   fried, **pasado por agua**   soft-boiled
huevos revueltos   scrambled egg
huir   to escape, to flee
humano/a   human

I

idioma (*m.*)   language
ilegal   illegal
ilegalidad (*f.*)   illegality
ilimitado/a   unlimited
iluminar   to light
impedir   to prevent
importante   important
importar   to matter, to import
imprescindible   vital
impresora (*f.*)   printer
impresos (*m.pl.*)   printed matter
incendio (*m.*)   fire
inclinación (*f.*)   taste, pleasure

incluido/a included
incluir to include
incluso even
incorporarse to join; to sit up
incrementar to increase
indefinido/a undefined, vague
independencia (*f.*) independence
individuo (*m.*) person
infección (*f.*) infection
inflamación (*f.*) swelling
informática (*f.*) computer science
informativos (*m.pl.*) news
infusión (*f.*) fruit tea
ingeniería (*f.*) engineering
ingeniero/a (*m./f.*) engineer
inglés(a) *n, adj* English
iniciar to begin
injusticia (*f.*) unfairness
injusto/a unfair, unjust
inmejorable excellent
inmueble (*m.*) building
inolvidable unforgettable
insolación (*f.*) sun stroke
instalarse to settle, to install oneself
instituto (*m.*) state secondary school
intentar to try to
interesante interesting, good value
interesar to be interested in
interferir to interfere in
internado (*m.*) boarding-school
interno/a (*m./f.*) boarder
interrupción (*f.*) interruption, break
invalidez (*f.*) invalidity
invitar to invite
ir to go
ir de bares to go on a pub crawl
ir de copas to go on a pub crawl
izquierda left

J

---

jarabe (*m.*) syrup
jardín (*m.*) garden
jefe/a (*m./f.*) boss, head
jornada completa (*f.*) all day, (work) full-time
joven *n* (*m./f.*) young man/woman *adj* young
joya (*f.*) piece of jewellery
joyería (*f.*) jewellers' shop
jubilado/a (*m./f.*) retired person
judías verdes (*f.pl.*) green beans
juego (*m.*) game, set
jueves Thursday
jugar *irreg* to play
junio (*m.*) June

junto(s) together
justicia (*f.*) justice
justo/a fair, right, just
juvenil young, youthful

K

---

kilometraje (*m.*) mileage

L

---

lado (*m.*) side; **al lado de** next to
largo/a long; **de largo** long, in length
lavadora (*f.*) washing machine
lavarse el pelo to wash one's hair
lechuga (*f.*) lettuce
leer to read
legalización (*f.*) legalisation
legumbres (*m.pl.*) vegetables, legumes
lejía (*f.*) bleach
lejos (de) far (from)
lengua (*f.*) language
lente gran angular (*m./f.*) wide-angle lens
lente (*m./f.*) camera lens
lentillas (*f.pl.*) contact lenses
lento/a slow
levantarse to get up
libertad (*f.*) freedom
libras esterlinas (*f.pl.*) pounds sterling
libre free
librería (*f.*) bookshop
librero/a (*m./f.*) bookshop owner
libreta (*f.*) notebook, bank-book, pass book (for bank account etc.)
libro (*m.*) book
ligar to pull, to be on the make
ligero/a light, slight
limpiar to clean
limpio/a clean
lindo/a lovely
línea (*f.*) line
listo/a ready
llamada (telefónica) (*f.*) telephone call
llamar to call
llamarse to be called
llegar to arrive
llegar a to manage to do something
llenar to fill
llevar to take; to carry; to wear
lloviendo raining
lo que that which
local (*m.*) premises
loco/a (*m./f.*) mad person
locura (*f.*) insanity
lotería (*f.*) lottery
luego later, then; (Mex) soon, quickly

---

lugar (*m.*) place, site
luminoso/a light
lunes (*m.*) Monday
luz (*f.*) (*pl* **luces**) light

M

madrileño/a *n, adj* native of Madrid
malas digestiones (*f.pl.*) bad digestion
maleducado/a rude
maleta (*f.*) suitcase
malísimo/a very bad
manchar to stain
maniobras (*f.pl.*) manoeuvres
mano (*f.*) hand
manta (*f.*) blanket
mantel (*m.*) tablecloth
mantener to keep, to maintain
manzana (*f.*) apple
manzanilla (*f.*) dry sherry, camomile tea
mañana (*f.*) morning
mapa de carreteras (*m.*) road map
maquillaje (*m.*) make-up
máquina (*f.*) machine; **escribir a máquina** to type
maravilloso/a wonderful
mareado/a sick
marido (*m.*) husband
marisco (*m.*) seafood
mármol (*m.*) marble
martes (*m.*) Tuesday
más o menos more or less
más more
masticar to chew
matriarcado (*m.*) matriarchy
matrícula (*f.*) registration, licence
mayor older
mayoría (*f.*) majority; **mayoría de edad** full legal age
media jornada (*f.*) part-time
mediano/a middle-sized
medicamento (*m.*) medicine
médico (*m.*) doctor
medio/a medium-sized
mediodía (*m.*) midday
mejicano(a) *n, adj* Mexican
mejor better; **a lo mejor** perhaps
mejorar to improve
melancolía (*f.*) melancholy
menor younger
menos de less than; **a menos que** unless; **por lo menos** at least
mentira (*f.*) lie
menudo/a small
mercancía (*f.*) merchandise
mercería (*f.*) haberdashery
merecer to deserve
mesa (*f.*) table
mezclarse to mix
miércoles (*m.*) Wednesday
mil thousand
minuto (*m.*) minute
mirar to look, to watch
misa (*f.*) Mass
mismo/a same, very
mitad (*f.*) half
módem (*m.*) modem
módico/a reasonable, moderate
molestar to bother, to disturb
momentáneamente momentarily
moneda (*f.*) currency, coin
monja (*f.*) nun
montaña (*f.*) mountain
moqueta (*f.*) fitted carpet
moreno/a brown, dark
morir(se) to die
morro (*m.*) snout, front of car
mostrar to show
motor (*m.*) motor
mover to move
muchísimas felicidades (*f.pl.*) congratulations
mucho a lot
mudanza (*f.*) move
mudarse to move house
mujer (*f.*) woman
mundo (*m.*) world; **todo el mundo** everyone
música popular (*f.*) pop music
música clásica (*f.*) classical music
música grabada (*f.*) recorded, taped music

N

nacer to be born
nacimiento (*m.*) birth
nada nothing
nadar to swim
nadie nobody, anybody
naranja (*f.*) orange
nariz (*f.*) nose
natación (*f.*) swimming
natural natural
náuseas (*f.pl.*) sickness
Navidad (*f.*) Christmas
necesidad (*f.*) necessity
necesitar to need
negocio (*m.*) business
nervioso/a nervous
nevar to snow
nevera (*f.*) fridge
ninguno/a no, none, nobody

nivel (*m.*)   level
noche (*f.*)   night
nocturno/a *adj*   night, evening
nombre (*m.*)   (first) name
normalmente   normally
nosotros/as   we
noticias (*f.pl.*)   news
novela policíaca (*f.*)   detective novel
noviembre (*m.*)   November
nubes (*f.pl.*)   clouds
nunca   never
nuevo/a   new

O

objetivo (*m.*)   objective, aim, camera lens
obra (*f.*)   deed, play, building site
obstáculo (*f.*)   obstacle
obtener   to obtain, to get
ocupado/a   busy, (telephone) engaged
ocurrir   to occur, to happen; **lo que ocurre**   what happens
odiar   to hate
odio (*m.*)   hate
oficina (*f.*)   office
ofrecer   to offer
oído (*m.*)   inner ear
oír   to hear, listen to
ojo (*m.*)   eye
olvidar   to forget
opcional   optional
operación (*f.*)   operation
opinar   to judge, to make a judgement
oración (*f.*)   prayer
(en) orden   (in) order
ordenador (*m.*)   computer
oscuro/a   dark
otitis (*f.*)   ear infection
otro/a   other, another

P

padres (*m.pl.*)   parents
paga (*f.*)   pay, wage
pagar   to pay for
página (*f.*)   page
país (*m.*)   country
paisaje (*m.*)   landscape, countryside
palabra (*f.*)   word
palo (*m.*)   stick, mast, golf club
pan (*m.*)   bread
pánico (*m.*)   panic
pantalla (*f.*)   screen
papel (*m.*)   role
paquete (*m.*)   package, parcel
para   for

para   (+ infinitive) in order to
para bien   for the better
para mal   for the worse
para que   in order that
parado/a   unemployed
parar   to stop, to turn off
parecer   to seem, look
pareja (*f.*)   pair, couple
parlamento (*m.*)   parliament
parte (*f.*)   part
partido (*m.*)   match, game
partir   to leave; **a partir de ahora**   from now on
pasado   after
pasar   to spend (time); **lo que pasa**   what happens
paso (*m.*)   step, crossing
pastel (*m.*)   cake
pastilla (*f.*)   pill
patata (*f.*)   potato
pausa (*f.*)   break
pavo (*m.*)   turkey
payaso (*m.*)   clown, comedian
pedir   to ask, to order
pelar   to peel
película (*f.*)   film
peligroso/a   dangerous
pelo (*m.*)   hair
pensar   to think; **pensar en**   to think about; **pensar de**   to think of
peor   worse
pequeño/a   small
perder   to lose
periódico (*m.*)   newspaper
permiso de conducir (*m.*)   driving licence
pero   but
perro (*m.*)   dog
persona (*f.*)   person
personal (*m.*)   staff
personalizado/a   personal, personalised
perspectiva (*f.*)   perspective, view
peruano/a *n, adj*   Peruvian
pescado (*m.*)   fish
pésimo/a   dreadful, terrible
petróleo (*m.*)   oil
picadura (*f.*)   bite, sting
picante   spicy
picar   to bite (of an insect)
picores (*m.pl.*)   rash, irritation
pie (*m.*)   foot; **a pie**   on foot
piedra (*f.*)   stone
piel (*f.*)   skin
pierna (*f.*)   leg
pimienta (*f.*)   pepper (spice)
pimiento (*m.*)   pepper (vegetable)
pintar   to paint

piscina (*f.*) swimming pool
piso (*m.*) floor, apartment, flat
pista de baile (*f.*) dance floor
pista de esquí (*f.*) ski slope
planchar to iron
plano de la ciudad (*m.*) city map
plata (*f.*) silver
platina (*f.*) deck
plato (*m.*) plate, dish
platos (*m.pl.*) dishes, crockery
playa (*f.*) beach
plaza (*f.*) (car) seat
plaza de mercado (*f.*) market place
plazo (*m.*) period, space (of time); **un plazo
de un mes** the space of a month
pobre (*m./f.*) poor man/woman
poco/a little, few
poder *irreg* to be able to, can
poesía (*f.*) poetry
pollo (*m.*) chicken
pomada (*f.*) cream
poner *irreg* to put
ponerse to become
ponerse a to begin to
por by, for, because of
porque because
poseer to possess, to own
potente powerful
practicar to practise, to play
precio (*m.*) price
precioso/a beautiful, precious
preferencia (*f.*) preference
preferir to prefer
pregunta (*f.*) question
preguntar to ask
preocuparse to worry
preparar to prepare
prestar to lend, to provide
prevenir to prevent
primo/a (*m./f.*) cousin
primero/a first
principio (*m.*) beginning
prisa (*f.*) hurry
problema (*m.*) problem
problemático/a difficult
proceso (*m.*) process
procurar to try to; to obtain
profesor(a) (*m./f.*) teacher
programa (*m.*) program, programme, syllabus
prohibir to forbid
pronto soon, early
propaganda (*f.*) publicity
propietario/a (*m./f.*) owner
propio/a own
protección (*f.*) protection
protegerse to protect oneself

próximo/a next
prueba (*f.*) proof
público public
pueblo (*m.*) town, village
puentes festivos (*m.pl.*) holidays on the
working days between two normal holidays
puerta (*f.*) door, gate
pues then
puesto que given that
puesto (*m.*) job
puntualmente punctually

Q

que which, that
quedar(se) to stay
queja (*f.*) complaint
quejarse to complain
querer *irreg* to love, to want; **no querer**
to refuse
quince fifteen
quitar to take/switch off, to take away
quizá(s) perhaps

R

radio (*f.*) radio
radiocasete (*m.*) radio cassette player
rápido/a fast
rápidamente quickly
rapidez (*f.*) speed
raro/a odd
ratón (*m.*) (computer) mouse
razón (*f.*) reason
razonable reasonable, moderate
reacción (*f.*) reaction
realizar to achieve
realmente really
recado (*m.*) message
recalentar to reheat
receta (*f.*) recipe
rechazar to reject
reciente recent
reclamar to claim, to complain
recoger to collect, to pick up
recomendar to advise
recordar to remember
red (*f.*) network, power supply; **la
Red** the Internet
redactar to write
redondo/a round
referencia (*f.*) reference
referirse to mean, to refer to
regalo (*m.*) present, gift
régimen (*m.*) diet
regular so-so, poor

regularidad (*f.*)   regularity
reina (*f.*)   queen
reír(se) *irreg*   to laugh
relacionar   to relate
relajado/a   relaxed
rellenar   to fill in
relleno (*m.*)   filling
remedio (*m.*)   cure
repelente (*m.*)   repellent
reponerse   to recover (from illness)
representar   to represent, to perform, to play
reprimir   to repress
requerir   to require
resfriado (*m.*)   cold
residencia (*f.*)   residence, hostel
respetar   to respect
respirar   to breathe
responsabilidad (*f.*)   responsibility
restaurante (*m.*)   restaurant
resultado (*m.*)   result
retirar   to remove, to move away
reunión (*f.*)   meeting, gathering
reunirse   to meet
revalorizar   to revalue
revista (*f.*)   magazine
rico/a   rich, sweet, cute
riesgo (*m.*)   risk
riñon (*m.*)   kidney
río (*m.*)   river
riqueza (*f.*)   wealth
ritmo (*m.*)   rhythm
rito (*m.*)   rite, ceremony
robar   to steal
rodaja (*f.*)   slice
rodilla (*f.*)   knee
rojo/a   red
romántico/a   romantic
romper   to break, tear
ropa (*f.*)   clothes
ropa interior (*f.*) underwear
rozar   to rub
ruido (*m.*)   noise

S

sábado (*m.*)   Saturday
saber a   to taste of
saber *irreg*   to know
saborear   to taste
sacar   to take out, to put out
sagrado/a   holy
sal (*f.*)   salt
saldo (*m.*)   payment, balance
salida (*f.*)   departure
salir de   to leave (from)
salón (*m.*)   living room, reception room

salsa (*f.*)   sauce
salud (*f.*)   health
saludar   to greet
santo/a   holy
santuario (*m.*)   shrine
sede (*f.*)   headquarters, head office
seguir   to go on, to continue
seguir adelante   to go forward
segundo   second
seguramente   certainly
seguridad (*f.*)   safety, security, certainty
seguro (*m.*)   insurance
selección (*f.*)   team
selecto/a   choice, chosen
semáforo (*m.*)   traffic light
semana (*f.*)   week
Semana Santa (*f.*)   Holy Week
sentir *irreg*   to feel
señal (*f.*)   tone, beep (answer phone)
señalizar   to indicate
separar   to separate
ser humano (*m.*)   human being
servicio (*m.*)   service
servicio militar (*m.*)   military service
servir   to serve, to be used for
si   if
sí   yes
siempre   always
sien (*f.*)   temple
sifón (*m.*)   draught beer (in South American
     Spanish), soda water (peninsular Spanish)
siglo (*m.*)   century
siguiente   following, next
símbolo (*m.*)   symbol
simplificar   to simplify
sin   without
sinceramente   sincerely
sintonía (*f.*)   tuning
sintonizar   to tune
sistema (*m.*)   system
sitio (*m.*)   place, room, seat
situación (*f.*)   situation
sobre *n* (*m.*)   envelope; *prep*   on, above,
     about
sobre todo   above all
sobrevivir   to survive
sociedad (*f.*)   club, society
socio/a (*m./f.*)   business partner
sofisticado/a   sophisticated
solamente   only
soldado (*m.*)   soldier
soler   to be usual, normal
solicitar   to apply for, to request
solista (*m./f.*)   soloist
solo   alone
soltar   to let go, to let out

soltero/a (*m./f.*)   single person
solución (*f.*)   solution
sombrero de paja (*m.*)   straw hat
sonreír *irreg*   to smile
sopa (*f.*)   soup
soporte (*m.*)   support
sorprendido/a   surprised
sospechar   to suspect
suave   soft, smooth, gentle
subir   to go/come up, to put up
suceder   to happen
sucio/a   dirty
sudar   to sweat
sueldo (*m.*)   wage, salary
suelo (*m.*)   floor
sueño (*m.*)   dream
suerte (*f.*)   luck, fortune
suficiente   enough
sufrir   to suffer
superficie (*f.*)   surface
supermercado (*m.*)   supermarket
por supuesto   of course
suponer   to suppose
suspender   to fail
sustancia (*f.*)   substance
sustituto (*m.*)   substitute, replacement

T

tabaco (*m.*)   tobacco
taberna (*f.*)   pub
tal vez   perhaps
talón (*m.*)   cheque
talonario (*m.*)   cheque book
también   also, too, as well
tampoco   neither
tanto   a bit
tarde *n* (*f.*)   afternoon, evening; *adv*   late
tarea (*f.*)   task
tarifa (*f.*)   price (list)
tarjeta (*f.*)   card
té (*m.*)   tea
teatro (*m.*)   theatre
tebeo (*m.*)   comic
teclado (*m.*)   key-board
tejano/a   Texan
tejanos (*m.pl.*)   jeans
telediario (*m.*)   television news
teleobjetivo (*m.*)   telephoto lens
televisión (*f.*)   television
tema (*m.*)   subject, topic
temas deportivos (*m.pl.*)   sports programmes
temblar   to tremble
temor (*m.*)   fear
temporada (*f.*)   period of time
temprano   early

tener que *irreg*   to have to
tener lugar   to take place
tensión (alta) (*f.*)   (high) blood pressure
teórico/a   theoretical
tercero/a   third
terminar   to finish, end
terraza (*f.*)   balcony, terrace
tez (*f.*)   complexion, skin
tibio/a   warm
tiempo (*m.*)   time, weather
tiempo parcial (*m.*)   part-time
tienda (*f.*)   corner shop, store
tierra (*f.*)   land, earth
tinto/a *adj*   red; *n* (*m.*)   red wine
tío/tía (*m./f.*)   uncle/aunt
típico/a   typical
tipo (*m.*)   kind, sort, body, figure
tirar   to throw, to pull, to spill
título (*m.*)   title, degree
tobillo (*m.*)   ankle
tocar   to touch; to knock, to play an
   instrument, to win (the lottery)
todavía   still, yet
todo/a   all; **de todas formas**   in any case
tomar   to take
tomar una copa   to have a drink
tortilla (*f.*)   omelette
tos (*f.*)   cough
toser   to cough
tostador (*m.*)   toaster
tóxico/a *adj*   toxic; *n* (*m.*)   poison
trabajar   to work
trabajo (*m.*)   job, work
traducir   to translate
traer   to bring, to cause, to have
traición (*f.*)   treason
tramitación (*f.*)   processing
tranquilo/a   quiet
transporte (*m.*)   transport
trasero/a   back, rear
tratamiento (*m.*)   (course of) treatment
tremendo/a   tremendous
tren (*m.*)   train
tribunal (*m.*)   court
tú   you
tumba (*f.*)   grave, tomb
turismo (*m.*)   tourism

U

últimamente   recently
último/a   last, latest
una vez   once
único/a   only, unique
unir   to bring together
unirse a   to join

usted *sing*   you
ustedes *pl*   you
utilizar   to use
uvas (*f.pl.*)   grapes

V

vacaciones (*f.pl.*)   holidays
vacío/a   empty
vago/a (*m./f.*)   lazy person
vale la pena   it's worth while
variedad (*f.*)   variety
varón (*m.*)   man, male
vasco/a *n, adj*   Basque
vaso (*m.*)   glass
vecino/a (*m./f.*)   neighbour
vega (*f.*)   meadow
vehículo (*m.*)   vehicle
vendimia (*f.*)   grape-harvest
veneno (*m.*)   poison
venir *irreg*   to come
venta (*f.*)   sale
ventaja (*f.*)   advantage
ventana (*f.*)   window
ventanilla (*f.*)   window in a bank or office
ver *irreg*   to see, watch
verano (*m.*)   summer
verdad   truth; **de verdad**   really
verdadero/a   true, real

verde   green
verdura (*f.*)   vegetable
vestido (*m.*)   dress
vestir(se)   to dress
vez (*f.*)   time; **a veces, algunas veces**
    sometimes; **de una sola vez**   at one go
viajar   to travel, to voyage
viaje (*m.*)   voyage
vida (*f.*)   life
viejo/a   old
viernes (*m.*)   Friday
vino (*m.*)   wine
visitar   to visit
vista (*f.*)   sight, view
vistoso/a   vivid, lively
viudo/a (*m./f.*)   widower/widow
volante (*m.*)   steering wheel
volver *irreg*   to go back, return
volver a (+ inf)   to do something again
vómitos (*m.pl.*)   sickness
vosotros/as (*m.pl./f.pl.*)   you
voz (*f.*)   voice

Y

y por eso   and because of this
ya   already
ya que   given that
yo   I

GRAMMAR
CONTENTS BY UNIT

	CONTENT	GRAMMAR
UNIT 1	Leisure activities; radio programmes; shopping	Impersonal verbs; nouns; adjectives; stem-changing verbs
UNIT 2	Talking about jobs; cooking a paella; fitness and beauty	Uses of **se** (reflexive, passive); negatives; stem-changing verbs
UNIT 3	Talking about cameras; describing fiestas; describing gestures and their meaning	Shortened adjectives; using **-ísimo**; present participles; position of adjectives
UNIT 4	Being a travel agent; talking about jobs; problem with learning languages; dining clubs in the Basque country	Continuous tenses in the present; **acabar de**; conjunctions
UNIT 5	Renting a flat; opening a bank account; talking about other jobs	Infinitives; using **se** (reciprocal, passive); comparison and superlatives of adjectives and adverbs
UNIT 6	Problems with travel; problems with cars and accidents; travelling by air	Preterite tense; personal pronouns
UNIT 7	Life before baby; living in Barcelona; life at boarding school	Imperfect tense; **acababa de**; continuous tenses
UNIT 8	Talking about meals; food hygiene; health problems; at the doctor's; remedies at the chemist's	Imperfect and preterite together; imperative with **tú** and **vosotros**
UNIT 9	A horrible morning; federalism in Spain	Past participles; perfect tense; summary of past tenses
UNIT 10	Fortune telling; news bulletins; hiring a car; buying a radio cassette	Future tense revised; conditional tense; making suppositions

GRAMMAR INDEX

Have you enjoyed this course? Want to learn more?

Breakthrough Languages

Ideal for self-study . Practise and develop your skills . Learn a new language

Level 1 beginner's courses

Easy-to-use book and cassette or CD* courses.

Available in French, Spanish, German, Italian, Greek and Chinese.

* CDs for French and Spanish only.

Also available online for French and Spanish Level 1:

For students:

Multi-choice grammar exercises

For teachers:

Photocopiable exercise sheets, teacher's notes and tapescripts

For all courses:

A free site licence is available on request permitting duplication of audio material for classes (conditions apply.)

Taking it further

Level 2 in Spanish, French and German
Level 3 in French

Increase your vocabulary, fluency and confidence with these higher level book and cassette courses.

Extra practice

Activity Books with imaginative and varied exercises

Available for Level 1 French, Spanish and German

www.palgrave.com/breakthrough